Dictatorship in
South America

Viewpoints/Puntos de Vista
Themes and Interpretations in Latin American History

Series editor: Jürgen Buchenau

The books in this series will introduce students to the most significant themes and topics in Latin American history. They represent a novel approach to designing supplementary texts for this growing market. Intended as supplementary textbooks, the books will also discuss the ways in which historians have interpreted these themes and topics, thus demonstrating to students that our understanding of our past is constantly changing, through the emergence of new sources, methodologies, and historical theories. Unlike monographs, the books in this series will be broad in scope and written in a style accessible to undergraduates.

Published

A History of the Cuban Revolution
Aviva Chomsky

Bartolomé de las Casas and the Conquest of the Americas
Lawrence A. Clayton

Beyond Borders: A History of Mexican Migration to the United States
Timothy J. Henderson

The Last Caudillo: Alvaro Obregón and the Mexican Revolution
Jürgen Buchenau

A Concise History of the Haitian Revolution
Jeremy Popkin

Spaniards in the Colonial Empire: Creoles vs. Peninsulas?
Mark A. Burkholder

Dictatorship in South America
Jerry Dávila

In preparation

Mexico Since 1940: The Unscripted Revolution
Stephen E. Lewis

Dictatorship in South America

Jerry Dávila

WILEY-BLACKWELL

A John Wiley & Sons, Ltd., Publication

For Alex

Contents

List of Illustrations   viii
Series Editor's Preface   xi
Preface and Acknowledgements   xiii

Introduction   1

1   Dependency, Development, and Liberation: Latin America
    in the Cold War   9

2   Brazil: What Road to Development?   20

3   Argentina: Between Peronism and Military Rule   55

4   Chile: From Pluralistic Socialism to Authoritarian Free
    Market   82

5   Argentina: The Terrorist State   112

6   Brazil: The Long Road Back   137

7   Chile: A "Protected Democracy"?   156

Conclusion   179

Sources   185
Index   201

Illustrations

Figures

I.1   Medical Students at the University of Buenos Aires being
      marched to jail, August 1972   3
1.1   Soldiers marching beneath a Chevrolet advertisement
      during the Brazilian military coup, 1964   14
2.1   The constitutionalist armored column sent to stop General
      Mourão's advance   30
2.2   General Luzeno Sarmento Ferreira proclaims Institutional
      Act I, witnessed by naval officers. The formal proclamation,
      which puts the decree into effect, is further formalized by the
      audio recording being made. Note the extension cord at the
      bottom left, which reflects the improvised nature of the new
      authority asserted by the armed forces   32
2.3   Delegation of wives and mothers at the Correio da Manhã
      newsroom, drafting a letter petitioning for the release of
      their husbands and sons, detained by the dictatorship, Rio
      de Janeiro, 1964   33
2.4   Commission of Military Inquiry confiscates books on
      communism and socialism, as well as books on racial
      inequality, at the University of Brasília Library, 1964   34
2.5   Costa e Silva front row, fourth from left. Delfim Neto is
      behind him, in glasses   36
2.6   Demonstrator being arrested in Belo Horizonte   38
2.7   Costa e Silva, in uniform, meeting with his cabinet in
      December 1968   39
2.8   Military Task Force searching for MAR guerrillas near
      Angra dos Reis, Brazil   42
2.9   Military Task Force searching for MAR guerrillas near Angra
      dos Reis, Brazil   43

3.1   Photo released by the ERP of Oberdan Sallustro   56
3.2   Police close a roadway to search vehicles for ERP members
during the Sallustro kidnapping   57
3.3   The Army suppresses a protest in Mendoza, 1972   65
3.4   Jailed members of ERP, Montoneros, FAL, FAP and other
groups, awaiting release after Héctor Cámpora's election
in 1973   69
3.5   Right-wing Peronists   70
3.6   Right-wing Peronists   71
3.7   Montoneros, Peronist Youth and other leftists celebrate
Perón's election in the Plaza de Mayo, 1973   71
3.8   Armed right-wing Peronists described as "police employees"
in Córdoba   74
4.1   Communists celebrate victories in municipal elections, 1971   88
4.2   Conservative women bang pots and pans in opposition to
Allende, 1971   89
4.3   The Moneda Palace in flames, September 11, 1973   92
4.4   Workers detained for violating the curfew after the coup,
November 1973   92
4.5   Prisoners being taken to the Air Force Academy for
execution, April 1974   93
4.6   At a desk in front of the Ministry of Defense, a woman
searches lists to see if her husband has been detained, 1973   94

Table

3.1   Political violence in Argentina, 1973–6   79

Series Editor's Preface

Each book in the Viewpoints/Puntos de Vista series introduces students to a significant theme or topic in Latin American history. In an age in which student and faculty interest in the Global South increasingly challenges the old focus on the history of Europe and North America, Latin American history has assumed an increasingly prominent position in undergraduate curricula.

Some of these books discuss the ways in which historians have interpreted these themes and topics, thus demonstrating that our understanding of our past is constantly changing, through the emergence of new sources, methodologies, and historical theories. Others offer an introduction to a particular theme by means of a case study or biography in a manner easily understood by the contemporary, non-specialist reader. Yet others give an overview of a major theme that might serve as the foundation of an upper-level course.

What is common to all of these books is their goal of historical synthesis. They draw on the insights of generations of scholarship on the most enduring and fascinating issues in Latin American history, while also making use of primary sources as appropriate. Each book is written by a specialist in Latin American history who is concerned with undergraduate teaching, yet who has also made his or her mark as a first-rate scholar.

The books in this series can be used in a variety of ways, recognizing the differences in teaching conditions at small liberal arts colleges, large public universities, and research-oriented institutions with doctoral programs. Faculty have particular needs depending on whether they teach large lectures with discussion sections, small lecture, or discussion-oriented classes, or large lectures with no discussion sections, and whether they teach on a semester or trimester system. The format adopted for this series fits all of these different parameters.

In this seventh volume in the Viewpoints/Puntos de Vista series, Professor Jerry Dávila of the University of Illinois at Urbana-Champaign analyzes a fascinating, yet sordid chapter in Latin American history: the Cold War-era dictatorships, with a focus on Argentina, Brazil, and Chile. The book offers a fascinating and ambitious comparison of military rule in three different countries. It focuses on several significant themes: the relationship between ideologies of economic development and political rule; the strategies of these dictatorships to maintain and expand their power; the cost of dictatorship in human terms; the nature of resistance movements; the ways in which race, class, and gender affected the lived experience under military rule; and the return to civilian rule in each of the three countries during the mid- to late 1980s.

This book is unique in its succinct comparison of military rule in South America during the period 1955 to 1989. This comparison reveals the significant differences among the three countries and allows the reader to understand the historical complexities that are often obscured by the use of labels such as "dictatorship" and "democracy." However, Dávila sees a common pattern amidst these complexities, as the dictatorships shared "a modernist belief that the state was both capable and obligated to fundamentally transform society to meet specified goals." Thus, ironically, the right-wing dictatorships of Argentina, Brazil, and Chile shared one fundamental belief with most of its critics on the left, whether social democratic or communist: the faith in government as the purveyor of modernization.

Jürgen Buchenau
University of North Carolina, Charlotte

Preface and Acknowledgements

In 1989, I worked for *The Washington Post* at the Oliver North trial, the culmination of investigations into the Reagan administration's secret sale of weapons to Iran to generate funding to back the Contra faction fighting the leftist Sandinista government in Nicaragua.

While that sentence is technically correct, it makes my job sound more formidable than it was. In reality, I had been liberated from the mailroom by the *Post* reporters covering the trial, who volunteered me to operate the photocopier the press pool, as part of the newspaper's cost-sharing for the press coverage of the trial. My job was to copy and distribute the mountains of declassified documents that were being released as trial evidence. Aside from a well-known television reporter's habit of using the paperclip tray on my copier as an ashtray, it was one of the greatest learning experiences a copy aide could have.

One lesson was immediate: a handful of the reporters in the press pool – lead *Post* reporter, George Lardner, Jr., reporters for the Associated Press, Pacifica Radio, CBS, and researchers the National Security Archive, stand out in my recollections – spent long hours poring over the documents. Together they reconstructed the declassified fragments of a wide-ranging clandestine collaboration between the Reagan administration and foreign governments that used secret arms deals to fund covert and possibly illegal policies. Congress had prohibited funding the Contra insurgency in Nicaragua, and this conspiracy allowed the Reagan administration to make some cash to spend on the side to arm the Contras. Another part of the scheme involved high-ranking U.S. officials offering U.S. aid or loans to foreign governments in exchange for discreet contributions to the Contras. The time the reporters spent with the documents, as well as their willingness to share information with each other, helped them decode a story the Reagan administration had worked hard to conceal.[1]

The other lesson became clear with time. For years during the 1980s, the investigations into Iran–Contra scandal were front-page news and anchored television newscasts. Congressional hearings displaced television programs. During the trial, the U.S. Federal District Courthouse in Washington, DC, had the vibe of the celebrity trials that would grip public attention in later years. Oliver North parlayed the attention to his trial into an unsuccessful senate campaign in Virginia and a successful career as a television personality. It was not clear then, but the trial was the end of an era in which events in Latin America, and U.S. policy toward Latin America, commanded the attention of a broad section of the public in the United States.

This era began with the Cuban Revolution in 1959. Castro's charisma, his defiance of the United States, the brinksmanship over nuclear missiles stationed by the Soviets in Cuba, and the brisk socialist transformation of the island captured the attention of people and policymakers in the United States, as it did in Latin America and the rest of the world. In the polarizing environment of the 1960s, some saw a socialist utopia being built, others saw a communist nightmare unfolding. This fascination took many forms. Between 1968 and 1972, 90 planes were hijacked from the United States to Cuba, an event that had become so common that airliners carried approach plans for the airport in Havana.[2]

This fascination was matched by U.S. government and university investments in "Area Studies": research that focused on regions of the world that were potential flash-points of the Cold War, but which were little studied by Americans. Latin American Studies programs in U.S. universities are fruit of this investment. The generation of scholars who emerged during this first impulse of building a new area of study called themselves "Fidel's children," since it was Castro's revolution that created this new attention to Latin American Studies.[3]

In the later 1960s and 1970s, military coups swept the continent. Latin America had become a laboratory of both radical reform and reaction where Argentina, Bolivia, Brazil, Chile, Ecuador, Paraguay, Peru, and Uruguay fell under military rule. In the shadow of the Watergate scandal, Congressional investigations began to uncover and document the details of U.S. government efforts to overthrow democratic regimes and support not just dictatorships but even their systems of repression. Congress passed several laws requiring U.S. presidents to report on covert assistance programs, and barring military assistance to regimes that violated human rights.

Though Jimmy Carter changed the U.S. approach to these dictatorships by criticizing their violating human rights, the election of Ronald Reagan in 1980 returned to supporting dictators and their methods as proxies in the fight against communism. In the 1980s, the United States fought the Cold War in Central America, where civil wars raged in Guatemala, El Salvador, and Nicaragua. U.S. financial and military support of one faction over another in each of these wars intensified their violence. By the end of the Cold War, peace agreements (negotiated in defiance of U.S. policy) resolved conflicts in Central America, and the generals yielded power in South America. The sense that the United States mattered in Latin America and that Latin America mattered to the United States dissipated.

The idea behind this book is to look back at a recent yet distant moment when the themes in this book loomed large. It is written with the goal of making the stakes and salience of these experiences with dictatorship make sense to contemporary readers. The stakes were enormous, and so were the costs. My hope is that this book captures the urgency of those moments.

There are many people who made this book possible. Colleagues, friends, and students shared insights, read chapters, pointed out sources, shared their work, and carried conversations that drove the project forward. Among them are Desmond Arias, Greg Childs, Ralph Della Cava, John French, Robert Funk, Daniel Cozart, Adrian Gorelick, James Green, Adam Hall, Audrey Henderson, James Hogue, Lyman Johnson, Miriam Jorge, Amy Kennemore, Victoria Langland, Jeffrey Lesser, Joe Love, Gregory Mixon, Satiro Nunes, Angela Randolpho Paiva, Anivaldo Pereira Padilha, Raanan Rein, Thomas Rogers, Karl Erik Scholhammer, Thomas Skidmore, Rachel Watts, Gregory Weeks, James Woodard, and Alexandra Lemos Zagonel. The University at North Carolina at Charlotte provided generous support for research and writing. History Department administrator Linda Smith invaluably kept the gears turning. I also thank Liv Dávila for her support at every step and her keen eye on the text, as well as Ellen and Alex for sharing their time. Finally, I thank Jürgen Buchenau, editor of the Puntos de Vista series for encouraging this project from the beginning, sustaining a lively conversation about this history, and reading several versions of the manuscript. I also thank Wiley-Blackwell editor Peter Coveney and the two generous readers whose comments made this a better book.

A few years after the Oliver North trial, I returned to the same courthouse on behalf of the *Post*, to camp out overnight for tickets to the public gallery at the trial of DC Mayor Marion Barry, so that additional *Post* reporters could sit in on the trial. Getting paid to sleep on a lawn chair in front of a federal courthouse, as if I were trying to score tickets to The Who, was its own thing. But that is a story for another preface.

Notes

1 The National Security Archive maintains collections of declassified U.S. foreign policy documents, including a collection of documents on the Iran Contra Affair, which are available both online and in print, www.gwu.edu/~nsarchiv/NSAEBB/NSAEBB210/index.htm, accessed October 14, 2012.

2 Robert T. Holden, "The Contagiousness of Aircraft Hijacking," *American Journal of Sociology*, 91:4 (1986), 879, 881.

3 Richard Graham, "Fidel's Child: A Half-Century of Doing Latin American History," *The Americas*, 68:1 (2011), 1–6.

Introduction

April 1, 1964.
September 11, 1973.
March 24, 1976.

These dates are tears in the fabric of history in Brazil, Chile, and Argentina. They are the day the armed forces of each country overturned their governments and seized power. Though these military coups reflected the culmination of years or even decades of growing political conflict, and even though each country had a long history of military interventions in politics and government, these dates inaugurated wholly new eras in these countries. In each case, this was the longest the military would hold power (between eight and twenty years), indicating a new depth in the military's distrust and resentment of politicians and civil institutions. Each of these dates opened the doors to the greatest state violence in these countries' histories. Detention, torture, murder and disappearance became tools of government. And each of these dictatorships imposed the most radical political and economic projects of these countries had seen.

It is striking that the military regimes of Argentina, Brazil, and Chile not only occurred during a shared time period, but that they also shared an excess of violence along with radical social and economic experimentation. Their shared historical moment was one in which a radical generation inspired by events like the Cuban Revolution, as well as the wars of liberation and decolonization in Africa and Asia, embraced the possibility of instant and profound national transformation. The military regimes that fought against (and sought to exterminate) these

Dictatorship in South America, First Edition. Jerry Dávila.
© 2013 Jerry Dávila. Published 2013 by Blackwell Publishing Ltd.

radicals, acquired from them a sense of the boundless possibility of profound change.

If a generation of radicals sought control of government in order to transform the country, now the military in government would attempt the same, giving radical expression to their own beliefs. Members of the armed forces and the political right were also emboldened by U.S. Cold War ideology, from which they drew the moral authority to attack their opponents. These dictatorships were products of a moment in which the left and the right shared a belief that almost anything was possible, and in which the right prevailed (at least temporarily). Both sides used the rhetoric of revolution, reorganization, and salvation.

These military dictatorships shared traits that placed them in a similar straitjacket. The armed forces were not organized to function as a national government or as the channel of political debate, yet they assumed both of these roles. What resulted were regimes that were inherently unstable and narrow-minded. Competition within the armed forces substituted traditional political competition. Shielded from oversight, the dictators and their subordinates exceeded even self-imposed limits to their authority and inevitably degenerated into corruption. These were societies in which anyone in uniform believed, with considerable impunity, that he was the dictatorship. Was the general who served as president the actual commander of the armed forces, or the representative of the armed forces? Though this question was resolved differently in each country, it loomed as a central contention about the nature of each regime.

And these regimes' nature made it inevitable that they would systematically violate the human rights of their citizens. Each came to power by defining the radical left as its foe. Each chalked up clear victories in liquidating that left. But even once the left had been decimated, each regime's national security doctrine and machinery of repression lived on, constantly looking for new targets, and etching its violence ever deeper into society. As the saying goes, if all you have is a hammer, every problem looks like a nail.

What's in a Number?

The number of victims that were tortured, killed, or disappeared by these regimes varied a great deal. In Brazil, the number is comparatively

Figure I.1   Medical Students at the University of Buenos Aires being marched to jail, August 1972.
Source: © Arquivo Nacional, Brazil.

modest: there is official recognition of 356 people killed by the regime.[1] In Chile, the number murdered ranges from 3,000 to 14,000.[2] In Argentina, the number starts at 8,960 but more frequently, 14,000 and 30,000 disappeared is invoked.[3] In Argentina one-third were women, half were between 20 and 30, and 12% were under 20. In turn, the lives taken by men in uniform in Argentina, Brazil, and Chile were part of a larger Cold War pattern in which hundreds of thousands were killed by their regimes across South America, particularly Guatemala, where 250,000 are estimated to have died, and Mexico, an ostensibly democratic country but one where counterinsurgency campaigns led to a larger number of deaths than in Brazil. So what is in a number?

The violence behind these numbers was not just an outcome of these regimes' policies. To the contrary, the violence was integral to the dictatorships: they applied their goals of national transformation by deliberately torturing, jailing, and killing their foes. The regimes transacted their internal politics on the bodies of the opposition, whether alive, missing or dead. In this context, judging the regimes on the basis of the relative numbers of deaths they inflicted is misleading. The loss of each life was significant to the victim and their relations, to the regime, and to the society the regime sought to remake by means of that violence.

The official numbers of victims are also misleadingly low: these were the number of people whose death at the hands of state agents could be fully documented by commissions of inquiry which published reports that are widely available, under the title *Nunca Más* (*Never Again, Argentina, Brazil: Never Again,* and *Never Again in Chile*). The burden of documentation in the *Nunca Más* reports meant that the number of disappeared that they reported serves simply as a starting point. These regimes often denied the existence of their crimes. The *Nunca Más* reports foreclose that fiction by presenting irrefutable evidence. By way of making sure these crimes would never happen again, as the reports' titles imply, they make unambiguously clear, often in unsettling detail, that these crimes occurred.

Disappeared

There is chilling news footage of Argentina's dictator, General Jorge Videla, answering a reporter's question about whether he would conduct an investigation into reports of disappearances perpetrated by his government.[4] In his rejection of the question, Videla revealed both the cynical machinations of a coldly bureaucratic mind and the meaning of disappearance to those who carried it out. With his arms gesturing in vague circles and speaking with circumlocution, Videla asserted that there was no investigation to be made because the people have disappeared. How could you investigate something that did not exist? No person, nothing to investigate.

This is what authoritarianism entails. Disappearance was not simply murder, since murder involves a body, a cause of death, a motive. And a murder concedes to the victim's relations the emotional and moral reprieve amid loss that comes from laying a body to rest. Disappearance was really three kinds of crimes at once. It was murder, but it was also the crime of erasing that crime. The victim and the act were both disappeared. Since the crime's existence was denied, its perpetrators, their actions, and the state's role were concealed. The sense of loss borne by the survivors of the victim was twisted into a special kind of terror brought by uncertainty over the victim's fate: could she still be alive? Where might he be? Who might be next?

Not every death was a disappearance. If the act of disappearance was a kind of message that signaled the power of the regime over its perceived enemies, there were other ways in which the regime would convey that message, and these sometimes involved a body. It was common to array the bodies of those killed in ways that suggested they were engaging in armed actions when they were killed. This exercise conveyed the message that the regime engaged in just defense against a violent threat. At other times, a body appeared in order to silence protest, or the body was a message from one faction of the regime to another: that they were the ones in control. Disappearance was one of many tools of terror in these regimes' arsenals. They learned to use torture, not just to obtain information, but to inflict terror. They carried out countless detentions unsupervised by civilian courts. At times thousands, or tens of thousands of people were detained at once. The violence was not a product of the politics, the violence was the politics.

How to Read This Book

These dictatorships share striking similarities, so it is natural to seek common threads among them. And there is much that we gain from considering these regimes together, as this book does. But the opposite is also true: the more closely we look, the better we see that these dictatorships were the fruit of national historical trajectories that were quite distinct.

An example of the ways these regimes can be taken together, and yet were profoundly different, is the role the judiciary played within them, as Anthony Pereira shows in *Political (In)Justice*. Pereira distinguishes between the relationships of each nation's courts to their dictatorships, and this distinction helps explain the different degrees of political violence perpetrated by the regimes. At one end of the spectrum, Brazilian courts generally collaborated with the regime's national security laws, recognizing the regime's ongoing changes to the constitutional framework and frequently convicting individuals prosecuted by the regime. At the other end of the spectrum, the generals in Argentina's *Proceso* looked back with dismay at the manner in which the civilian government elected in 1973 released the prisoners convicted by the preceding dictatorship (1966–73). As a result, their security services tended to kill rather than prosecute perceived enemies of the regime. In between was the Chilean experience: since the military had few ties to the judiciary, it initially resorted to extrajudicial execution. As the Pinochet regime gained confidence in the judiciary's willingness to protect the regime's interests, the violence unleashed in 1973 diminished and prosecutions increased.

There are a few questions to keep in mind which help us understand these patterns:

- To what extent are regimes comparable? How does comparison help us understand the regimes?
- Despite their deep antagonism, do you see connections between leftist movements and right-wing dictatorships that bear scrutiny?
- How significant were political ideology and political culture to the inception and character of these regimes?
- How did these authoritarian regimes radicalize? And what factors drove "decompression"?
- How did economic factors shape the history of the dictatorships? Is this the area where we can best connect the three historical experiences?
- How do studies of the experience of racial and ethnic minorities, of gender, or of labor movements help us better understand the history of these dictatorships?

A good way to step into these questions is to consider the tension between politics and economics. An influential school of thought defined by Argentine political scientist Guillermo O'Donnell suggested that these regimes resulted from a stage of dependent capitalist development shared by each country. In this phase of development, pressure for redistribution from economically and politically marginalized popular classes were checked by dominant groups who protected the privileges they drew from their relationship with international capital.

The key to O'Donnell's analysis is his emphasis on the interactions of economic and political groups. The populist projects carried out under Juan Perón in Argentina (1946–55 and 1973), or João Goulart (1961–4) in Brazil, favored nationalization of industry, assertion of worker rights, price controls, and restrictions on foreign companies' ability to remit profits home. Foreign and domestic business, and members of the traditional economic elite, responded to the anxiety and uncertainty this created by shifting their investments from productive to speculative areas, producing what O'Donnell calls a "plunder economy," undermining national economies.[5] The crises faced in Brazil in 1964, in Argentina in 1966 and 1976, and in Chile in 1973 (where powerful economic groups reacted with even deeper anxiety to President Salvador Allende's socialist project), were examples of this kind of behavior by powerful groups who felt threatened.

The military interventions that followed these crises in Argentina, Brazil, and Chile were "bureaucratic-authoritarian," meaning that the armed forces established regimes that ostensibly gave autonomy to technocrats to restore political and economic order so that private enterprise could again invest safely and productively. O'Donnell cautions us that this stability was an illusion: that these regimes reflected their societies, were shaped by national political cultures, and were captive to powerful interest groups. And their economic policymaking resulted in crises deeper than those they sought to arrest: business groups and powerful families did not only resort to speculative plunder when leftist or populist politics produced anxiety, they responded the same to economic anxieties triggered by right-wing dictatorships as well. O'Donnell uses social class as an organizing element of his analysis, and sees the political context as being created by a country's economic situation.

A different way to understand the regimes is to unpack the generals' vision, as well as the mindset of the technocrats that were integral to bureaucratic-authoritarian regimes. When we do this, we see the dictatorships as the fruit of a modernist belief that the state was both capable and obligated to fundamentally transform society to meet specified goals. U.S. political scientist James Scott calls this "seeing like a state" by reordering natural, social, political, economic and cultural landscapes to reflect an ideal.[6] The economic factors explored by O'Donnell are of great significance, but these regimes are no less a product of the hubris of their leaders, who were emboldened by the radical utopianism of the Latin American left of the 1960s and 1970s that they endeavored to form utopias framed by their own world-views.

Transition governments at the end of military rule faced the largely disastrous consequences of the armed forces' belief that they could govern autonomously, generate stability and transform their nations. Civilian governments in Argentina in 1983 and Brazil in 1985 faced economic crises far deeper than the armed forces had reacted to in the first place, while the civilian government taking office in Chile in 1990 found itself in the free-market straitjacket bequeathed by dictator Augusto Pinochet. These civilian governments had to confront these

8   *Introduction*

challenges through governing practices and political institutions whose legitimacy had been battered by authoritarianism. Together, O'Donnell and Scott help us see not just the dictatorships, but also the democratic transitions, as a confluence of economic factors and radical ideology. These two readings of this history frame a classic debate over the primacy of social and economic factors versus the role of politics and ideology. *Dictatorship in South America* will surely not settle the debate (and it would not be fruitful to do so). But keeping the debate in mind is a good way to read the pages ahead.

Notes

1 The number comes from the Ministry of Justice Special Secretariat for Human Rights, *Direito à memória e à verdade* (Ministry of Justice, 2007), and revises the earlier report of the Archdiocese of São Paulo compiled in *Brasil Nunca Mais*, which documented 125. *Torture in Brazi: A Shocking Report on the Pervasive Use of Torture by Brazilian Military Governments, 1964–1979* (University of Texas Press [1979], 1998), 205.
2 *Nunca Más en Chile: Síntesis correigda y actualizada del Informe Rettig* (LOM, 1991, 1999).
3 Pilar Calveiro, *Política y/o violencia: Una aproximación a la guerrilla de los años 70* (Norma, 2005), 189; *Poder y desaparición: los campos de concentración en Argentina* (Colihue, 2006), 29; *Nunca Más: The Report of the Argentine National Commission on the Disappeared* (Argentine National Commission of the Disappeared, 1986), 284–5.
4 www.youtube.com/watch?v=9MPZKG4Prog, accessed October 14, 2012.
5 Cited in David Lehman, "A Latin American Political Scientist," *Latin American Research Review*, 24:2 (1989), 189.
6 James C. Scott, *Seeing Like a State: How Certain Schemes to Improve the Human Condition Have Failed* (Yale University Press, 1998).

1

Dependency, Development, and Liberation

Latin America in the Cold War

How does a country develop? Is economic development simply created by a free marketplace? Or is it possible to accelerate development by guiding the market? If so, how can a government engineer that development? In the twentieth century, these were among the most pressing questions facing Latin America, and the answers to them had enormous consequences.

At the beginning of the century, liberalism was the predominant political and economic ideology in Latin America. It entailed constitutional republican government whose role was to preserve order, protect private property, and promote free trade. In practice, this meant that a handful of people controlled farmland, mines, mills, and the labor to exploit them. This minority profited by exporting agricultural commodities and minerals, while importing manufactured goods. It was a system that placed great wealth in a few hands, and its critical integer was cheap labor. The patrons of the economic system were also the directors of the political system.

By the middle decades of the century, social groups including women, urban workers, and rural laborers, pressed for political and economic inclusion. At the same time, Latin Americans began to ask whether it was possible to catch up with wealthy, powerful, and industrialized nations like the United States, Britain, Germany, or Japan. The dual impulses of political inclusion and economic growth were interrelated, and a new kind of politician, populists, learned to tap the groundswell of new voters and the appeal of economic development. Populist politicians cultivated a mass following by promising rights to workers, access to health and

Dictatorship in South America, First Edition. Jerry Dávila.
© 2013 Jerry Dávila. Published 2013 by Blackwell Publishing Ltd.

education, industrialization, and rising wages. In Brazil, Getúlio Vargas played this role in the 1950s, building on the base of labor legislation and state sanctioned unions he created during 15 years of mostly dictatorial rule (1930–45). Argentina had one of the most charismatic populists, Juan Perón (1946–55). Chile, by contrast, had little populist experience because traditional political parties expanded their appeal to workers, producing electoral competition between its center Christian Democratic Party and leftist groups like the Socialist Party, which culminated in the presidential election of Salvador Allende (1970–3).

By the end of the Second World War, Latin Americans faced a transcendent question: what is the path to development? And this question begat two difficult ones: Who bears the costs? And who reaps the rewards? The answers to the first question reflected a broad consensus: the state must act where the market had failed to propel economic development. But the second set of questions were divisive: any development plan confronted the gulf between those who traditionally held wealth and political power, and those who did not.

What did development mean? It was the response to underdevelopment, which had many facets. Economically, underdevelopment meant reliance on export agriculture sustained by impoverished rural laborers, as well as reliance on imported technology, manufactured goods, and capital. It also meant deficient infrastructure. Take Brazil as an example: much of its territory was unreachable by road. Its rail lines and highways were inadequate and badly conserved. The reach of electricity, telephone, telegraph, as well as water and sewer treatment was restricted to urban areas in a country where the majority of the national territory and population were rural. Politically and socially, it meant weak institutions with a limited reach. Education and access to healthcare were restricted: in 1950, 57% of Brazilians were illiterate (and consequently lacked the right to vote). The armed forces lacked capacity, training, and equipment. Adding to these challenges, Brazil's population was exploding: Of 52 million inhabitants in 1950, more than half were under the age of 20.

"Developmentalism" was the art of correcting underdevelopment. Among 1950s U.S. intellectuals, modernization theory was an especially influential vision of development which was based on the assumption that underdeveloped societies faced a lag relative to developed societies. It presumed a linear path of evolution in which the United States sat hierarchically above Latin America. Under this model, which became the logic of U.S. foreign assistance programs during much of the Cold War (1945–90), societies like Argentina, Brazil, and Chile should embark on projects to become more like the United States. Understandably, this model appealed to mid-century U.S. intellectuals and policymakers. In Latin America, modernization theory and its colonialist implications, held less sway.

The most powerful diagnoses of underdevelopment and its remedies came from Latin America itself, especially the social scientists associated with the United Nations Economic Commission for Latin America (ECLA), headquartered in Santiago, Chile, and directed between 1950 and 1963 by Argentine economist Raúl Prebisch. Prebisch's approach, structuralism, interpreted the world as divided between a core (countries which were capital rich and industrialized), and a periphery (poor countries which relied on exports of raw materials, and were politically and economically vulnerable to the influence of core nations). For Prebisch, Latin American countries could not industrialize just by following liberal free-market rules. Instead, industrialization needed a push by the state through a process called import-substitution industrialization (ISI). This could be achieved through tariff barriers to keep imports out, as well as state financing or even ownership of industry. Prebisch's ideas were a located between liberal thought and more radical developmentalist thinking. For instance, he believed ISI had to be balanced with private ownership, free trade, and limited public spending.

Prebisch's approach became a springboard for a new interpretation of development and underdevelopment called dependency theory, pioneered by later generations of social scientists affiliated with ECLA. Dependency theorists offered a new diagnosis of the conditions that made that role necessary: industrialized countries in the northern hemisphere prevented the industrialization of countries in the southern hemisphere. Dependency theory was largely the opposite of modernization theory: it saw the terms of the relationship of countries like Argentina to countries like the United States as a perverse engine that inhibited development and reinforced inequality in Latin America. It was also pessimistic that development could be achieved under capitalism.

Dependency theorists drew from Marxism as well as from Prebisch's structuralism. They believed the relationship between core and periphery trapped Latin America in poverty and underdevelopment. Specifically, trade between the United States and countries like Argentina, Brazil, or

Chile was governed by "unequal exchange" between the low value of agricultural and mineral exports relative to the high value of manufactured imports. This unequal exchange was dynamic: over time, the value of agricultural goods continued to decrease relative to the value of industrial goods.[1] In other words, Chile would have to export many, many grapes in order for a few Chileans to afford a car imported from the United States. In turn, exporting cars meant that many more people in the United States could afford Chilean grapes. Dependency theory explained that this growing differential trapped these countries in underdevelopment.

The solution to this problem, according to structuralists and dependency theorists was to replace the free-market doctrine of promoting the export of commodities for which they had a comparative market advantage (like coffee or copper) with policies such as ISI, fostering the creation of domestic industry. Dependency theorists went further, stressing social and economic reforms to combat poverty, such as land redistribution. These perspectives were widely shared: Prebisch was Argentine, Chile was the host of ECLA, and many influential dependency theorists were Brazilian, including Celso Furtado, who would serve as minister of planning (1962–3) and Fernando Henrique Cardoso, who would be the first elected Brazilian president to serve his full term after the end of military rule (1994–2002), though by this point he had renounced the theories he pioneered. Not all Latin Americans were dependency theorists, and disputes about the path to development paved the road to dictatorship, as three examples show.

In Brazil, the debate over oil exploration exemplified divergent paths to development. Nationalists like populist Getúlio Vargas rallied around the slogan "the oil is ours!" and sought to create a state monopoly to control the new industry. Since oil was a strategic resource, it should not be owned by foreigners, nor should foreigners reap the profits from extracting and refining Brazilian oil for Brazilian consumers. Conservative opponents argued for foreign investment: it was foreign companies, not the state, which had the capital and the technology to develop the oil industry. The outcome was a compromise: a new state company, Petrobras, held a monopoly over extraction but shared refining and distribution with private (mostly foreign) companies. The debate over oil reflected the ongoing political struggle over the development.

In Argentina, populist Juan Perón nationalized industries and pushed ISI to a degree well beyond that advocated by structuralists and dependency theorists. Prebisch disagreed with Perón's takeover of the Central Bank (which Prebisch had directed from 1935 until 1943) and resigned his faculty position at the University of Buenos Aires in 1947 when the university refused to remove his name from a list of supporters of Perón's economic plans.[2] Peronists and leftists in Argentina disdained Prebisch's approach because of its emphasis on private ownership of industry, foreign investment, and economic stability.

Among these leaders, Salvador Allende took the most radical path to breaking economic dependency. His 1970 electoral program explained "Chile is a capitalist country, dependent on the imperialist nations and dominated by bourgeois groups who are structurally related to foreign capital and cannot resolve the country's fundamental problems."[3] Allende's approach went beyond the prescriptions of structuralists and dependency theorists like his friend Prebisch. He pursued socialization of the economy through nationalization of banks, utilities and the foreign-owned copper industry (which accounted for the 80% of Chile's exports and was primarily held by U.S. Anaconda Mining), as well as accelerated redistribution of land. Politically, these economic changes would be matched by a process of empowering workers and communities to make local decisions. This would be a new historical course, liberating Chile from dependency on foreign capital and its domestic allies. Allende called it the Chilean Road to Socialism.

The Cold War in Latin America

The debate over development was intensified by the U.S. Cold War doctrine of containment, which sought to prevent the spread of communism beyond Eastern Europe and the Soviet Union. The United States pressed Latin American countries to adhere to free-market policies, provide a supportive environment for U.S. business, and reject Marxism and Socialism. The United States counted on the support of traditionally wealthy and powerful social classes in Latin America whose fortunes were often tied to trade with the United States or to American business interests. The United States also cultivated Latin American armed forces by providing training, financing, and equipment. U.S influence was not just overwhelming, when necessary it was enforced with violence, either by supporting military coups or through occasional direct military intervention.

The United States and its allies within Latin America used a wide brush to paint populism, developmentalism, and nationalism red. Much of the Latin American political and economic spectrum – ranging from moderate developmentalists like Prebisch to populist nationalists like Juan Perón and Getúlio Vargas, to Socialists like Salvador Allende, and beyond them to the revolutionary Marxist left – faced U.S. antagonism. U.S. policymakers defended archaic social, economic and political orders that reflected legacies of exclusion and exploitation that were often inherited from the colonial era. This alliance resulted in the violent suppression of social movements and radicalization of those seeking social change.

U.S. Cold War policy in Latin America varied in its nature and degree. In the Caribbean and Central America, the United States often employed direct intervention, such as orchestrating the military coup that deposed the reformist president of Guatemala, Jacobo Arbenz (1954), and inva-

Figure 1.1   Soldiers marching beneath a Chevrolet advertisement during the Brazilian military coup, 1964.
Source: © Arquivo Nacional, Brazil.

sions of the Dominican Republic (1965), Grenada (1983), and Panama (1989), as well as a failed invasion of Cuba (1961). South American countries were not in the direct shadow of the United States. Since the United States could not impose its objectives as directly, it worked through allies among the armed forces as well as domestic and international business groups. U.S. companies became proxies for U.S. foreign policy: Ford and General Motors funded secret police and death squads in Argentina and Brazil. International Telephone and Telegraph (ITT) supported groups seeking to overthrow Chile's Allende.

The 1959 Cuban Revolution was a watershed. Cuba's economy was closely tied to the United States and its political system was shaped by repeated U.S. intervention. Fidel Castro's movement had a clear goal among its initial objectives: attaining autonomy from the United States Castro adhered to Marxism only gradually as his regime distanced itself from the U.S and carried out social and economic reforms. Since the Cuban economy was vulnerable to sanctions imposed by the U.S. government, Castro pursued a relationship with the Soviet Union that was cemented by the failed U.S. attempt to land a military force of Cuban exiles at the Bay of Pigs in 1961, followed 18 months later by the Cuban missile crisis. Yet Castro bristled at trading one form of dependency for another. Often in defiance of the Soviet Union, Castro supported revolutionary movements in Latin America and Africa in order to create a block of liberated nations that could become politically and economically autonomous from both the United States and the Soviet Union.

For the left, and particularly among university students, the Cuban Revolution suggested that the transformation of a society to alleviate historic injustices could be done with heroic speed. Underdevelopment could be vanquished through more direct means than those advocated by developmentalists like Prebisch. The revolutionary regime nationalized industries and large farms, implemented reforms protecting the poor from landlords, created a socialist economy, eliminated malnutrition by rationing and equitably distributing food, eradicated illiteracy, and made education and healthcare free and universally accessible. These achievements were the envy of social reformers across Latin America. What was more, the Cuban Revolution seemed to show that insurgency could be a successful path to power, and that once in power, leftists could quickly and decisively transform a society.

For the right, the Cuban Revolution inspired fear and intensified its willingness (present long before 1959) to violate the constitutional order to preserve the social and economic order. For the United States, it seemed to validate the Containment Doctrine. For Latin American armed forces, the revolution expanded the meaning of national security to incorporate action within national borders and against their own citizens, and intensified the stakes of that struggle. Castro had executed the officers of the president he deposed, so Latin American military officers saw their struggle against insurgencies as a fight to the death: they would not surrender to revolutionary groups out of fear they would be dealt the same hand.

The trajectory of Che Guevara reflects the dynamics of revolution. An Argentine doctor, Guevara traveled to Guatemala with an interest in Arbenz's reforms. He fled to Mexico after the U.S.-backed coup and met Fidel Castro. When Castro mounted his insurgency in Cuba, Guevara became the movement's strategist. In revolutionary Cuba, Guevara implement his far-ranging ideals for creating a more just society by seeking to eliminate the profit motive as an economic engine out of the belief that profit engendered exploitation. As minister of industry, Guevara's ideals proved ruinous. Guevara left to continue supporting movements for liberation, first in Zaire, then in Bolivia, where he was captured and killed by troops trained by the United States.

The methods of guerrilla war proposed by Guevara, and refined by French collaborator Régis Debray, called for the creation of rural *focos* (flash points) that, because of their isolation, made guerrilla groups hard to find and defeat. Their objective was not to defeat the regime in power through direct military confrontation (this was an unlikely prospect). Instead, guerrilla actions should educate the public about the nature of the struggle and build opposition to the regime. A guerrilla movement's goal was to induce the regime to resort to repressive actions that would undermine its legitimacy, lead to mass opposition, and induce its collapse. Movements using *foco* tactics proliferated. But if insurgents read Guevara's manual, *Guerrilla Warfare,* so too did soldiers training in counterinsurgency. As the methods became more common, the armed forces became better prepared and the chances for successful guerrilla campaigns dwindled.

The Cuban Revolution transformed U.S. policy in Latin America. It prompted U.S. officials to rethink the significance of development: if aid to development could alleviate social inequalities and poverty, perhaps support for radical movements in Latin America would diminish. The Kennedy administration created the Alliance for Progress program

(1961–73), which was influenced by structuralism and collaborated with ECLA. The Alliance for Progress invested billions of dollars in infrastructure projects, support for land redistribution, literacy campaigns, and the development of domestic industry, across Latin America. In the 1950s, Brazilian President Juscelino Kubitschek (1956–60) had urged the U.S. government to provide this kind of development aid to Latin America but was ignored. After the Cuban Revolution, the Alliance for Progress was too late and too limited to reshape the landscape of conflict.

Alongside development aid, the U.S. government increased military assistance such as counterinsurgency training, and supported military conspirators seeking to overthrow democratic governments. During the 1964 military coup in Brazil, for instance, the U.S. Navy sent fuel and supply ships to the Brazilian coastline to aid the conspirators if they encountered resistance. This support was followed by extensive financial and technical assistance to military regimes. The U.S. armed forces and CIA offered training in interrogation and torture. An infamous example was former FBI agent Dan Mitrione, who was sent to Brazil and Uruguay by the U.S. Agency for International Development to teach electroshock torture. His techniques, he said, inflicted "the precise pain, in the precise place, in the precise amount, for the desired effect."[4] He was kidnapped and executed by the Uruguayan Marxist guerrilla group Tupamaros in 1970. (The Tupamaros' kidnapping of Mitrione became the subject of a remarkable film by Costa-Gavras, *State of Siege*, which was filmed in Chile in the months before its military coup).

A key figure in the U.S. relationship with South American dictators was Henry Kissinger, the architect of U.S. foreign policy under presidents Richard Nixon and Gerald Ford (1969–77). Kissinger saw the dictatorships in Argentina, Brazil, and Chile as vehicles for promoting U.S. interests. He coordinated the "invisible blockade" against Salvador Allende's government in Chile (1970–3) and conspired to see him deposed. After the 1973 military coup, Kissinger privately reassured Chilean dictator Augusto Pinochet that his government was not concerned about the human rights abuses perpetrated by the new regime. When the military Junta seized power in Argentina in 1976, Kissinger urged the generals to conduct their wave of terror quickly before international opposition mounted. When Brazilian General Emilio Garrastazu Médici (1969–74) visited Washington at the height of the Brazilian dictatorship's repression of the opposition, Kissinger declared that where Brazil led, Latin America would follow.

Kissinger's support for these dictatorships was based on his assessment that U.S. power was receding. The Vietnam War, and the 1973 Oil Embargo and the impeachment process of Richard Nixon diminished the foreign influence of the U.S. government. In this context, stable, anticommunist regimes like those in South America provided relief for American foreign policy. For Kissinger, the human rights toll of these regimes' actions was incidental to the strategic and political significance the regimes represented for the United States.[5]

But the U.S. relationship with these regimes was more complex. As human rights violations mounted, Latin American political exiles, U.S. scholars, church groups and politicians applied pressure on the U.S. government for supporting these regimes. One outcome was the congressional investigation led by Idaho Senator Frank Church, which documented U.S. government and business support for the coup in Chile that resulted in Allende's death and the installation of that country's Junta. Public pressure also resulted in laws that tied U.S. military aid to human rights and required Congressional approval for covert military assistance (a law President Ronald Reagan skirted, triggering the Iran–Contra scandal in the early 1980s).

Opposition to dictatorships over the question of human rights became sufficiently extensive in the United States that Jimmy Carter made it a prominent part of his presidential campaign in 1976. As president, Carter changed the course of U.S. foreign policy in Latin America by advocating the defense of human rights. Latin American dictators were skeptical. Brazilian President Ernesto Geisel (1974–9) saw Carter's criticism of Brazilian human rights violations as a simple effort to re-assert influence. Geisel saw as proof of this the fact that Carter's willingness to criticize the regimes' human rights violations was not matched by criticism of his country's role in those abuses. In 1977, the U.S. Congress assumed the role of reviewing military agreements with foreign countries to ensure human rights were respected. Geisel responded by canceling the Military Assistance Agreement in place between Brazil and the United States since 1952.

The United States had played an important role in creating the conditions under which these dictatorships came into being, and provided critical support even to the most violent aspects of these regimes. Later, under pressure from human rights advocates at home, the United States government pressured the regimes to respect human rights. Yet in the case of each of these regimes, the United States' role was important but not decisive. These regimes' origins, their endurance, opposition to them, and their end were first and foremost, homegrown. What was more effective than U.S. foreign policy in undermining the dictatorships was the economic factor. The confluence of oil costs, high interest rates, and a global recession between 1979 and 1982, and Argentina's calamitous invasion of the Falkland Islands, were the most significant external factors in ending the dictatorships in Argentina, Brazil, and Chile. Internal factors were also critical: the increasingly effective ways in which the political opposition learned to contain and gradually roll back these dictatorships.

Notes

1 Joseph Love, "Raúl Prebisch and the Origin of the Doctrine of Unequal Exchange," *Latin American Research Review*, 15:3 (1980), 46.

2 Edgar J. Dosman, *The Life and Times of Raúl Prebisch, 1901–1986* (McGill-Queen's University Press, 2010).

3 Cited in Brian Loveman, *Chile: The Legacy of Hispanic Capitalism* (Oxford University Press, 2001), 246.

4 William Blum, *Killing Hope: U.S. Military and CIA Interventions Since World War II* (Common Courage, 1995), 203.

5 There is an extensive collection of declassified documents related to Kissinger's involvement in Latin America available online at the National Security Archive, www.gwu.edu/~nsarchiv/NSAEBB/index.html, accessed October 14, 2012.

2

Brazil

What Road to Development?

General Golbery do Couto e Silva, the intellectual architect of Brazil's dictatorship, laid out an ambitious goal: building "a healthy and strengthened economic sector that is better protected from adverse foreign pressures and which provides a solid infrastructure both for the greatness of Brazil as a twenty-first-century world power, and for the creation of a more just society in terms of income distribution, wealthier, and less vulnerable to cycles of corrosive crises."[1]

Nowhere did the ethos of developmentalism loom larger than in Brazil. It is hard to imagine a country with a deeper sense of making itself. The mindset of developmentalism permeated the visions of Brazilians across the ideological spectrum. The terms of development were the arena in which they acted out their rivalry. Behind the political upheaval Brazil experienced in the decades preceding military rule, and the dictatorship's violent struggle with its opponents, lay strikingly shared faith in the state as a catalyst. During the Second World War, Austrian refugee Stefan Zweig called his host country, Brazil: the "land of the future."[2] What remained was the question of who would guide the state, and how it would make the future.

When the armed forces seized power in 1964, the generals carried a set of tools that shaped the ways they governed: a sense of mission which held that the armed forces were a moderating power that would right Brazil's course in times of calamity; experience bringing that power to bear in national politics; and a belief that economic development and national security were entwined. Late nineteenth-century officers were

Dictatorship in South America, First Edition. Jerry Dávila.
© 2013 Jerry Dávila. Published 2013 by Blackwell Publishing Ltd.

among the most ardent proponents of positivism, an ideology that advocated national progress through scientific and technical innovation, as well as rationalization of society. The slogan on Brazil's flag, adopted in 1889, uses positivist language: "order and progress." In the twentieth century, these ideas materialized in two critical ways.

First, the armed forces adopted a broad definition of national security. Drawing lessons from the First World War, military strategists understood Brazil to be woefully unable to conduct "total war" which mobilized all of a nation's resources. Brazil's industry was nascent and war material was largely imported. The country depended on foreign capital. Land transportation was precarious or nonexistent in many areas. Brazil's soldiers struggled to suppress civilian revolts. Much of the population, including soldiers, was illiterate and addled by endemic diseases. The military saw these weaknesses as threats to national security.

Second, officers became restive over politics. The leaders of Brazil's Republican regime (1891–1930) seemed content to limit government to preserving order and the planter classes' exports. In the 1920s, junior officers known as the *tenentes* (lieutenants) revolted to protest a government that they saw as unwilling and unable to meet the nation's challenges. Their revolts fit a history of military intervention in politics that culminated in the 1964 coup. This role began in 1889 when the armed forces deposed Emperor Pedro II, who had ruled since 1840, to install a republican regime. The coup created a new model of action that drew the armed forces into a succession of interventions in politics (1889, 1930, 1937, 1945, 1954, 1955, 1961, and 1964).

The military interventions forced political changes reflected in redrafted constitutions. The 1889 coup led to the republican 1891 constitution. When the military installed Getúlio Vargas as president in 1930, it initiated a reform process culminating in the 1934 constitution. Reticent about the politics that ensued, the armed forces backed Vargas' *autogolpe* (a coup dismissing his own government and forming a dictatorship) and the promulgation of an authoritarian 1937 constitution. In 1945, the armed forces deposed Vargas, leading to the 1946 constitution, which restored the democratic system established in 1934. The generals that seized power in 1964 consolidated their regime through the 1967 constitution. The post-dictatorship constitution ratified in 1988 was the country's seventh (its fifth in the twentieth century alone).

A Military Mindset: Edmundo Macedo Soares

The generals coming to power in 1964 were part of a generation which had experienced the *tenente* revolts of the 1920s, the central state building under Vargas, combat experience in the Second World War, and finally, the series of interventions borne by Cold War mistrust of populism. They differed over key questions: some officers were disdainful of politicians and ready to act against the government, even if it meant breaking the military chain of command, while others valued the maintenance of constitutional legality and military hierarchy. They disagreed about models of development. For instance, some of the *tenentes* became leading members of Brazil's Communist Party, while others joined Brazil's fascist movements.

Still, the generals agreed on much. They favored infrastructure projects like road building to integrate the country, as well as heavy industry and energy production. They were pro-American (many forged personal ties within the U.S. armed forces while fighting in Europe), but they wanted their country to be less dependent on the United States They saw populism as demagoguery, so they favored the appearance of apolitical leadership and administration by technocrats. They believed in the free market and courted foreign investment, but subordinated these to industrialization and development that they saw as integral to national security.

General Edmundo Macedo Soares' career traces the life of this mindset within Brazil's armed forces, and its power over the generation of officers who governed after 1964. He had been a rebellious lieutenant in 1922, yet ended his career on the board of directors of General Electric in the 1980s. Like many in his cohort, Macedo Soares had an early immersion in a military culture, attending an Army high school in Rio de Janeiro and graduating from the national military academy in 1921. He took part in the first *tenente* revolt, an act for which he was sentenced to prison. In 1925, he escaped to France, where he studied metallurgy.

Macedo Soares returned to Brazil after the military installed Vargas as president in 1930. He became the main planner studying the development of a steel industry. Vargas leveraged a Second World War alliance with the United States to accelerate industrialization. In return for land leases for airbases, and the deployment of Brazilian troops alongside the

U.S. V Army in Italy, the U.S. government provided financing and technical expertise for building a national steel complex. Macedo Soares became technical director of the U.S.-financed steel complex being built in Volta Redonda and oversaw its construction.[3]

After the armed forces deposed Vargas in 1945, Macedo Soares served as federal Minister of Transportation and Public Works and was appointed governor of Rio de Janeiro state, where Volta Redonda was located. He became director of a new state-owned motor factory, a critical piece of Brazil's nascent automotive industry. After he retired from active duty in 1952, General Macedo Soares circulated through the boards of directors of the diversifying array of state companies that formed part of Brazil's growing steel industry. He participated in planning commissions and took on his first private sector role as vice-president of Mercedes-Benz of Brazil, a pioneer in domestic truck manufacturing.

Macedo Soares supported the 1964 coup and under military rule he continued to shape the realm of planning commissions, state-owned enterprises, private corporations and associations of industrialists that defined Brazil's industrial sector. In 1968, as minister of commerce, he was one of the signers of Institutional Act 5, the military decree that closed Congress and suspended civil liberties. In 1969, he returned to the private sector, becoming president of Mercedes of Brasil. For the remainder of his career, he would serve on the boards of many of the largest industrial manufacturers in Brazil, ranging from Mercedes to General Electric and Volkswagen.

Macedo Soares' trajectory resembled that of his generation of officers. They did not fully hew to either the liberal or leftist models of development. Unlike the Chilean dictatorship's free-market ideologues, Macedo Soares believed the state played a preeminent role in fomenting development through planning, administration, capitalization, and protection of industry. Even his private sector positions were in foreign firms that operated in Brazil because they participated in an industrial complex built and coordinated by the state. By pursuing foreign capital and technology, his nationalism also differed from the formula advanced by Brazil's left. Macedo Soares was the avatar of a distinct Brazilian form of state capitalism intended to accelerate industrial development. He subordinated free market to the goal of industrialization. In pursuing this goal, he brooked no challenge to Brazil's access to foreign capital, markets, and technology.

Development and Democracy

By the 1950s, Brazilian industrialization gained momentum, but a destabilizing political and military conflict over the path of development had also taken root. Was development best pursued through foreign investment, stable currency, and restrictions on wages, as the political right believed? Or did state-mandated increases in wage tables and national ownership of key industries result in more equitable development and a break in the cycle of dependency?

Under the rules of the 1946 constitution, literate men and women (except for enlisted servicemen) gained the right to vote. New voters, many organized by unions, favored populists who promised higher wages, social welfare, and development through state ownership of industries and utilities. For conservatives, who found common cause with many officers, populism and its appeal were threats: increased wages diminished profits, nationalization of industry repelled foreign investment, and inciting workers might spark a social revolution.

Getúlio Vargas returned to the presidency in 1951 as a populist. Mistrustful of populism, the armed forces and conservatives conspired to overthrow him. In 1954, the war minister presented Vargas an ultimatum: resign or be removed. Vargas shot himself, leaving behind a suicide letter condemning "the agents against the people, who have organized and unleashed themselves again upon me ... to keep me from continuing to defend, as I always have, the people, especially its most poor." He detailed his defense of wages and the nationalization of industries. He declared that because of his martyrdom, the people "will no longer be anyone's slave."[4]

The coalition against Vargas next tried to block the president elected in 1955 from taking office. Physician and governor Juscelino Kubitschek won the presidency with the same support that had elected Vargas. A legalist faction in the armed forces prevailed over officers mobilized against Kubitschek, allowing him to take office. Kubitschek was the last democratically elected president to leave office at the end of his constitutional term until 2002, so his path to development and his strategy for dealing with the armed forces are instructive. He pursued development that nurtured his popular appeal but met national security goals. He drew officers into management of his project and invested in modernizing military facilities and equipment. Though middle-rank officers rumbled with insurrection, none moved the military commanders.

Kubitschek's agility was evident in his purchase of an obsolete British aircraft carrier, renamed for his home state, *Minas Gerais*. Until then, Navy officers refused to even recognize him. Kubitschek remarked "With the aircraft carrier, I will cease to be the Navy's enemy."[5] More than placating the Navy, he precipitated a politically valuable debate about naval aviation: did carrier landing rights belong to the Navy or the Air Force? Both claimed it and fought over it for years – a dispute resolved only after the 1964 coup, when President Castelo Branco allocated the landing rights to the Air Force. The true tactical value of the carrier was political rather than military, and it ended its long life in 2004, when the Navy listed the obsolete hulk on eBay.

The savvy that Kubitschek demonstrated with the aircraft carrier defined his broader vision of governing. He campaigned on the slogan "50 years [of progress] in 5," through investments in infrastructure and industrialization. These would be executed through a plan that called for the creation of a new capital, Brasília, in the center of the country and the creation of new industries capable of producing cars, trucks, and tractors. Kubitschek's opponents responded that he would bring "50 years inflation in 5." There was truth to both interpretations.

Brasília was the centerpiece of Kubitschek's development project. Moving the capital from Rio de Janeiro to a new city in the interior placated the military by integrating territory it saw as vulnerable. The new capital also spurred development by serving as the hub of thousands of miles of new roads, a national electrical grid, and telecommunications systems. The frenzy of construction of the capital and the infrastructure connecting it to the rest of the country increased employment and consumption. Brasília's modernist architecture, and the bold names of its main features – the presidential residence was called the Palácio da Alvorada (Palace of the Dawn) – nourished a sense that Brazilians were mastering their destiny. The urban design featured an innovative road system that avoided traffic lights through the prolific use of ramps. From the sky, Brasília resembled an aircraft. Brasília was a capital befitting the "land of the future."

Kubitschek's projects were expensive, but they enabled him to manage the pressures on the presidency. He promoted this approach as an alternative to more radical solutions, and urged the U.S. government to create a program of development aid for Latin America akin to what he put into practice in Brazil. Eisenhower rebuffed the idea, though it later inspired the Alliance for Progress program. Still, development costs outpaced foreign investment and the revenue from Brazil's exports, which spurred inflation and depleted the government's currency reserves.

In 1959 the U.S. government refused to back a loan requested by Kubitschek, insisting he first implement a stabilization plan by the International Monetary Fund (IMF). The IMF proposed cuts in public spending, increased interest rates, and wage restrictions, which would tame inflation but induce a recession. Kubitschek refused: the plan would make it impossible to balance Brazil's political demands. But his unwillingness to absorb the costs of his policies placed succeeding governments at a disadvantage. His successors faced inflation, capital flight, and painful choices that could no longer be eased through the kind of lavish spending Kubitschek had employed.

Jânio Quadros, who succeeded Kubitchek in 1961, seemed suited to the challenge. He was the popular mayor and governor from São Paulo, where he claimed to have rooted out corruption. The UDN, the conservative party that been beaten in national elections by Vargas and Kubitschek, seized upon Quadros as a candidate who could win the presidency. His victory was a hollow win for the UDN: Quadros quickly fell out with its congressional leaders. Neither Quadros nor the UDN found a path toward economic stabilization. Quadros became more politically isolated and as his legislative agenda stalled. He drank heavily and behaved oddly. His foreign minister, Afonso Arinos, described an encounter that reflected his eccentricity:

> I was told the President wanted to see me immediately at the presidential palace. I explained that I could not go right away . . . I was again summoned by the President. [I] went right to the palace . . . thinking something serious must be happening. Jânio received me jovially . . . He said nothing that justified his insistence on meeting, which unnerved me. The President then asked if I wanted to go with him to the presidential residence to talk and have a glass of scotch before lunch. We left together and in the garage he smiled and refused to ride in the foreign ministry Cadillac, saying it was a luxury car. We instead got in his Chevrolet, me unsettled and him unworried. At the residence, the President led me to the library, poured our drinks, handed me a newspaper and started to read one himself . . . What did he want?[6]

Soon after, Quadros submitted a letter of resignation to Congress, boarded a plane for São Paulo and precipitated a constitutional crisis.

The armed forces refused to allow Vice President João Goulart to take office. When Quadros resigned, Goulart was on a trade mission to China, and the Air Force prohibited his plane from returning. Goulart was Vargas' protégé and had been minister of labor during the months of union pressure over wages that preceded Vargas' suicide. The armed forces saw Goulart as the political heir of a demagogue. Goulart's congressional supporters defused the crisis by crafting a compromise that allowed him to take office but with a cabinet appointed by Congress. He gained full presidential powers two years later.

Goulart faced daunting challenges. Since Kubitschek's break with the IMF in 1959, Brazil experienced inflation and public deficits. Foreign investment faltered amid the absence of a stabilization plan, the political crisis unleashed by Quadros's resignation, and mistrust of Goulart's aims. The U.S. government restricted aid to the armed forces and to states with conservative governors. By 1964, inflation neared 100% but Goulart lacked the political support to remedy it. During the succession crisis, his adversaries demonstrated their willingness to defy the constitution to block him. He faced a wall of congressional opposition. His political base among labor unions undermined the possibility of making unpopular economic decisions.

Goulart sought to overcome congressional opposition by waging a public campaign in favor of a slate of what he called Base Reforms. They were conceived by Minister of Planning and dependency theorist Celso Furtado and included rural land redistribution; nationalization of foreign-owned utilities; caps on rents and rent increases; doubling of worker wages; expansion of university slots; a campaign to eliminate illiteracy; and electoral reform extending the right to vote to illiterates and enlisted men. Goulart called these the "Brazilian Road" in reference to the more radical reforms being conducted in Cuba. His comparison signaled to the left his willingness to implement long desired goals, while seeking (in vain) to reassure the right, the armed forces, and the United States that his plan differed from the Cuban approach.

Goulart campaigned for his reforms through rallies in major cities. The first took place on March 13, 1964 in front of the Rio de Janeiro Central Rail Station that connected to the city's working-class suburbs. Unions, students, and leftist parties organized a turnout of at least 150,000. Goulart, impassioned, urged constitutional reforms, nationalization of refineries, and the expropriation of land on large estates.

Right-wing groups orchestrated their own rallies that brought conservative women to the streets banging pans to protest inflation.

Soon after Goulart's Central Station speech, naval sailors protested for the right to marry and vote, better shipboard conditions, as well as the right to organize. The last was the most controversial of these measures, but it reflected the frustrations of sailors who were denied rights available to other Brazilians, even to naval officers. Goulart expressed support for their demands. For military commanders this was the last straw: since the president defied military hierarchy to support a mutiny, he had forfeited his authority and deserved to be deposed. Intellectual Gilberto Freyre, a longtime advocate of military rule, had called the armed forces "a force above parties, with a highly national spirit, which transcends short term interests and factionalism."[7] Were Goulart's opponents prepared to put these beliefs into practice?

The conspirators counted on U.S. support: Ambassador Lincoln Gordon argued their case within the U.S. government, as did Military Attaché Vernon Walters, who had been the liaison between the U.S. Army and Brazilian forces during the Second World War, where he developed personal ties with leading conspirators. The outcomes were substantial: the United States was the first country to recognize the military Junta as Brazil's government, even as Goulart struggled to preserve his presidency. The U.S. Navy deployed a task force carrying fuel, medical supplies, and ammunition to back the conspirators in the event of resistance by supporters of Goulart.

Why couldn't opponents simply wait to replace Goulart via the ballot box? Presidential elections were scheduled for the following year. Economic conditions were dire. Goulart's policies seemed like desperate lunges rather than a plan of government. Three high-profile candidates in the center and the right were preparing to run for president, including Kubitschek. The odds seemed excellent that Goulart's foes could replace him with their choice of options.

The military's actions revealed their doubts over the outcomes of that election. Their mistrust was twofold. Goulart's reforms benefited the poor, who were the vast majority of the population. Granting people who were illiterate the right to vote would transform the political landscape: in 1960, 39% of Brazilians over age ten were illiterate. If Goulart could unlock and win their votes, he would be unbeatable. Alternatively, they feared Goulart would destabilize Brazil and spark a social revolution. His support for striking sailors fed that fear, which was made more palpable by the Cuban Revolution, which had succeeded just five years earlier. This mindset allowed the conspirators to believe they were preserving democracy – a perverse logic that permeated the dictatorship and conferred moral legitimacy. Within the dictatorship's National Intelligence Service (SNI), created by General Golbery do Couto e Silva, reams of wire tap reports and suspect files were fastidiously hand stamped with the slogan "The Revolution of 1964 is irreversible and will consolidate democracy in Brazil!" The stamp is bizarre: these were classified documents that were to be seen by a handful of the regime's secret police, and the stamp served no administrative function. Did the stamp offer some kind of absolution to the handlers of these documents for the human rights violations they contained?

"The 1964 Revolution is irreversible and will consolidate democracy in Brazil!"

On March 31, 1961, General Olympio Mourão Filho, an army commander in Minas Gerais, unleashed the operation to depose Goulart by sending a column of tanks to neighboring Rio de Janeiro to seize the old presidential palace. The act was precipitous: the conspirators planned to stage the coup on April 5. Still, the conspirators were well organized and Goulart was in a weak position. One by one, regional army commanders joined the conspirators. The commander of an armored battalion in Rio de Janeiro dispatched a tank column to stop General Mourão, but just before the armored columns met, he changed his mind and ordered the tanks back to their base, preserving valuable military hardware from damage over a political dispute.

Goulart turned to the safety of his home state, Rio Grande do Sul, along the southern border with Uruguay. Here, Goulart's brother-in-law, populist former governor Leonel Brizola, urged resistance. They counted on the loyalty of the commander of the Army division based there. By this point, the armed forces had detained leading leftists and supporters of Goulart. Congressional leaders supported the coup and declared the presidency vacant, which allowed them to swear into office the constitutional successor, President of the Chamber of Deputies Ranieri Mazzilli. U.S. President Lyndon Johnson publicly conveyed his "warmest wishes" to the new government, while the U.S. press presented the coup as a

Figure 2.1   The constitutionalist armored column sent to stop General Mourão's advance.
Source: © Arquivo Nacional, Brazil.

"severe blow to Cuba."[8] Goulart chose not to resist and crossed into Uruguay, where he spent the rest of his life in exile.

Though Deputy Mazzilli was formally president, power was really held by a Junta called the "Supreme Revolutionary Command," headed by the commanders of the Navy and the Air Force, as well as Army General Artur da Costa e Silva, a key conspirator who became Minister of War after the coup. They had no intention of keeping Mazzilli in the presidency: his presence was merely theater that allowed the Junta to depict the new government as legal, and Mazzilli was a willing actor. The armed forces quickly consolidated power and struck out at their foes.

Rural labor leaders who advocated redistribution of lands were detained, tortured, or killed.

Over the next two weeks, the Supreme Revolutionary Command consolidated its rule. On April 9, it promulgated an Institutional Act (AI-1), a decree that – by the authority the Junta granted itself, and that congressional majorities supported – superseded the 1946 constitution. AI-1 allowed the new regime to suspend the political rights of its perceived foes for a period of ten years, and was followed by a succession of lists of people being purged. The lists included governors, congressmen, university presidents, officers, journalists, professors, and diplomats: wave after wave of perceived foes across federal and local government. Celso Furtado was on the first list issued. Any politician who criticized the regime could expect to be on the next list.

Being purged was a heavy burden: aside from being expelled from their function and losing their livelihood, the purged lost their right to vote (as it turned out, a less valuable right after 1964), publish or teach. More, they were dragged into an unending maze of interrogations and inquiries that were intimidating, humiliating, and ruinously costly. During the term of the first military president, General Humberto Castelo Branco (1964–7), over 3,500 met this fate.[9] Among them, Juscelino Kubitschek was singled out for humiliating interrogation until being allowed to leave the country. In Paris, "JK" as he was commonly known, grew increasingly depressed and demoralized, signing letters to friends "ex-JK."

Under AI-1, the Junta accorded itself the power to name a candidate for president that would be sent to Congress for ratification. Within the Junta's logic, this was a democratic act: with AI-1 the Junta had granted itself the right to modify constitutional procedures, and its designated candidate would be ratified by an elected and representative congress. This logic was absurd: no clause in the 1946 constitution allowed for the armed forces to depose Goulart, nor did the constitution allow for the military to name a new candidate for president in the place of Goulart's constitutional successor, Ranieri Mazzilli, regardless of Mazzilli's personal willingness to allow it. What is more, the Congress was no longer a representative body: the Junta purged forty members the day before it submitted its candidate for congressional approval. The remaining congressmen, whether they supported the coup or not, understood the Junta's power over them.

Figure 2.2 General Luzeno Sarmento Ferreira proclaims Institutional Act I, witnessed by naval officers. The formal proclamation, which puts the decree into effect, is further formalized by the audio recording being made. Note the extension cord at the bottom left, which reflects the improvised nature of the new authority asserted by the armed forces.
Source: © Arquivo Nacional, Brazil.

The Junta's candidate, General Humberto Castelo Branco one of the architects of the coup, was elected with 361 votes and 72 abstentions. The first test his government faced was the economic crisis of inflation and capital flight. Castelo Branco's economic strategy reflected a renewed alignment with the United States. His foreign minister proclaimed that "what is good for the United States is good for Brazil."[10] When the United States occupied the Dominican Republic in 1965, Brazil sent troops. In turn, the U.S. government restored aid and access to credit frozen during the Goulart presidency (this aid now included training in interrogation and torture). In the first year alone after the coup, the United States provided $1 billion in aid and loans.

Castelo Branco's economic team, Planning Minister Roberto Campos and Finance Minister Octavio Bulhões, developed a stabilization plan

Figure 2.3   Delegation of wives and mothers at the Correio da Manhã news-room, drafting a letter petitioning for the release of their husbands and sons, detained by the dictatorship, Rio de Janeiro, 1964.
Source: © Arquivo Nacional, Brazil.

that followed IMF recommendations. Both had studied in the United States and critics on the left disparagingly called Campos by the English translation of his name, "Bobby Fields." Campos and Bulhões' plan cut inflation by freezing wages and reducing public spending and subsidies for public services and utilities. As if to the validate the nickname "Bobby Fields," a U.S. ambassador described how "in almost every Brazilian office involved in administering an unpopular tax, wage, or price decisions, there was the ubiquitous American advisor." The Campos–Bulhões Plan set cost-of-living wage increases below the rate of inflation, which in practice reduced the value of those wages. Though the plan deliberately eroded salaried worker wages, it subsidized the wealthy by easing financing for cars and appliances to sustain manufacturing. Worker losses along with the reductions in public spending curbed inflation, but the reduction of consumer demand made the economy stall. In 1965, economic growth was lower than the rate of population growth.[11]

Figure 2.4   Commission of Military Inquiry confiscates books on communism and socialism, as well as books on racial inequality, at the University of Brasília Library, 1964.
Source: © Arquivo Nacional, Brazil.

Politically, Castelo Branco struggled to balance his intention to cede power to a civilian successor with the expectations of hardline officers who wanted to prolong military rule. The dictatorship had both political allies and opponents in Congress and in local politics. The occasional successes of these opponents rendered Castelo Branco vulnerable to pressure from hardliners who feared losing power. In turn, hardliners constantly pressed for more severe political restrictions that inflamed the opposition. This cycle unfolded when opposition candidates won several important governorships in the 1965 elections (the presidential election was postponed until 1967). Hardliners compelled Castelo Branco to issue AI-2, which suspended the 1946 constitution, canceled direct presidential elections, dissolved political parties, and gave the regime authority over the judiciary. Believing that a two-party system like that of the United States would produce a more stable and effective political system, the regime now allowed two parties, ARENA (Alliance for National Renewal), allied to the regime, and the MDB (Brazilian Democratic Movement), which comprised the legal opposition.

Despite Castelo Branco's re-engineering of the party system, the cycle repeated itself in 1966 when elections again yielded symbolic victories for opposition MDB candidates. Under pressure, Castelo Branco issued AI-3, which suspended congress and mandated indirect election of governors and mayors of major cities. Castelo Branco acquiesced to the hardliners' choice for president, General Artur da Costa e Silva, but he sought to bind the next regime by enacting a new constitution. To do so, he issued AI -4 to reconvene the congress that was suspended since AI-3. Legislators who criticized the proposal were purged, and the constitution of 1967 was ratified. It reinforced the arbitrary powers created by the institutional acts, and gave the president authority over congress and the judiciary. The new constitution also defined a range of activities as threats to "national security and the political order" subject to military justice.

There is an irony to Castelo Branco's presidency: he aimed to preserve legality and constitutionality, and wanted to yield the presidency to a civilian. But to preempt the hardliners, he departed from these goals and created the regime he sought to prevent. When he left office, Brazil had a new constitution, another general as president, a harsh national security law, indirect elections, and purges that reached deep into society. He imagined that the new constitution would bind his successors, but there was no reason to believe this. His successors would continue to use to the same tools, imposing institutional acts, changing political rules, or modifying the constitution at every turn.

The Hard Line: Costa e Silva and Médici (1967–74)

By the end of Castelo Branco's presidency, economic growth had begun to pick up. Brazil's GDP increased 6% in 1966 and 4% in 1967. Costa e Silva applied the political space afforded by a recovering economy to easing controls on political and labor activity, believing he could rely more on consent than on coercion. He quickly learned that beneath these restrictions lay mounting social unease about a dictatorship that now

Figure 2.5   Costa e Silva front row, fourth from left. Delfim Neto is behind him, in glasses.
Source: © Arquivo Nacional, Brazil.

gave no sings of returning to civilian rule. In the summer of 1968, when Costa e Silva relaxed restrictions on union activity, workers responded with a wave of strikes across Brazil's major industrial cities, seeking to recover their considerable losses in earning power. These strikes foreshadowed wider tensions.

These tensions erupted when police shot and killed a student participating in a protest over cafeteria conditions at the Federal University of Rio de Janeiro. Edson Luis de Lima Souto became a martyr whose death catalyzed student opposition to the dictatorship.[12] In the week after his death, students across the country went on strike and engaged in confrontations with police. At the memorial service for Edson Luis in downtown Rio de Janeiro, police attacked the gathering students. What started as a complaint about cafeteria food became a denunciation of the dictatorship and a call for a return to democracy. By mid-1968, marches and confrontations spread across Brazil, echoing protests around the world, from Mexico City to Paris, Prague, and across the United States. Protests in Rio de Janeiro culminated in the March of the Hundred Thousand, which mobilized students, members of the clergy, musicians, and artists.

The presence of clergy among the protesters reflected the diversity of the Brazilian Catholic Church in the 1960s. Though it included clergymen who supported the regime, many members believed that their role was to support the victims of exclusion and oppression through support for land redistribution, labor rights and human rights. Archbishop Helder Câmara was a leader of this contingent who voiced criticism of the regime since the coup, when the soldiers murdered and tortured rural labor leaders in Pernambuco, part of his archdiocese. The generals called him the "Red Bishop" and prohibited the press from mentioning him. But Câmara was influential within the Brazilian Church's governing body, the National Council of Bishops, and he counted on the support and protection of São Paulo's Cardinal Evaristo Arns, which gave him the latitude to speak out on human rights.

Catholic progressives found common cause with other Latin American clergy who embraced the doctrine of liberation theology. A centerpiece of this movement was the 1968 Conference of Latin American Bishops, which expressed a "preferential option for the poor." This meant advocating on behalf of poor, excluded, and marginalized peoples, aiding them in challenging the sources of their exploitation and oppression. The Bishops Conference issued a statement describing the means to achieve this. These included land redistribution, recognition of peasants' and worker's unions, as well as a discussion of capitalism, industrialization and the world economy that drew from structuralism and dependency theory. Clergy pursued these goals through conscientization – consciousness-raising – teaching the nature of exploitation based on methods pioneered by exiled Brazilian educator Paulo Freire.[13] This social and political engagement of liberation theologians had a lasting impact, particularly in Brazil and Central America.

Amid the protests of 1968, students conspired to reconstitute the National Student Union (UNE), disbanded immediately after the coup. Student activists organized a secret national congress at a farm in São Paulo where they planned to elect a new leadership that would give national voice to students opposing the dictatorship. The 400 students who turned up at the rain-drenched farm were arrested en masse (the student movement was widely infiltrated by agents and informants, so

Figure 2.6   Demonstrator being arrested in Belo Horizonte.
Source: © Arquivo Nacional, Brazil.

the meeting was no secret). Nonetheless, this effort to engage in clandestine political activity foreshadowed the guerrilla war that would follow the crackdown on student protests. Each new degree of repression spurred a more radical response from opposition groups, which in turn justified intensified repression. A cycle of violence was about to begin.

Over the course of 1968, the regime met mounting dissent with escalating repression. The pot boiled over when opposition congressman Márcio Moreira Alves took to the floor of the Chamber of Deputies and denounced the regime as violent and oppressive. He invoked the classic Greek play by Aristophanes in which the heroine Lysistrata calls on women to deprive their husbands of sex until the men ended an interminable war, and he asked wives and girlfriends to boycott men in

Figure 2.7   Costa e Silva, in uniform, meeting with his cabinet in December 1968.
Source: © Arquivo Nacional, Brazil.

uniform until democracy was restored. The generals felt that Alves had crossed a line. Rather than simply purging him from Congress, Costa e Silva demanded that the Congress itself impeach Alves. After intense debate, Congress refused. Costa e Silva responded by issuing Institutional Act 5 (AI-5).

AI-5 shut Congress, gave the regime authority over state and local governments, and eliminated *habeas corpus*, allowing the police and armed forces to detain civilians without charges. After AI-5, the regime decreed a harsher National Security Law. The new law broadened the list of crimes subject to military tribunals, lengthened sentences and introduced the death penalty for many violations. It subjected media to censorship and outlawed political meetings, strikes and demonstrations. Non-violent acts such as publicly criticizing the regime or speaking favorably of a banned opposition group, were subject to imprisonment. Part of the new law was seemingly written with Marcio Moreira Alves' speech in mind: "morally offending anyone in a position of authority for reasons of factionalism or politico-social nonconformity" was now punishable by 2 to 4 years in prison.

At the end of August 1969, Costa e Silva suffered a stroke and soon died. A military Junta comprised of the chiefs of the three branches of the armed forces assumed power and refused to allow the civilian vice president to succeed Costa e Silva. In keeping with the practice initiated by Castelo Branco, the vice president was a civilian ally of the regime. Vice President Pedro Aleixo demanded that the constitution be respected and that he assume the presidency. The Junta responded by abolishing the office of vice-president. When it became clear Costa e Silva would not recover, the Junta polled the senior officer corps to arrive at a consensus candidate for president, General Emilio Garrastazu Médici.

Médici brought the regime to its greatest extremes, politically and economically. He waged a ruthless war against the armed opposition movements that proliferated after the promulgation of AI-5, while silencing political criticism and maintaining a heavy hand on press censorship. At the same time, he continued to pursue the rapid economic expansion that had begun under Costa e Silva. U.S.-based businesses like Union Carbide ran advertisements congratulating Brazil on its growth, echoing the regime's slogans like "No one holds this country back."

Opposition by Other Means

By stifling dissent and criticism, the regime forced its opponents to choose between powerless silence or illegal and dangerous action. Throughout the 1960s radical students had idolized Che Guevara, but had avoided the revolutionary path he had pioneered. The Communist Party shunned armed uprising and sought political engagement. But with peaceful protest and political dialogue foreclosed, growing numbers of the regime's opponents resorted to *luta armada*, "armed struggle." These groups were primarily urban, often comprised of middle-class students who lacked military training. They waged actions intended to build awareness of opposition to regime in defiance of its enforced silence, as well as bank robberies and seizures of weapons from military garrisons in order to sustain their struggle. They mostly sought a socialist revolution inspired by Cuba, and relied the on theories and strategies defined by Guevara.

The regime responded by building a network of intelligence services that gave ubiquitous and violent expression to the national security state. The struggle between guerrilla groups and the bureaucracy of repression was brutally one-sided. Though the guerrilla groups had some successes, such as the kidnapping of the U.S. ambassador in 1969, followed by the German and Swiss ambassadors and the Japanese Consul in São Paulo by 1972, the struggle was short lived. Armed resistance gave military hardliners justification to build a system of repression that outlived the dreams of a socialist revolution. The machinery of repression ultimately served a political project: after it vanquished the guerrilla movements, it continued to invent targets in order to maintain a climate of fear that strengthened the hand of military hardliners and marginalized the civilian political opposition. Through the threat of force and the illusion that the country still faced "subversion" from ill-defined "dangerous elements," the members of what journalist Elio Gaspari calls the "basement" would shape the edifice of military rule.[14]

The emergence of armed insurrection against the regime had two causes. First, it was a natural expression of the youth and labor radicalism that had grown since the Cuban Revolution. The second was AI-5. Between 1964 and 1968, opponents of the regime underwent a tutorial in discretion as even mainstream organizations like the National Student Union were suppressed, so after 1968 they felt prepared to take the step into guerrilla struggle.

The experience of Popular Action (AP) was emblematic. Formed in 1962 by members of Catholic youth movements, AP conducted projects that its members deemed revolutionary but were not violent nor aimed at overthrowing the government. Instead, AP members engaged in adult literacy campaigns and organized in support of Goulart's Base Reforms. After the AP was banned in 1964, its membership shrank from several thousand to several hundred who were now members of a clandestine organization. Members of AP went to work in factories or in the countryside with the goal of raising worker consciousness. In 1966, AP carried out its first large attack: a bomb planted at the Recife airport timed to detonate upon the arrival of President Costa e Silva. The bomb killed an admiral and a government official. Like other groups, the AP was ideologically fragmented: its members differed with each other over the nature of the revolution and the society it was to create. By the early 1970s the AP was decimated by repression, and its surviving members had splintered into smaller groups or affiliated with other movements.

The participation of purged soldiers and officers in the revolutionary groups proved vital as few guerrillas possessed military training. One of the earliest guerrilla groups, the Nationalist Revolutionary Movement

(MNR), was comprised of purged soldiers and coordinated by Leonel Brizola from his exile in Uruguay. The MNR carried out actions across the border in southern Brazil in 1966 and 1967. It was succeeded by the Movement for Revolutionary Action (MAR), formed by imprisoned soldiers who escaped and formed a *foco* near Angra dos Reis, in southern Rio de Janeiro, where a decade later the regime would build Brazil's first nuclear power plant.

The most notorious of the soldiers turned guerrillas was Carlos Lamarca, an army captain who had served in the UN peacekeeping mission after the Suez Crisis in 1956. After the promulgation of AI-5, he defected to the Marxist Popular Revolutionary Vanguard (VPR), one of the main guerrilla organizations operating in Rio de Janeiro and São Paulo, which merged with other groups to become the Revolutionary Action Vanguard – Palmares (VAR-Palmares), that took the name of a defiant runaway slave community in the seventeenth-century Brazilian northeast. Lamarca was particularly reviled by military leaders, who regarded him as a traitor and focused relentlessly on killing him. Similar

Figure 2.8   Military Task Force searching for MAR guerrillas near Angra dos Reis, Brazil.
Source: © Arquivo Nacional, Brazil.

Figure 2.9 Military Task Force searching for MAR guerrillas near Angra dos Reis, Brazil.
Source: © Arquivo Nacional, Brazil.

efforts were expended to capture Carlos Marighella, the leader of the Communist Party's armed wing, the National Liberation Alliance (ALN).

Repression

From the start, the military regime had many tools at its disposal for spying on opponents, conducting arrests, and carrying out interrogations. Three months after the coup, Castelo Branco created the National

Intelligence Service (SNI) and appointed General Golbery do Couto e Silva as its director. It became the main domestic espionage organization, conducting wiretapping, maintaining networks of informants, and managing the mountains of data compiled by a proliferating array of intelligence and security services. The SNI became so powerful that when General Ernesto Geisel became president in 1974, he named the SNI director ambassador to Portugal in order to get him out of the country, since the knowledge he had from years of domestic spying had made him into Geisel's principal rival for the presidency. In turn, Geisel's SNI Director, General João Baptista Figueiredo, would succeed him as president.

Beyond the SNI, each branch of the armed forces had its own spy service: CENIMAR, the Center for Naval Intelligence; CISA, the Air Force Intelligence Service; and CIE, Army Intelligence. Each participated in detention and torture, but their main role was processing intelligence. Enforcement fell first and foremost to the Department of Political and Social Police (DOPS), which had been created under Vargas and existed in each state as a special investigative police force controlled by the governor. After 1964, state DOPS agencies were coordinated with the armed forces intelligence services. By 1969, a mosaic of police and military task forces combated subversion. The pioneering entity was Operation Bandeirantes (OBAN) in São Paulo, which combined members of the Army intelligence service and the DOPS, and was privately funded by business groups including General Motors and Ford. OBAN carried out espionage and detentions, systematically employing torture and disappearance, as well as invented causes of death to explain the high mortality rate of its detainees.

The Médici regime built OBAN into a national network of army detachments known as DOI-CODI. In each state or city there were now multiple security agencies carrying out similar tasks, sometimes in collaboration, sometimes in competition. This competition was particularly intense in São Paulo, where the DOPS included a ruthless death squad led by detective Sergio Fleury. DOI-CODI was responsible for finding and killing Lamarca, while the São Paulo DOPS assassinated Marighella. When Fleury's DOPS captured VPR militant Mário Osawa, who was hospitalized for injuries from a car crash, OBAN agents demanded he be turned over. Fleury wanted to interrogate Osawa before OBAN did in order to be the first to learn Lamarca's whereabouts, so he kept him in the hospital by jumping on his chest to break his ribs.[15]

Fighting for the Revolution

The experiences of three militants, Dilma Rousseff, Maria do Carmo Brito, and Suely Yumiko Kamayana, help illustrate the experience of participating in these movements.

In 1964, high school student Dilma Rousseff, joined the Revolutionary Marxist Workers Political Organization (POLOP). The POLOP was not itself a guerrilla organization, but for Rousseff and many others it served as a conduit from student activism to armed militancy. While she studied economics at the Federal University of Minas Gerais, Rousseff joined a guerrilla organization called the National Revolutionary Command (COLINA), which operated in Minas Gerais and Rio de Janeiro. By this time, Rousseff lived clandestinely and adopted the code name "Estela." COLINA carried out several actions including the killing of a Bolivian officer believed to be involved in the manhunt and execution of Che Guevara.

When the Minas Gerais cell of COLINA was suppressed by police in 1969, Rousseff went on the run, rejoining the organization in Rio de Janeiro. The remaining members of COLINA merged with Carlos Lamarca's VPR, becoming VAR-Palmares. Rousseff's transit from POLOP to COLINA to the VAR-Palmares reflected the fluidity of these organizations. They were created, merged or disintegrated as the authorities decimated their ranks. Like other revolutionary groups that resorted to bank "expropriations," the VAR-Palmares faced the challenge of raising large sums of money with which to sustain not only its campaign, but to maintain its very existence through costly networks of safe-houses, cars, and even daily stipends to buy meals. VAR-Palmares found creative financing: it broke into the home of the mistress of notoriously corrupt São Paulo politician Adhemar de Barros, and robbed his safe containing $2.5 million, the largest "expropriation" by a revolutionary movement to date.

Rousseff was captured in São Paulo in 1970 by OBAN agents. Held by OBAN, she was tortured for weeks with the methods OBAN most frequently used: the "parrot's perch" by which the victim was suspended by their knees with their wrists bound to their ankles, and the "dragon's chair" which delivered bruising electrical shocks. She was convicted by a military tribunal. After her release in 1972, Rousseff completed her degree in economics and in the 1980s became a key administrator in a succession of state government posts as a member of the leftist Brazilian

Workers Party (PDT) and Workers Party (PT). In 2005, she became chief of staff to President Lula da Silva (PT). In 2010, she became the first woman elected president of Brazil.

Maria do Carmo Brito was also member of POLOP in Minas Gerais, and helped establish COLINA in 1967, living under the codename "Lia." Like Rousseff, she survived the suppression of COLINA in Minas Gerais and moved to Rio de Janeiro joining VAR-Palmares. Under the force of repression and ideological differences, VAR-Palmares was dismantled and Brito became a commander of the recreated Popular Revolutionary Vanguard, the VPR, becoming one of the few women to hold such a leadership role. By 1970, the VPR had been reduced to a struggle for survival, punctuated by actions intended to keep opposition visible or to secure the release of jailed fellow guerrillas. Brito was captured by the DOPS in 1970 as she and the VPR were planning to kidnap the German Ambassador. DOPS agents tortured her to obtain information about the organization and its members. Realizing that she would break under torture, the VPR precipitated its kidnapping of the ambassador, and now included her name on the list of prisoners ransomed for his release. Though VPR gained the release of Brito and 39 other guerrillas, they failed to draw attention to their struggle since the accelerated timing of the kidnapping meant its news was drowned out by Brazil's victory in the 1970 soccer World Cup.

Banished from Brazil, Brito was received by Algeria. She convalesced from torture at a former French colonial resort that Algerian authorities used to help exiles like her recover. Brito went on to Chile during the Allende period, where she met and married exiled VPR member Mário Osawa. Also captured in 1970, he was ransomed for the Japanese consul in São Paulo. After the 1973 coup, Brito and Osawa fled Chile and in 1976 settled in newly independent Angola, where they worked in education and journalism alongside the country's Marxist regime. After the 1979 amnesty, they returned to Brazil, where Brito became a school social worker and Osawa practiced journalism. Back home, Brito reflected: "Brazil's misery is a kettle for brewing rebellion. I did not become politically active for theoretical reasons, it was because I deeply uncomfortable about violence and hunger. Just that. It was never an attempt to make history. Misery disturbs me deeply. I still carry that today. The question of curable human suffering. But direct intervention for change, I think that has ended for many of us."[16]

Like Mário Osawa, Suely Yumiko Kamayana was part of the large ethnic community of Japanese descent in São Paulo. She had studied at the University of São Paulo and become a militant in the Communist Party of Brazil (PCdoB). The PCdoB sought to avoid the fate of urban guerrilla groups, which were easy prey, by carrying out the principal effort in Brazil to create a rural *foco*. In 1966, it established a presence in a remote impoverished region of north central Brazil along the Araguaia River. The PCdoB received Cuban training and patiently worked to reproduce the conditions that made the Cuban Revolution successful, such as earning the support of the local population. Kamayana, code-named "Chica," arrived in 1970. The Army learned of the *foco* soon after, but it too worked patiently to build a counterinsurgency task force which, between 1972 and 1974, eradicated the PCdoB contingent. A central feature of the Army's footprint was a building used for interrogations, flanked by mass graves. The area counted little more than 80 guerrillas, of whom at least 64 were killed. Kamayana was killed near the end of the operation in 1974.

The government kept the existence of the guerrilla group and its destruction secret. After the military operation in Araguaia was complete, the counterinsurgency force eliminated the remains of the group and of the action, disinterring the killed guerrillas and burning their bodies. A curious story about Kamayana would later emerge. In 1993, an Air Force officer involved in disappearing the guerrillas declared to a popular news magazine:

> Suely had been killed at the end of 1974. Her body was buried in a place called Bacaba where cells and interrogation chambers had been built under the command of the Army Intelligence Center. During operation cleanup, Suely's body was disinterred. It was intact, unclothed, with very white skin that showed no sign of decomposition, just the bullet wounds. Suely's body was placed in a plastic bag and taken to my helicopter. It was transported to a location . . . where it was put in a pile of other disinterred bodies. It was then covered with old tires and gasoline and the bodies were incinerated.[17]

The president, the educator, and the martyr mapped the difficult and uncertain outcomes students living under the dictatorship faced as the regime suppressed opposition.

The Economic Miracle, 1968–73

The Médici years combined the most intense repression with the highest rate of economic growth. Was there a link between authoritarianism and development? The conditions for stimulating the economy were ripe: the Campos–Bulhões plan had righted public finances and created an environment of increasing foreign aid and investment. When he took office in 1967, Costa e Silva charged his new finance minister, Antonio Delfim Neto, with accelerating economic growth while controlling inflation. When Médici became president in 1969, he kept Delfim Neto in place. Delfim Neto saw an opportunity in the economic conditions created by the Campos–Bulhões Plan: the economic slowdown caused by plan left surplus productive capacity and pent-up consumer demand which Delfim Neto could tap by easing credit. He added to the mix an innovative mechanism to balance growth and inflation: indexation.

"Crawling-Peg" indexation was the practice of making constant small devaluations of Brazil's currency, the cruzeiro, in keeping with projected inflation. The devaluations achieved two aims: first, they facilitated long-term contracts for foreign trade, since the final market price and exchange rate could be set at the time the contract was first made, eliminating considerable uncertainty and risk from trade deals. Second, indexation allowed businesses to adjust prices and payrolls constantly, helping wage earners and consumers retain earning and purchasing power, and allowing banks to continually adjust interest rates on deposits. These measures made inflation generated by rapid economic growth virtually invisible. Transactions ranging from a contract to export coffee to a paycheck, a trip to the store, or opening a savings account now happened on a stable and predictable platform, protected from the inflationary undercurrents. Before, inflation had been an all-consuming problem: workers relentlessly sought to regain the lost value of wages, merchants were uncertain about the terms for contracts, consumers worried about what they could afford and when, and the government faced constant pressure to take painful measures to tame inflation at the expense of other economic goals – and losing credibility for failing to do so. Now these concerns seemed to drift effortlessly away.

With inflation pressures neutralized (something very different than resolved), Delfim Neto focused the government's attention on stimulating growth, drawing on a wider set of tools than would otherwise have been available, given their inflationary nature. Neto eased credit in different areas of the Brazilian economy, including farm credit, home financing, lending to industry and commerce, as well as financing of exports. The National Economic Development Bank, created fifteen years earlier to finance infrastructure and state-owned businesses, ramped up its lending for public projects, and it extended its lending to include private businesses.

The flood of credit increased demand and stimulated production. Companies could borrow easily to build capacity. The large sector of state-owned companies, ranging from utilities to heavy industry, and development agencies in the northeast and the Amazon region, took advantage of increasingly easy foreign loans to expand their activities. Meanwhile, the regime deployed a raft of social programs to show its commitment to combatting social inequality – programs like the MOBRAL adult literacy project, or the construction of the Trans-Amazonian highway, intended to both integrate national territory while making land available to impoverished northeasterners beset by drought. These projects further stimulated the economy.

The result was explosive economic growth: between 1968 and 1973, the economy grew at an annual rate of 11.3%. Much of this was expanded industrial production. The production of intermediate and consumer goods driven by expanding internal markets began to spill over Brazil's borders: a rising proportion of Brazil's exports were manufactured products. The Brazilian foreign and finance ministries worked furiously to cultivate new markets for these goods, promoting trade in Africa and the Middle East. Accelerating industrialization, expanding markets and the stability created by indexation made Brazil an attractive target for multinational companies that raced to establish subsidiaries or to buy domestic companies.

Alongside trade and transportation, the government also invested in telecommunications as a means of promoting national integration. At the height of the Miracle, the regime developed a national color television standard (one of the first countries outside of the United States, Japan, and Europe to do so). The first Brazilian color transmission was the soccer World Cup held in Mexico City in 1970, where the Brazilian national team won its third championship. The accomplishment befitted the outsized economic accomplishments of the Miracle. The regime promoted it heavily and declared a three-day national holiday.

The generals saw television as a means of building national unity: people living far from each other would be drawn together by watching the same news and soap operas. They built a network of transmitters and eventually launched a broadcast satellite. The beneficiary of this investment was Globo, a company with a newspaper and television and radio stations in Rio de Janeiro whose owner, Roberto Marinho, was willing to meet the regime's goals in cultural programming and the tone of news coverage. He was rewarded with access to the transmission network that made Globo one of the world's largest media conglomerates, with a continental reach in its transmissions, a national advertising base, and public subsidies which permitted it to become the country's largest producer (and exporter) of television programming.

As the Miracle generated new conceptions of life and leisure in Brazil, the growing middle and upper classes pulled away from the poor. The regime subsidized the life of the urban middle class in southeastern Brazilian cities like São Paulo and Rio de Janeiro through easy credit for housing, cars, and other durable goods, as well as investments in higher education at the expense of public primary and secondary education. This was by design: the regime rewarded the social classes whose consumption propelled industrialization. At the other end of the social scale, conditions were bleaker. The regime suppressed industrial wages in order to keep business costs low. It did this discretely by failing to honestly account for inflation in the indexation of salaried wages. The 1973 adjustment of the minimum wage was an egregious example: the government defined inflation at 15%, while outside observers like the World Bank assessed it at 20–25%.[18] Repressive wage practices were common in an environment in which workers could not strike. Beyond the government's desire to conceal inflation in indexation, businesses found freedom to disregard pressure from their employees over wages.

Formal wages (from salaried jobs) tell only part of the story. Most Brazilians labored informally and in poverty, be they in sprawling urban *favelas* (shanties) or in the countryside, where the concentration of land tenure relegated many to the roles of subsistence farming or working as day laborers on the fields of large landowners. Médici addressed this poverty by building the Trans-Amazonian highway, which connected the northeast to the Amazon. The highway served two aims: on the belief that less populated regions posed a security risk, Médici integrated national territory by road so that poor farmers could flood into the

Amazon and farm new lands. Many did, though their prospects were bleak: the soil was poor, and clearing the forests led to desertification as the moisture cycle that forests had sustained dissipated. Settlers faced violence from *grileiros*, thugs who seized their land. Violence spurred a cycle of deforestation as displaced settlers were constantly forced to seek virgin lands.

Racial minorities faced disproportionate disadvantages under the miracle. Indigenous peoples were displaced by road building, logging, settlement, and the expansion of the agricultural frontier. Brazil became a leading soybean producer thanks to farm credit and the promotion of exports. But the spread of industrialized agriculture came at the expense of subsistence farming communities that had depended on those lands. The same was true for communities formed by descendants of runaway slaves, known as *quilombos*. Located far from developed areas but near bodies of water, many were displaced by hydroelectric projects. Lacking title to their land, they had little recourse.

Black and racially mixed Brazilians were also sidelined. Racial inequalities produced by informal discrimination meant that black and mixed-race Brazilians earned less than half of what white Brazilians earned. Despite systematic inequality, the dictatorship promoted the idea that Brazil was a "racial democracy" that did not have discrimination. The national security laws defended this idea, and university faculty who conducted research on racial inequalities were purged. Adding substance to its assertion that racial inequality did not exist in Brazil, the regime removed the category of race from the 1970 census. Activists challenging racism in Brazil were exiled or spied upon. Dance parties featuring "black music" from the United States, such as soul and rhythm & blues, were monitored by the DOPS.[19]

The Miracle was a political product that the regime held up like a trophy. By the same measure, the regime became dependent on the miracle. The prosperity experienced by privileged groups, along with the notion that Brazil was becoming a developed nation helped distract from the repression the regime meted out to its opponents. Its logic could be distilled into a common bumper sticker: "Brazil – love it or leave it!" That the character of Brazil's economic expansion magnified income inequalities was nonetheless politically problematic, compelling Medici to acknowledge that "the economy is doing fine but people aren't."[20] The answer was to continue to pursue high levels of growth on the grounds that the rising tide would eventually lift all ships.

The choice to hang the legitimacy of the regime on the perpetuation of an economic bubble was unsound. Rapid growth resulted from conditions that were not inherently durable. First, the Campos–Bulhões plan had suppressed demand and industrial output. As credit eased, production rebounded. The international context contributed as well: the global economy was buoyed during the years of the miracle by high levels of growth in Western Europe and Japan, as well as a gamut of increased spending on expanding social programs and military spending in the United States. Fatefully, the expansion depended upon the cheap and stable cost of importing oil. Brazil imported 80% of its oil, and increasing demands for energy by both producers and consumers during the miracle meant not just continued but steadily increasing demand.

The international conditions that supported the Brazilian miracle disintegrated under he weight of the Yom Kippur War in the Middle East. After Syria and Egypt invaded Israel in October 1973, the government of the United States supplied weapons to Israel, turning the tide of the war. Though the war lasted less than three weeks, its effects were felt far longer. Arab leaders punished nations that had supported Israel during the war by withholding oil. The main target of the OPEC Oil Embargo was the United States. As Arab leaders courted support from African oil exporters, the latter asked that Brazil be included in the embargo. Just as it had realigned itself toward the United States since 1964, the Brazilian military regime had supported Portugal in its wars to retain its African colonies. African countries, which cooperated to eradicate European colonialism on the continent, sought to compel Brazil to break with Portugal. Brazilian diplomats narrowly succeeded in evading the embargo.

Brazil still faced ruinously higher oil prices. The war and the embargo caused the international market price for a barrel of oil to quadruple from $3 to $12. The cost of Brazil's oil imports climbed to $710 million for 1973 and $2.8 billion in 1974. This cost fed a $4.5 billion trade deficit despite the government's push to double the value of exports. Though it was not immediately apparent, Brazil had just transitioned from the end of the Miracle to the beginning of its debt crisis. Economically dependent on oil and politically dependent on the Miracle, the military regime subsidized domestic fuel prices. While other nations faced upheaval created by rising oil prices, fuel shortages and simmering inflation caused by energy costs, the Brazilian government's borrowing created the illusion of stability.

The regime was at a curious crossroads. In 1964, the armed forces charted a course toward free-market reforms, deficit, and inflation reduction, as well as closer alignment with the United States. A decade later, the regime was on a very different trajectory. It shepherded an ambitious economic project that pursued artificially high levels of economic growth sustained by rising indebtedness, state planning, and suppression of inflation through price and wage controls. With growing state command of the economy along with increased borrowing from abroad, the regime sustained economic growth even after the peak years of the miracle. In 1974, in the midst of the aftershocks of the oil embargo, the Brazilian economy grew at a rate of 7%, while the United States, Japan and much of Europe faced recession.

Conclusion

The economic miracle (1967–73) marked the culmination of the generals' attempt to impose their vision of the proper functioning of the economy, society, and politics in Brazil. The regime's economic policies contained elements of the modernizing republicanism that the armed forces pitted against the monarchy in the nineteenth century, the Positivist doctrine that evolved into the disaffection of the *tenentes* in the 1920s, and the uneasy sharing of development goals with a fractious and unstable civilian political system. In 1964, the generals resolved to sweep civilian politicians aside and apply the kind of technocratic, state-guided development they had long envisioned. If the resulting economic development was dramatic, it was also becoming clear that these gains were built with unsustainable premises and terrible costs.

Notes

1   Golbery do Couto e Silva, *Conjuntura política nacional: O poder executivo e geopolítica do Brasil*, 3rd edn. (José Olympio, 1981), 37.
2   Stefan Zweig, *Brazil: A Land of the Future* (Ariadne Press, 2007).
3   See Oliver Dinius, *Brazil's Steel City: Developmentalism, Strategic Power, and Industrial Relations in Volta Redonda, 1941–1964* (Stanford University Press, 2010).

4   Thomas Rogers, "'I Choose This Means to Be With You Always': Getúlio Vargas' *Carta Testamento*," in Jens Hentschke (ed.), *Vargas And Brazil* (Palgrave, 2006), 247–8.

5   Maria Victoria de Mesquita Benevides, *O governo Kubitschek: Desenvolvimento econômico e estabilidade política* (Paz e Terra, 1976), 172.

6   Afonso Arinos, *Planalto* (José Olympio, 1968), 161.

7   Gilberto Freyre, "As Forças Armadas no Brasil," *O Cruzeiro*, January 1, 1963; Fundação Gilberto Freyre, Artigos de Jornal de Gilberto Freyre, AJ-13, 1963–4 (O Cruzeiro).

8   "Washington Sends 'Warmest' Wishes to Brazil's Leader," *The New York Times*, April 3, 1964; "Upset in Brazil Is Blow to Cuba," *The New York Times*, April 3, 1964.

9   Daniel Aarão Reis, *Ditadura militar, esquerdas e sociedade* (Jorge Zahar, 2000), 43.

10   http://cpdoc.fgv.br/producao/dossies/AEraVargas1/biografias/juraci_magalhaes, accessed October 14, 2012.

11   Thomas Skidmore, *Politics of Military Rule* (Oxford University Press, 1990), 39, 55, 62, 68.

12   On student protests and opposition culture, see Victoria Langland, *Speaking of Flowers: Student Movements and the Molding of 1968 in Military Brazil* (Duke University Press, 2013).

13   See Andrew Kirkendall, *Paulo Freire and the Cold War Politics of Literacy* (University of North Carolina Press, 2010).

14   Elio Gaspari, *A Ditadura Derrotada*, 397–8, from the series *A Ditadura Envergonhada, A Ditadura Escancarada, A Ditadura Derrotada, and A Ditadura Ecurralada* (Companhia das Letras, 2002–4).

15   Jeffrey Lesser, *A Discontented Diaspora: Japanese Brazilians and the Meanings of Ethnic Militancy* (Duke University Press, 2007), 134.

16   Interview with Maria do Carmo Brito and Mário Osawa, May 25, 2006.

17   Comissão Especial Sobre Mortos e Desaparecidos Políticos, *Direito à Memória e à Verdade* (Secretaria Especial dos Direitos Humanos, 2007), 261; Lesser, *A Discontented Diaspora*, 110–11.

18   Skidmore, *Politics of Military Rule*, 205.

19   Paulina Alberto, "When Rio was *Black*," *Hispanic American Historical Review*, 89:1 (2009), 3–39.

20   Jan Knippers Black, *The Politics of Human Rights Protection* (Rowman & Littlefield, 2009), 53.

3

Argentina
Between Peronism and Military Rule

On March 21, 1972, police stopped the car of Fiat of Argentina president Oberdan Sallustro as he drove to work. The "police" were disguised members of the Revolutionary Army of the People (ERP), a Marxist guerrilla organization. The kidnapping was part of a tide of violence by left-wing and right-wing groups. Over the preceding week, guerrillas from different organizations had kidnapped and ransomed a winery executive, and killed a former finance minister as well as a former police chief who had been accused of committing torture.

Why kidnap Sallustro? The ERP applied Guevara's ideas about "popular war," waging actions meant to sway public opinion and discredit the regime and its allies. The ERP kidnapped Sallustro after the military regime then in power (1966–73) had helped Fiat suppress strikes at its tractor and locomotive plants. Sallustro's kidnappers released a photo and a list of demands. The photo showed a resigned captive seated before an ERP flag bearing the slogan "win or die." They demanded the release of jailed Fiat workers and rehiring of workers fired during the strike; the withdrawal of police who had been stationed inside the plant; the release of 50 imprisoned guerrillas to Algeria; and a donation by Fiat of $1 million in public school supplies bearing a message from the ERP that the supplies were "the riches that the fathers of all poor children produce but that is stolen by the exploiters."[1]

Fiat agreed. The government refused, declaring "we are not going to let these criminals play Robin Hood." Instead it mounted a manhunt, seeking ERP members and the "People's Jail" where Sallustro was held.

Dictatorship in South America, First Edition. Jerry Dávila.
© 2013 Jerry Dávila. Published 2013 by Blackwell Publishing Ltd.

Figure 3.1   Photo released by the ERP of Oberdan Sallustro.
Source: © Arquivo Nacional, Brazil.

Soldiers blocked roads and highways at rush hour, stranding motorists while soldiers searched every car. The ERP's deadline passed, as did an extended deadline. Police found the "People's Jail," and when they raided it, Sallustro's captors executed him.

Fiat of Argentina memorialized its slain director by naming a new truck the "Sallustro." Ironically, the truck's engine had debilitating design flaws, prompting truckers and mechanics to nickname it "Sallustro's revenge." Soon "Sallustro's revenge" referred to any problem a Fiat owner had with their vehicle. The bad engine was the most benign way in which Sallustro's kidnapping and death marked an era of violence. On the day Sallustro and his captors died, members of the ERP and the Revolutionary Armed Forces (FAR) assassinated the commander of a military task force in the city of Rosario who had (prematurely) boasted that he had eliminated 85% of the area's guerrillas. In 1974, two years after the death of Sallustro, gunmen killed Fiat's personnel manager, seemingly to com-

Figure 3.2   Police close a roadway to search vehicles for ERP members during the Sallustro kidnapping.
Source: © Arquivo Nacional, Brazil.

memorate the Sallustro's assassination. How did this kind of violence become Argentina's political language?

Enthralled by Peronism

Between 1955 and 1983, Argentina experienced three periods of military rule, lasting a total of 18 years (two additional military dictatorships preceded this period). Argentines turning 28 in 1983 would have spent two-thirds of their life governed by the armed forces. The episodes of military rule punctuated years of turbulent and often violent politics. These decades shaped by military rule culminated in the 1976 military coup, which began an era of unbridled state violence unleashed by the armed forces' *Proceso de Renovación Nacional*, the Process of National Renewal, or Proceso (1976 to 1983). Through the Proceso, the armed forces sought to eradicate the roots of political unrest and economic stagnation in order to create a stable new national order. The Proceso resulted in the death of at least 14,000 Argentines.

During the decades culminating in the Proceso, Argentina faced a clash between rival economic models and the political framework to implement them. Populist Juan Perón set the terms of this debate. Elected in 1946 and re-elected in 1951, Perón pursued development driven by nationalizations and increased wages. In 1955, the armed forces deposed him and installed a dictatorship that lasted until 1958. The armed forces resented Perón's influence over the period of civilian rule that followed and in 1966 took power again. In 1973, the military relented and allowed Perón to return. He was re-elected president in 1974, but died nine months later.

By the time the armed forces allowed Perón to return from exile, Peronism had scrambled the traditional polarization between left and right. Because of his popularity, political groups on both the left and the right called themselves Peronists and fought each other over their claims to Perón. There the unions had mostly become channels of political organization loyal to Perón. Beyond them, there were the armed forces, which for decades had sought to suppress Peronism. And there was a radical left (including the ERP) that had no allegiance to Perón. These groups attacked each other in a cycle of violence that consumed Argentine politics. At some point every political party and movement advocated violence against its rivals or advocated dictatorship as a means to impose their vision. Sallustro's kidnapping, and the government's decision not to negotiate reflected the way politics had come to function in Argentina.

Argentina's economic arc was equally dramatic: at the beginning of the century it had the highest per capita income in Latin America. Its prosperity came from an export boom in beef and grains. The advent of canning and refrigeration stimulated the creation of vast meat-processing facilities in around Buenos Aires. During the boom, Argentina received over 3 million European and Middle Eastern immigrants, swelling the country's increasingly urban and unionized working class. Since the Depression, Argentina's economy stagnated, first due to the collapse of demand for Argentina's agricultural exports, and later as those exports faced increased foreign competition. During the 40 years preceding the 1966 military coup, the Argentine economy grew at an annual rate under 1%. Though in 1929 per capita income in Argentina was almost equal to that of Australia, by 1960, it was just over half that amount.[2]

Argentina's urban working class was the largest in Latin America and had the highest standard of living in the mid-twentieth century, but this standard of living was besieged both by economic stagnation and attempts by businesses and successive military governments to suppress wages to increase competitiveness. The historic experience of prosperity yielding to anxiety turned Argentina's labor unions into powerful political organizations. As unions became the conduits of political competition, they were met both by civilian politicians eager to tap their political potential, and the armed forces and conservative groups, who sought to stifle them.

Argentina enacted universal male suffrage in 1912, drawing workers into politics. The Radical Civic Union (UCR) party cultivated workers' votes through reforms such as regulation of factory conditions, and elected party leader Hipólito Yrigoyen to the presidency twice (1916–22, 1928–30). In 1930, anxiety over worker politics and the impact of the Depression provoked the first of six twentieth-century military coups in Argentina. Generals inspired by Italian fascism deposed Yrigoyen. During the "Infamous Decade," a succession of generals and their civilian allies held power through elections won by banning the UCR and leftist parties.

The Infamous Decade culminated in a 1943 coup by which the armed forces took power again. Seeking the support of workers, the generals created a Department of Labor to establish a dialogue with union leaders. The director of the department, Colonel Juan Perón, appreciated the political potential held by the working class and learned to capitalize upon it. The generals grew uneasy about the political base Perón was building and jailed him. Actress Evita Duarte, Perón's girlfriend (they soon married) mobilized the unions to secure Perón's release.

Juan Perón was elected president in 1946 with the support of the urban working class. Perón met with labor leaders as he took office, wearing an undershirt in symbolic unity with the working class, whom he called the *descamisados* – shirtless (manual) laborers. He presented an economic plan to increase employment and wages through nationalization of industries, import substitution, increased consumer demand, and control over commodity exports. Perón would make the workers prosperous, and the workers would make Perón powerful. Social groups that had prospered through the old free trade model felt threatened by this program. They supported more moderate programs of development like the one advocated by Raúl Prebisch.

Perón's formula benefited from the role played by his charismatic wife, Evita, who became an intermediary between Perón and the *descamisados*, nourishing a cult of personality around Perón. He formed a political party, the *Partido Justicialista*, which translates to Party for Social Justice and reflected the rhetoric of providing a fairer deal for workers. Behind the scenes, Perón reassured Argentina's conservative elite that, at the end of the day, he was one of them, and that he was their best hope because he and his reforms stood between the workers and truly radical leaders. As Perón expressed it, "the masses don't have value just because of their numbers or their abilities. Their value lies in the leaders they have before them."[3]

Perón nationalized banks, railroads, telephone, telegraph and electric utilities, airlines, and the merchant fleet. He also created an institute to redistribute of capital within the economy. The Argentine Institute for Promotion of Trade (IAPI) purchased the country's entire export production of beef and grains, and negotiated its sale abroad. IAPI invested its profits in industries that manufactured consumer goods workers could purchase with their higher earnings. In theory, this scheme would create self-sustaining internal markets by which consumption would sustain production. At first, Perón's scheme succeeded. Workers with more purchasing power increased consumption of textiles, beef and consumer goods. The formula depended on commodity prices, which were high after the Second World War but declined as European farming recovered and with competition from the U.S. Marshall Plan. As commodity prices and export markets dwindled, the capacity for IAPI to eke out profits to invest in industry depended on lowering its purchase prices to the point where producers withheld their products.

Assessments of Argentina's historical trajectory often revolve around ascribing blame over its stagnation. Perón's critics contended that his development plan distorted the economy, created unmanageable worker expectations, undermined the export sector, triggered inflation, and drove away investment. Perón was responsible for Argentina's decline. Perón's supporters argued that he arrested a worse decline: agriculture-based development had peaked and those who profited from exports had failed to reinvest to the benefit of the economy until Perón stepped in. The nationalization of British-owned railroads nourished both views. Paying $50 million for obsolete and ill-maintained railroads could be seen as pound-foolish: a costly propaganda opportunity for Perón to claim sovereignty over a foreign-owned industrial sector. But it was penny-wise to assume the railroads in exchange for wartime exports that Britain now struggled to pay. The debate characterized a dependent nation's struggle to transition from reliance on agricultural exports to sustainable industry. And they show how Perón's attempts to speed industrialization served his prestige, relied on overly optimistic expectations, and deepened political divisions.

Perón's political fortunes turned on an economy weakened by lower commodity prices and Evita's death from cancer in 1952. Evita's charisma had been a cornerstone of Perón's political power. After she shepherded the bill granting women's suffrage in 1947, she organized a Peronist Feminine Party that swelled the ranks of supporters of Peronism. The first women elected to office were Peronists. In the 1951 election, slightly more than half of men voted for Perón, but nearly two-thirds of women did. Still, Evita had been frustrated in her wish to stand for vice-president because the military objected to her candidacy. Juan Perón struggled in her absence to balance opposition by landowners and the military with the demands of workers who had tasted greater prosperity in the late 1940s but saw employment and spending power recede. An expanding economy and a messenger like Evita helped Perón close the gap between these groups. Now Perón found the gap growing along with the ranks of his foes. Though he had been an Army officer and participated in the last military government, many officers mistrusted him. So did the Catholic Church: he was excommunicated in 1955 over a dispute with Argentine priests. Perón relied increasingly on force, seizing newspapers and jailing opponents.

The Failure of De-Peronization, 1955–73

While Perón's reversal of fortune might have been adjudicated by the 1957 elections, the opportunity never arose. In September 1955, he was overthrown by the armed forces. He fled to Paraguay and settled in Spain as a guest of dictator Francisco Franco. The military called its coup the "Liberating Revolution" and ruled for three years, mostly under General Pedro Aramburu (1955–8). Inspired by the de-Nazification conducted in Germany after the war, the new regime conducted de-Peronization, seeking to erase Juan and Evita Perón's influence over public life. Aramburu barred Perón from returning, outlawed Peronist parties, removed Peronists from union leadership, and expelled them from the military. It struck Peronist holidays from the calendar and forbade public mention of him. Aramburu had Evita's cadaver removed from the Ministry of Labor, where it was being embalmed for public display. Public schools faced a problem: textbooks had become saturated with Peronism and could not be used.[4] During the 1956 school year, students were relegated to using textbooks published in the 1930s.

This was the second time the military sought to reshape politics by banning the main political party (as it had during the Infamous Decade with the UCR). But the armed forces' and conservatives' distaste for Peronism could not simply be imposed by decree. De-Peronization led to a backlash: Perón's support had been diminishing, but workers and the poor now rallied to him. This created a distorted political arena and forced politics out of normal institutional channels. If Perón or Peronist candidates could run for national or local office, they would win. Because of their exclusion, political institutions and public policies lost legitimacy. A sign of this crisis of legitimacy was the high rate of spoiled ballots: denied the ability to vote for Perón, many would cast their vote for no one at all.

The Liberating Revolution regime allowed elections in 1958, but without Perón or openly Peronist candidates. The elected president, Arturo Frondizi (1958–62), had discretely sought Perón's endorsement from exile. He struggled to build a viable political coalition in the Peronist vacuum, and pursued a project of infrastructure building and promotion of heavy industry that resembled the approach that succeeded for his contemporary, Juscelino Kubitschek, in Brazil. With a more fragile political base than Kubitschek's, Frondizi also courted the radicalizing left, for instance by meeting with fellow Argentine Che Guevara. Frondizi's flirtation with Peronism and leftists fueled mistrust by the armed forces. They forced Frondizi to resign in 1962 after he overturned the ban on Peronist candidates for provincial elections.

Senate President José Maria Guido succeeded Frondizi until elections were held in 1963. The newly elected president, Arturo Illia, was also forced by the military to resign in 1966 after allowing Peronists to run in congressional elections. Though the military allowed no political formula to include Perón, no political formula could succeed by excluding him. After Perón's first term in office, from 1946 to 1951, no elected president would remain in office until the end of his constitutional term until Carlos Menem, a member of the Justicialist Party founded by Perón, did so in 1999. Argentina's economic project foundered on the political crisis. Governments lacked the cohesion and continuity to sustain policies, maintain a stable economic environment, attract foreign investment, or control inflation. Historian Paul Lewis explains "The real problem of Argentine business in the 1960s was not, strictly speaking, a shortage of capital, but a lack of willingness to invest." Bankers and businessmen did all they could to sequester money abroad rather than place it at the mercy of the country's political and economic turbulence.[5]

In 1966, the armed forces again took control. Frustrated with the failure of civilian rule to support de-Peronization and to arrest an ongoing wave of strikes, a new armed forces movement called the "Argentine Revolution" installed General Juan Carlos Onganía in the presidency. The Argentine Revolution was a political turn that both shaped and foreshadowed the *Proceso* a decade later. It differed from earlier military governments in its expressed intention to retain power, and lasted over seven years. Onganía and the armed forces disbanded political parties and dealt harshly with striking workers. The dictatorship was the first to substantially interfere in university life, arresting students suspected of involvement in opposition politics. And the regime pledged to sanitize and stabilize the country's government and its economy through a program of currency stabilization and deficit reduction akin to Brazil's Campos–Bulhões Plan (1964–7). The regime restricted workers' right to strike, suppressed wages to curtail inflation, opened the country to more direct foreign investment and reduced trade barriers. The results were diminished inflation, greater profits for businesses, and a lowered standard of living for workers.

While in its first years the regime suppressed political dissent, stabilized the economy, and quelled worker demands, the blanket of control it maintained was upset in 1969 by strikes in the industrial city of Córdoba, the *Cordobazo*. The mounting opposition to the Argentine Revolution regime also echoed events in Brazil, where strikes and protests resulted in the Brazilian dictatorship's promulgation of AI-5 in 1968. As in Brazil, the sequence of events culminating in the Cordobazo began when police shot and killed three university students participating in demonstrations against an increase in cafeteria prices.

The killings unleashed student protests that drew the support of unions, which joined the unrest to protest wage controls that, again as

in Brazil, had been used to control inflation by stifling wages. The protests culminated in a nationwide general strike led by the national labor
federation (CGT, Confederación General del Trabajo). Autoworkers in
Córdoba began the strike a day early, turning the city, with its large
industrial worker and university student populations, into the flashpoint
of social unrest. Students and workers occupied the downtown quarter,
and Onganía deployed the army to retake the city. The Cordobazo
resulted in the death of thirty strike participants and left hundreds
wounded. It became a lightning rod for opposition to the dictatorship.
Opposition groups mounted demonstrations and strikes in other cities
over the course of the year, and initiated a second uprising in Córdoba
in 1971, called the *Viborazo*.

This upheaval revealed yet again the unintended consequences of the
military's intervention, which recalled the larger failure of de-Peronization.
By shutting down the constitutional and institutional channels for political action, the armed forces inspired increasingly radical and violent
opposition. Beyond general strikes and student protests, a new wave of
armed guerrilla groups seeking to overthrow the regime, and replace it
with a variety of different models of government and economy, flour-
ished. Particularly inspired by the Cuban Revolution, these groups
believed that armed action would not just topple the dictatorship, but
unleash a complete transformation of society. While similar groups proliferated in other parts of Latin America during these years, the Argentine
revolutionary groups had a peculiarly national character: within a political context defined by the exclusion of Perón and the official erasure of
the memory of Evita, the majority of these groups defined themselves as
Peronists.

The *Montoneros*, a leading leftist political and military organization,
established itself through a dramatic act. In 1970, the Montoneros kidnapped General Aramburu, who had helped topple Perón and governed
from 1955 to 1958. The group placed him on trial for "crimes against
Argentina," and sentenced him to death. In the course of his trial, they
demanded that he reveal the location of Evita's body, which he had
removed and disappeared as president. He revealed that he did not know
the location, which was registered in a letter in possession of the executor
of his will, and could be revealed only after his death. When his body
appeared on a roadside shortly afterward, the Montoneros took credit
for rescuing Evita's remains.[6] In the years following this symbolic act, the

Montoneros grew from the handful of members who carried out the kidnapping to a political movement with millions of members.

General Onganía took power in 1966 with promises of a return to order, and the creation of a stable environment for economic growth. He produced neither. The 1969 Cordobazo and the 1970 kidnapping and execution of Aramburu so heightened the country's political crisis and Onganía stepped down in 1970. He ceded the presidency to another General, Roberto Levingston. Levinsgston held office for less than a year before the second Córdoba uprising, the *Viborazo*, compelled his resignation. The generals were unable to dampen the social unrest fueled by radicalizing Peronist unions and students. Their powerlessness eroded the regime's popularity. A third general, Alejandro Lanusse, assumed the presidency (1971–3) and negotiated a return to civilian rule. Perhaps he could achieve in the transition what his predecessors had failed to accomplish in the dictatorship. His government continued to suppress

Figure 3.3   The Army suppresses a protest in Mendoza, 1972.
Source: © Arquivo Nacional, Brazil.

labor unions and leftist groups like the Montoneros, but he conceded that de-Peronization was a failure that resulted in political instability and ungovernability. Lanusse lifted the restrictions on Peronist political activity and the ban on Perón's return. He scheduled elections through which Peronist dentist Héctor Cámpora won the presidency on the campaign slogan "Cámpora in Government/Perón in Power." All attempts at governing without Perón having failed, the military Junta played its last card.

Argentine Left and Perón's Return, 1969–74

As in Chile, Brazil, or the United States and Europe, a generation gap in the 1960s yielded youth movements that were increasingly radical. But in Argentina, the political vacuum created by de-Peronization and military rule intensified this youth radicalization. Like other social and political movements, this new Argentine left reflected the contours of Argentina's political culture by declaring itself Peronist, championing the return of an aging Juan Perón and celebrating Evita as a martyr to the people. This left, like other parts of Argentine society, was balkanized into separate, often overlapping organizations. The largest and most influential by the early 1970s were the Montoneros and the Peronist Youth (*Juventud Peronista*). These were mass social and political movements that at their peak had millions of adherents.

At their fringes, these movements had armed branches that clashed with right-wing Peronist groups, the armed forces, and the police in a cycle of violence that created an atmospheree of siege and instability in Argentina. Among this radical left there was a host of smaller groups that were more wholly committed to social revolution through armed guerrilla struggle. The largest of these was the ERP (Ejército Revolucionário del Pueblo), which kidnapped Sallustro. Numerous other groups existed for shorter periods, and in many cases merged into the two larger movements, Montoneros and ERP. Among them were the ELN (Ejército de Liberación Nacional), which merged into the FAR (Fuerzas Armadas Revolucionárias, which merged with the Montoneros), as well as the FAP (Fuerzas Armadas Peronistas), and the FAL (Fuerzas Armadas Libertadoras), which both joined into the ERP.[7] These groups were more or less influenced by the guerrilla methods and tactics promoted by Che Guevara.

Members of these groups shared much in common. They were mostly young, mostly urban, and often from the middle class. They were inspired by the Cuban Revolution – both the act of seizing power and the brisk pace of social and economic transformation in Cuba after 1959. For them, the Cuban Revolution was a repudiation of the caution and gradualism of older generations of Marxists: profound national transformation was possible *now*. Poverty, illiteracy and exploitation could – and must – be immediately eradicated. The "oligarchic state" serving bankers, landowners, bosses and the military must be replaced by a "popular state" that represented the will of the people and addressed popular needs. Journalist Horacio Verbitsky defined the broad goals of this left. They:

> Included a planned economy, the elimination of monopolies, the control of foreign trade and the diversification of markets. The nationalization of the banking system, the repudiation of the foreign debt drawn on the backs of the people, agrarian reform so that the land belongs to those who work it . . . They envisioned protecting domestic industry, the development of a heavy industrial sector, the integration of regional markets, the nationalization of basic economic sectors (steel, oil, electricity, meatpacking), an independent foreign policy that builds common cause with oppressed peoples . . . dignified salaries and stable work for all, homes for the homeless, hospitals for the sick, justice for those who were born or aged amid injustice.[8]

They did not see themselves as taking power, they saw themselves as liberating the nation. A byproduct of this idealism was also ideological division among militants, who had small but seemingly profound differences of opinion about the path to revolution and the society to be created.

These movements were organized into small tactical units called cells, each largely blinded to the existence and composition of other cells in order to prevent the interrogation of individual members from threatening the coherence of the overall organization. They carried out armed actions that avoided civilian casualties, directing their efforts against institutions such as the police and the armed forces. These armed actions were not intended to seize control outright, but rather to build capacity by raiding arms and cash, and to undermine the legitimacy of what their proponents saw as the repressive institutions that stood in the way of a true dialogue between the state and the people that would result in the creation of the "popular state" that expressed the will of the people rather than the interests of capitalists and "gorilas" (as they disparagingly termed members of the armed forces). Each year, Argentina's guerrilla movements carried out a growing array of armed acts, ranging from assassinations of political figures or members of the police, kidnappings, bank robberies or bombings, averaging more than two acts of violence per day by the mid-1970s.[9]

These approaches netted spectacular successes and frequent failures. The armed wing of the Montoneros scored some dramatic victories, like the 1970 kidnapping, clandestine trial and execution of the former dictator General Aramburu, or their 1974 kidnapping Aramburu's body from its vault to demand the repatriation of Evita's to Argentina (both of which allowed the Montoneros to lay claim to Evita's legacy); and later with the 1974 kidnapping of Juan and Jorge Born, scions of one of Argentina's wealthiest industrial and finance families, who they ransomed for $60 million to fund their revolutionary operations. But there were equally failed operations, such as the spectacular 1972 Trelew prison break, in which guerrillas dressed as guards took over the prison and sprang over 100 jailed members of the FAR, the ERP and Montoneros. Six – all movement leaders (including ERP leader Mario Santucho) – made it to a hijacked airliner waiting for them at a nearby airport, with which they fled to Chile and eventually Cuba. The rest were recaptured, and many were assassinated at a nearby army base, their bodies arranged to make it seem they were killed trying again to escape. Even if General Lanusse recognized the futility of continued military rule and was preparing to yield power to Peronists, his government continued to use this kind of violence against the radical left.

The political high-water mark of the Argentine left was the brief presidency of Peronist Héctor Cámpora. Horacio Verbitsky suggests that at the moment of Cámpora's election, the left "had no brakes," seeking a full social revolution and missing its opportunity to consolidate the gains it had achieved by forcing an end to the dictatorship of the Argentine Revolution and electing Cámpora.[10] Cámpora sought a governing accord that bridged the radical (Peronist) left, the old-line Peronist unions, and the restive and often violent Peronist right, while orchestrating Perón's return from exile. He governed over a fractious and expectant moment in which popular organizations from far across the political spectrum imagined themselves victorious and held continuous marches and rallies to demonstrate their respective strength in relative numbers, while quietly fighting each other at the margins.

In Argentina's peculiar political landscape, young, urbane members of the left looked to Perón's return as the means to transform Argentina into a socialist state. At the same time, members of Argentina's far right, many with openly fascist ideas, looked to Perón's return as a means of seizing power and crushing the left. Beneath the simmer of competing expectations, the Peronist right laid claim to Perón and his political circle. As Perón prepared for his return to Argentina, the elderly and increasingly infirm leader and his wife Maria Estela (Isabelita) fell under the influence of their thuggish astrological guide, José López Rega, a retired policeman who had formed part of Perón's private security detail in Spain and insinuated himself into a role as Perón's chief political and spiritual advisor. López Rega was known as *el brujo*, the sorcerer, for his occult practices. He ingratiated himself with Perón by weaving a bizarre version of freemasonry into the belief that Perón was the spiritual savior of Argentina.

At Perón's behest, Cámpora appointed José López Rega as Minister of Social Welfare, a job far less benign than it sounds. The ministry, which

Figure 3.4   Jailed members of ERP, Montoneros, FAL, FAP and other groups, awaiting release after Héctor Cámpora's election in 1973.
Source: © Arquivo Nacional, Brazil.

Figure 3.5   Right-wing Peronists.
Source: © Arquivo Nacional, Brazil.

received and expended funds collected through Argentina's (largely Peronist) labor unions, served as a perch from which López Rega could organize a network of corrupt police, vigilantes, and right-wing Peronists who would seize control of the Peronist movement and help push Cámpora aside once Juan Perón returned. A signature act in López Rega's campaign came on June 20, 1973, the very day Perón returned from his 18-year exile.

As Juan Perón's plane approached Buenos Aires' Ezeiza airport, historically large crowds marched to the stage set up on an overpass on the airport road, from which Perón was to greet his supporters. The stage and rally were organized by López Rega's Ministry of Social Welfare, under the direction of one of his deputies, Secretary of Sports Jorge Osinde, a retired Army colonel who had been Perón's intelligence chief in the 1950s. The leadership of the Montoneros and leftist Peronist Youth understood that they were being edged aside. They responded by

Figure 3.6 Right-wing Peronists.
Source: © Arquivo Nacional, Brazil.

Figure 3.7 Montoneros, Peronist Youth and other leftists celebrate Perón's election in the Plaza de Mayo, 1973.
Source: © Arquivo Nacional, Brazil.

organizing a massive turnout to greet Perón, hoping to use their numbers to assert their influence to the returning leader. The government estimated that 3 million people attended the rally. The Montoneros, Peronist Youth, and CGT union members marched toward the stage, carrying banners equating Peronism to socialism.

As the leftist marchers approached, Osinde's men opened fire on them from the stage. The crowd panicked and dispersed, under fire from sharpshooters hidden in nearby trees. Thirteen marchers were killed and hundreds wounded. Osinde's men occupied the airport's hotel, which they used to round up members of the leftist groups and beat them.[11] Perón's plane landed at another airport. The next day, Perón issued a statement condemning his leftist supporters and siding with the perpetrators of the massacre. From that moment on, the situation of Argentina's left grew increasingly difficult. With Perón back and the government unable to manage the growing violence between its left and right factions, Cámpora resigned under pressure from Perón's right-wing allies, paving the way to new elections.

Perón won and returned to the presidency in October 1973, holding office until his death nine months later. This time, he secured the vice-presidency that had eluded Evita for his third wife, Maria Estela (known as Isabelita). This was a bizarre and unfortunate choice: Isabelita Perón was a native of Panama who Perón met during his exile. She accompanied him to Spain, and aside from a few short trips to Argentina in the years preceding Perón's return, she had never even spent time in the country. Now she was the first in line of succession to a 78-year-old president in rapidly failing health. Not since the age of the colonial viceroys was Argentina led by someone with such a limited connection to the country.

Even many of Perón's critics held out hope that the return of Perón might heal the growing social and political chasm in Argentina – certainly no one else had been able to. Perón's challenges were twofold: he had to find a way of stabilizing an economy that faced stagnation, inflation running at nearly 100%, and capital flight, and he needed to bridge the political divides that had deepened since he was deposed. Of these, the deep economic troubles were the easier to confront. Perón and Finance Minister José Gelbard negotiated an economic agreement between the mainstream political parties, major employers, and the labor unions. The "Social Pact" established fixed government expenditures, wages, and prices. If adhered to, the agreement would tame inflation and create a pathway to economic growth.

Initially, the Social Pact seemed to work. Wages stabilized, strikes lessened, inflation diminished from 100% to nearly 30%.[12] Still, establishing a consensus to hold costs, wages and deficits in place was easier than carrying it out, and the agreement had the misfortune of coinciding with the fourfold increase in oil prices during the 1973 OPEC Oil Embargo, which made it impossible to meet the goals for inflation, reduce the country's trade deficit, or balance government expenditures. If the Social Pact was not doomed to fail on its own accord, international events made it impossible to succeed. Still, the dominant characteristic of the past quarter century of Argentina's economy had been instability and it was unrealistic to expect sufficient will and agreement to keep the Social Pact glued together.

The Social Pact was far more successful than the attempt to bridge Argentina's political divide. The political differences between Peronism and the other political parties were not the main challenge. Instead, the problem was within the Peronist movement itself, which incorporated much of Argentina's radical left and right, groups that were now at war with each other. The far right, comprised mainly of longtime Peronists, including members of the more conservative unions and the police, were far fewer in number than the left, but they tenaciously tightened their grip on power. Their effective leader was Perón's political and astrological advisor, José López Rega. Gradually, and with the cooperation of Isabelita, López Rega succeeded in limiting access to Perón to those whom López Rega trusted and supported – members of the Peronist far right.

As Minister of Social Welfare, López Rega continued the war on the Peronist left that began at the Ezeiza airport massacre. He formed a death squad that acted out of the Ministry: a paramilitary group called the AAA (Argentine Anticommunist Alliance). Under the direction of Osinde, the AAA assassinated not just members of radical leftist groups, but also journalists and politicians that López Rega saw as a threat.[13] Though the AAA should not be confused with the U.S. automotive association that that shares its acronym, it is worth noting that its equivalent, the Argentine Auto Club, was a privately owned organization whose Peronist director provided vehicles, communications equipment, and volunteers to operate them for the Ministry of Social Welfare group that staged the Ezeiza massacre.[14]

Figure 3.8   Armed right-wing Peronists described as "police employees" in Córdoba.
Source: © Arquivo Nacional, Brazil.

The AAA was comprised of current and former members of the police and the armed forces, as well as figures emerging from the rightist Peronist labor groups and even organized crime members. It was initially headed by Federal Police Chief Alberto Villar, who had been trained in counterinsurgency techniques at the U.S. Army's School of the Americas in Panama.[15] The Montoneros killed Villar in 1974, though the organization survived him. Between 1973 and 1976, it conducted over 1,000 assassinations and disappearances. Much like the militant left, the far right was comprised of a spectrum of paramilitary groups beyond the AAA. The federal police, and city and provincial police forces, particularly in Buenos Aires, Santa Fé, and Córdoba, organized "task forces" whose goal was to suppress the armed left extra-judicially.

Perón's return to Argentina failed to bridge the country's divisions. His decision, under the influence of Isabelita Perón and López Rega, to favor the Peronist right and crush the Peronist left, only deepened the country's political crisis and prompted an escalation of violence. While by 1973 the Montoneros had conducted numerous armed and violent actions, such as the execution of General Aramburu, they were predominantly a national political movement with hundreds of thousands of members, and an even larger number of sympathizers. Its goal remained turning Argentina into a socialist state, and its leaders believed that Perón would naturally align himself with the movement once he returned.

The Montonero leadership was confident that Perón was ideologically sympathetic to their goals, but even if he were not, he would be practical enough to recognize in their numbers the political benefits of adhering to the movement. Perón was neither. In the aftermath of the Ezeiza massacre, the Montonero leadership repeatedly tried to establish dialogue with Perón, only to be told their interlocutor would be López Rega. The break finally came May 1, 1974, when hundreds of thousands of Montoneros marched on the Casa Rosada, Argentina's presidential palace. Perón addressed the tense gathering, called the Montoneros "idiots," and expelled them from his Justicialist Party. Two months later, Perón died.

During his 9-month presidency, Perón failed to find a formula to reconcile Argentina's left and right. The task was increasingly complicated as the two sides fought each other with escalating violence. And in the twilight of his life, Perón no longer possessed the energy or creativity needed to achieve reconciliation. At any rate, his choice was to side with the right supported by López Rega and Isabelita, and one of his last political acts was to shut down political dialogue with the Montoneros and their hundreds of thousands of supporters. More troubling, his political legacy was Isabelita Perón's ascent into the presidency, inauspiciously becoming the first woman head of state in the Americas. Isabelita was flanked (and overshadowed) by López Rega. He purged the cabinet of political moderates, replaced them with his followers among the Peronist right, regardless of their ability or experience, and he stepped up the paramilitary war against the left.

Isabelita Perón governed from July, 1974 until the military seized power in March, 1976. Her presidency was an especially erratic period in Argentina's political history. Forty-three years old when she was sworn in, and with little experience either in politics or with Argentina, Perón depended almost completely on López Rega, who in turn was guided by raw ambition and esoteric beliefs. Her government faced daunting challenges. Inflation accelerated to 74%, en route to a dizzying 954% in 1976.[16] The Social Pact unraveled under pressure from workers whose frozen salaries did not keep up with prices that rose in the aftermath of the 1973 Oil Embargo. Access to foreign investment and loans withered under the weight of the country's economic and political crises, making it difficult to finance imports or service the government's foreign debt. Government administration suffered under the incoherence of policy directions from the presidency.

A jarring example of policymaking under Isabel Perón was the ill-conceived 1975 financial stabilization plan dubbed the *rodrigazo* for its creator, Finance Minister Celestino Rodrigo. Before being named finance minister by López Rega, Rodrigo had been an engineer working in López Rega's Ministry of Social Welfare. Faced with an inflation rate of over 100%, capital flight, and the exhaustion of the government's foreign currency reserves, Rodrigo imposed a set of measures one journalist called "an economic heart attack."[17] His solution to Argentina's long and increasingly grave economic crisis was a devaluation of the peso against the dollar that more than doubled fuel costs, utilities and groceries, while limiting worker wage increases to no more than 50%. The immediate result was a profound crisis in purchasing power. Many families struggled to buy enough to eat in what some called a "hunger program." The main workers' organization, the CGT (General Worker's Confederation), which was one of Isabelita Perón's few remaining supporters, sought higher salary adjustments, which the president first conceded and then quickly revoked. A spontaneous national work stoppage ensued, culminating in a general strike coordinated by the CGT. Perón had lost the last remnant of her political base.

Workers marched in Buenos Aires and other cities, demanding that Perón dismiss López Rega, whom they held responsible not just for the *rodrigazo* but the general political chaos and much of the violence besieging the country. In a sign of the moment's crisis, as union leaders arrived in Buenos Aires seeking to dialogue with the president, they would be met by armored cars filled with armed bodyguards to protect them against the epidemic of political assassinations. Meanwhile, as the *rodrigazo* unfolded just as the Montoneros released the kidnapped Born brothers, and their first act was to use some of the $60 million ransom to distribute food in working-class neighborhoods. The crisis forced Perón to dismiss López Rega, Rodrigo and the rest of her cabinet. After his departure, the discovery of a large arsenal used by the AAA inside the Ministry of Social Welfare building triggered a corruption investigation against her government. Utterly dependent on López Rega, Isabelita Perón now found herself without a political compass and announced she was taking a month-long medical leave from the presidency to cope with nervous exhaustion.

The *rodrigazo* had the opposite of its intended effect. Workers struck for wage increases that could meet inflation. These increases fed the inflationary spiral. Business owners, large ranchers, bankers, and anyone else with much money resorted more than ever to the creative spectrum of means they had developed to hide money and sequester it overseas, sapping domestic investment and further pushing inflation. Between July 1975 and March 1976, inflation surpassed 900%. The economic crisis deepened by the *rodrigazo* and its aftermath only confirmed the impression any observer would have of the Isabelita Perón government: within it, there was no plan and no control. Growing numbers of Argentines now spoke openly – and often longingly – of the probability of a military coup.

The Spiral of Violence

After their rejection by Juan Perón in 1974, the Montoneros, under the leadership of Mário Firmenich, made a fateful decision between remaining a political movement, and becoming a revolutionary movement. With their political channels closed by Perón and his political heirs, the Montoneros turned to insurrection, believing they could build their political movement into a massive popular army. They lashed out at military and police targets, killing two successive Buenos Aires police chiefs and infiltrating Buenos Aires police headquarters to set off a bomb in the cafeteria. The attacks triggered fierce reactions from police and the armed forces. The Montoneros' new strategy made its militants easy targets for the police and paramilitary death squads. Members of the Montoneros who joined it as a political movement, and who had no connection to its armed actions, were targeted. In an indication of the disproportionate cost to the left of the campaign it waged, in the year after Perón's death 504 political assassinations were recorded. Of them 54 were police, 22 were members of the military, and the remaining 427 were leftists.[18]

A similar fate befell the ERP. Smaller than the Montoneros, the ERP committed to guerrilla warfare after it coalesced from other radical groups in 1969. It adhered to Guevarist strategies and continued to attack police and military targets after Perón returned. After Perón's death, under the leadership of Mario Roberto Santucho, the ERP implemented a classic Guevarist approach: establishing a rural area under its own control – a *foco* – from which it could build a national insurrection. The ERP sough to establish its *foco* in the remote northwestern province of Tucumán, an impoverished rural area. Under *foco* theory, Tucumán was ideal: the terrain was rugged, which favored small guerrilla bands over regular military forces; the poverty of its inhabitants meant they would likely understand that the ERP was fighting to free them from oppression, so they would support and protect the ERP guerrillas. Under Santucho's reasoning, this approach had succeeded for Guevara in Cuba, and now it would be the basis of the ERP's campaign in Argentina.

Like the Montoneros' embrace of armed resistance, the ERP's *foco* in Tucumán was a fateful decision. After they relinquished power to the Peronists in 1973, the Argentine armed forces had avoided confrontation with the radical left. But as the ERP sought control over a growing area of Tucumán, claiming to have liberated a third of the province, Isabelita Perón called on the Army to suppress the movement. "Operation Independence," led by General Jorge Videla (who became the leader of the military Junta which took power in 1976) eradicated the ERP guerrillas in Tucumán. Like *focos* in Brazil and Chile, the ERP's numbers were quite limited: at its peak, it had fewer than 200 guerrillas in Tucumán, and its claim that it controlled a third of the province's territory was ephemeral. They were met, however by thousands of soldiers, under orders to liquidate them. General Videla declared that "as many people will die in Argentina as are necessary to achieve peace in our country."[19] Videla used the operation in Tucumán as a training ground, rotating army units through the province to give them counterinsurgency experience that they applied when Operation Independence was expanded in July 1975 to include the entire country, with orders to "annihilate" leftist "subversives."

The Montoneros' and ERP's military campaigns exposed their members to the full force of the military and paramilitary death squads, and it created a pretense for building the state machinery of repression which dominated Argentina in the coming years. The people taking up arms in the Montoneros' and ERP's campaigns imagined that their idealism, combined with some limited training, would enable them to repeat the breathtaking successes of Che Guevara and Fidel Castro in Cuba. In reality they were outmatched by the police and military. Since 1959, the latter had studied counterinsurgency techniques, with training by the United States and France. The armed forces were ready to apply harsh lessons learned from the U.S. and French failures in Cuba, Algeria, and Vietnam, so they were prepared for Guevara's tactics in ways that the Cuban military had not been.

Like its Brazilian and Chilean counterparts, Argentina's armed left experienced far more failure than success. The police, the armed forces, and right-wing paramilitary groups learned to fight the guerrillas, and violently dismantled the revolutionary movements. As in Brazil and Chile, the revolutionary groups' legacy could be measured most by the justification they provided for the violence carried out by men in uniform and their vigilante allies, and in the state machinery of surveillance, detention, repression, and disappearance which outlived the revolutionary groups and cast its gaze on wider and wider segments of society (see table 3.1).

There was a curious exception to this dismal legacy: the $60 million "liberated" by the Montoneros in ransom for the Born brothers in 1974. Montoneros in Argentina and abroad disagreed about how the money should be used and who should hold it. They resolved their differences by placing it in the hands of the Cuban government, which meted it out in support of the Montoneros' revolution. Once the Argentine dictatorship destroyed the Montoneros, the Cuban government weighed what to do with the orphaned money and resolved to continue to apply in support of Latin American revolutions. It became a kind of grants program that funded revolutionary projects far afield of Argentina, particularly in Central America.[20]

Table 3.1 Political violence in Argentina, 1973–6

	May 1973– April 1974	May 1974– April 1975	May 1975– March 1976
Armed actions	1,760	2,425	4,324
Associated deaths	754	608	1,612

Note: 66% of the deaths listed were of leftist militants.
Source: Pilar Calveiro, *Política y/o Violencia: Una aproximación a la guerrilla de los años 70* (Norma, 2005), 63.

Preparing the Return of Military Rule: Argentina in 1976

On New Year's Day, 1976, Commander of the Armed Forces General Jorge Videla issued a public ultimatum to Isabel Perón and her government to quickly address the country's economic and political troubles or be replaced. In the previous week, 14 political assassinations, mostly of suspected leftists, had been reported.[21] A week earlier, a large and well-armed ERP force attacked an army base seeking to capture its large arsenal. The 5-hour battle left 7 soldiers dead and cost the lives of between 62 and 156 guerrillas, depending on police or newspaper accounts of a nearby mass grave. Seemingly no one was taken alive.[22]

By this point, the commanders of the armed forces bided their time. When the armed forces yielded power in 1973, they had little public support. The generals' unpopularity not only made it difficult to govern but also stung an officer corps that believed it acted with unequalled commitment to the national interest. But the economic instability and political failure that followed Perón's return in 1973 restored the credibility of the military's management of state affairs, while the violence perpetrated by right-wing death squads and leftist guerrillas seemed impossible to suppress without a strong military hand. The armed forces planned their return.

Notes

1   "Argentina Again Rebuffs Kidnappers," *The New York Times*, March 28, 1972, 3.
2   Guillermo O'Donnell, *Modernization and Bureaucratic Authoritarianism* (University of California Press, 1973), 132.
3   Maristella Svampa, "El populismo imposible y sus actores, 1973–1976," in Daniel James (ed.), *Nueva História Argentina IX: Violencia, proscripción y autoritarismo (1955–1976)* (Sudamericano, 2003), 416.
4   Monica Esti Rein, *Politics and Education in Argentina, 1946-1962* (M.E. Sharpe, 1998).
5   Paul Lewis, *The Crisis of Argentine Capitalism* (University of North Carolina Press, 1990), 362, 365.
6   Nicholas Fraser and Marysa Navarro, *Evita* (Norton, 1996), 189.
7   Paul Lewis, *Guerrillas and Generals: The "Dirty War" in Argentina* (Praeger, 2001), 38.
8   Horácio Verbitsky, *Ezeiza* (Contrapunto, 1985), 11.

9   Lewis, *Guerrillas and Generals*, 51–2.
10   Verbitsky, *Ezeiza*, 13.
11   Verbitsky, *Ezeiza*, 95–8.
12   Lewis, *Crisis of Argentine Capitalism*, 429.
13   Lewis, *Crisis of Argentine Capitalism*, 433.
14   Verbtisky, *Ezeiza*, 71.
15   Calveiro, *Politica y/o violencia* (Norma, 2005), 54.
16   Lewis, *The Crisis of Argentine Capitalism*, 429.
17   Juan Yofre, *"Nadie Fue"*: *Crónica, documentos y testimonios de los últimos meses, días y horas de Isabel Perón en el poder* (Sudamericana, 2008), 161.
18   Calveiro, *Politica y/o violencia*, 58.
19   Lewis, *Crisis of Argentine Capitalism*, 436.
20   Jorge Castanñeda, *Utopia Unarmed: The Latin American Left after the Cold War* (Vintage, 1993), 16.
21   Andrew Graham-Yool, *Tiempo de tragedias y esperanzas: Cronologia histórica 1955–2005, de Perón a Kirchner* (Lumiere, 2006), 802.
22   Juan B. Yofre, *"Nadie Fue,"* 310, 328; Graham-Yool, *Tiempo de Tragedias*, 802.

4

Chile

From Pluralistic Socialism to Authoritarian Free Market

In October 1998 Chilean senator-for-life and former dictator Augusto Pinochet was arrested in London, where he was undergoing medical treatment and visiting his friend, former British Prime Minister Margaret Thatcher. He was detained in fulfillment of an extradition request made by a Spanish judge seeking to try him for the murder of Spanish citizens under the dictatorship over which he had presided from 1973 to 1990. Soon after, prosecutors in other European counties pressed their own indictments of Pinochet for the murder of their citizens by agents of the Chilean state under his rule. This was a remarkable denouement for the leader of a regime whose violence spilled over Chile's borders with unusual zeal, including the car-bombing of a political opponent in Washington, DC, in 1976, border conflicts with Argentina and Peru, as well as the creation of Operation Condor, a syndicate of intelligence services from other South American dictatorships that acted as an espionage and assassination ring. The arrest presented a paradox for Chilean President Eduardo Frei. His father was a former president who was possibly poisoned to silence his opposition to the dictatorship. Yet Frei fought the extradition requests and secured former dictator's return to Chile. The arrest and the manner of Pinochet's release closed the cycle of military rule and re-democratization in Chile under Pinochet and the Junta.

Drawing a distinction between Pinochet and the military Junta is crucial to understanding the distinct character of Chile's dictatorship. Unlike the regimes in Argentina and Brazil, Chile's dictatorship had a

Dictatorship in South America, First Edition. Jerry Dávila.
© 2013 Jerry Dávila. Published 2013 by Blackwell Publishing Ltd.

single public face throughout its almost 18 years: Augusto Pinochet. As a result, it is tempting to think of this as a personalist – as rule by a strongman – as was the case under Rafael Trujillo in the Dominican Republic, Papa and Baby Doc Duvalier in Haiti, Manuel Noriega in Panama, Anastasio Somoza in Nicaragua, and Alfredo Stroessner in Paraguay.

The "Pinochet regime" describes a period rather than one man's rule. Pinochet was both powerful and politically gifted. He negotiated with the Junta to be its front man and eventually president. But the other members of the military Junta also succeeded in asserting their own authority, albeit behind the scenes, as Carlos Huneeus and Robert Barros show.[1] The Junta consolidated a system that had Pinochet serve as its public representative, and shielded its debates and divisions from view. But behind this facade, the regime's radical ambitions and internal debates echoed those of the dictatorships in Argentina and Brazil.

The character of military Chile's political culture reflected both the senior military's antipathy toward Allende's reforms as well as the comparative political stability in the decades before the 1973 coup. Similarly, the Argentine and Brazilian dictatorships reflected those countries' political cultures. In Argentina, a disorderly succession of military heads of state reflected that country's political disintegration as well as the almost messianic faith in magical solutions to political crises in the years since Perón was first ousted by the armed forces in 1955. In Brazil, the generals holding the presidency echoed long-held developmentalist aspirations, and the generals' fixed presidential terms reflected the armed forces' compulsion to present arbitrary measures as democratic and constitutional. By contrast, Chile's Junta managed to maintain political and administrative cohesion, shield their decision-making behind Pinochet's public shadow, and chart a consistent economic and legal path across nearly 18 years in power.

The regime's signature project was to make Chile a laboratory of radical free-market reform. This went beyond reversing the socialization promoted by Allende: they replaced decades of policies that had prevailed in Chile since the Second World War, erasing what Marcos Novaro and Vicente Palermo call the "democratic industrialist system" of promoting economic development along the lines defined by ECLA, which was headquartered in Santiago.[2] The Pinochet regime transformed Chile from a leading example of policymaking inspired by dependency theory, into a society that represented a radical free-market alternative.

Chile under Allende

Chile's history before the 1973 coup differed from that of Argentina and Brazil in critical ways. First, there was less of a tradition of military intervention in politics, outside of a period of military rule in the 1920s. Second, Chile did not have a history of populism. Instead, Chilean national politics in the mid-twentieth century was divided into three political coalitions: on the right, the Conservative and Liberal Parties, which represented landowners and large investors in the nitrate and copper mining industries; at the center, the Christian-Democratic Party, modeled on the political parties of the same name in post-war Western Europe, was a party that combined aversion to Communism with progressive social policies; and on the left, there was an amalgam of parties allied to the Socialist and Communist Parties, called Popular Unity (UP).

Through the late 1950s and 1960s, electoral politics in Chile moved leftward, reflecting the general tendency in Latin America by which increasingly universal suffrage gave voice to historically and economically marginalized groups such as women, urban and rural laborers as well as, in the Chilean case, copper and nitrate miners who worked in the most important sector of the national economy. In the countryside, laborers who were often of indigenous descent pressured for the redistribution of land by breaking up *latifundios*. Urban workers pursued higher wages, improved housing, healthcare, education, and a stronger political voice.

While in Brazil and Argentina, populists capitalized on the growing political voice of these workers to build their power bases, mainstream political factions in Chile competed for those voters without the emergence of a charismatic figure like Perón. The left's reform proposal included nationalizing foreign-owned mining companies, so that the profits from copper and nitrates would remain in Chile and could fund social reforms and industrial development. In the 1960s, the right-wing parties lost ground, and the center Christian-Democratic Party moved leftward, promoting land redistribution and social reforms. Chile became a major site of developmentalist economic reform in the 1960s. By the 1970 elections, the popular diagnosis of Chile's social inequality and underdevelopment, as well as its preferred remedies had radicalized to the point where the leftist coalition under Popular Unity (UP) was best positioned to win the presidency.

In 1964, Christian Democrat Eduardo Frei received covert financial support from the U.S. government and business and defeated Marxist physician Salvador Allende by a large margin. In 1970, the U.S. government and business groups provided over $1 million in covert financial support to prevent Allende's election. This time, Allende and his coalition of leftist parties (UP) won a plurality of the vote – 36% over the 35% garnered by the Christian Democratic candidate and the 28% of the Conservative candidate. (This was not unheard of: Richard Nixon won the 1968 presidential election with a plurality of the vote.) Allende charted a course of reforms intended to create a "Chilean road to Socialism," which would be peaceful and lawful, in comparison to the manner in which socialist states had been established through revolution or imposition in Cuba and Eastern Europe. The Chilean road contrasted with the Soviet crackdown on the reform movement in Czechoslovakia in 1968: flower power in place of Stalinist thugs. Seeking to avoid a backlash, Allende took pains to keep the reform program strictly within the legal realm of the 1925 constitution, and even signed a promise demanded by Congressional opponents that he would govern within constitutional bounds.

In 1971, Allende nationalized the foreign mining companies, a move with such broad appeal that the law was passed by the Chilean senate unanimously. He accelerated the rural land reform program already in place, expropriating *latifundios*. Though Allende's intention was for redistribution to be peaceful and gradual, this was one of several areas of state policy that slipped out of control: the reform program inflamed long simmering tensions. Emboldened rural laborers and tenants seized land in advance of the redistribution process while landowners hired armed gangs to beat them back. The land reform process prevailed, but the upheaval resulted in food shortages, rising prices, and anxiety among wealthy Chileans that Popular Unity would unleash radical mobs to grab their assets as well.

Allende presided over a fractious coalition of leftist groups. Among them, the Communist Party was one of the most cautious and conservative: an older party whose members had faced a long history of repression, they were wary of a backlash against socialist reforms. Among the more radical allies were Allende's Socialist Party, and left of it, the Revolutionary Leftist Movement (MIR) and the Popular Unity Action Movement (MAPU). Though MIR and MAPU collaborated with Allende, they envisioned a social revolution and encouraged the more ambitious ideals of radical youths and workers. Allende sought to temper this grassroots radicalism, seeking an orderly transition to a socialist economy in which government programs and regulations could raise the standard of living of the working class (worker wages rose 50%), complete the redistribution of land, and accelerate development.

Allende conducted a national campaign of building public housing, schools, and health clinics. Many reforms focused on working women's issues, which were engaged by a new Ministry of the Family. These included community daycare centers, milk distribution to low-income families, neighborhood grocery cooperatives, and price controls. Allende pursued nationalization of foreign-owned businesses, but not domestic ones. Yet he struggled to temper the enthusiasm of his more radical supporters, who saw little difference between foreign and domestic bosses. Workers conducted labor actions including the seizure and nationalization of the country's largest textile complex, the Yarur mills, a process of consciousness-raising and labor action richly detailed by Peter Winn in *Weavers of the Revolution*.

The challenges Allende faced within his own coalition were small compared to the pressure brought by powerful conservative opponents both in Chile and abroad. Allende's opposition included rural landowners, bankers, business owners, most of the armed forces and police, large sectors of the Catholic Church, most television and radio stations, most newspapers, all weekly magazines, and a majority of the national congress and senate. Allende's opponents also included U.S. multinational corporations and the Nixon administration. When President Nixon learned that Allende had been elected, he pounded his desk, repeatedly muttering "That son of a bitch!"[3] National Security Advisor Henry Kissinger remarked "I don't see why we have to let a country go Marxist just because its people are irresponsible."[4]

Chilean and U.S. businessmen as well as the U.S. government tried to prevent Allende's assumption of the presidency. When Army Chief of Staff René Schneider insisted that the military's role was to uphold the constitution under which Allende would take office, he was assassinated. This opening act of violence set the tone by which Allende's opponents would fight his government. When the effort to prevent Allende from taking office failed, his Chilean and U.S. foes worked to depose him and succeeded with the September 11, 1973 coup that left Allende dead and General Pinochet in power.

Factory owners stalled production and withheld goods from the market as a means of undermining Allende's economic reforms. Merchandise disappeared from store shelves, both in response to lower profit margins caused by price controls and in an attempt to sabotage the economy and again undermine Allende. Right-wing groups, such as the fascist Fatherland and Freedom organized constant protests, and armed groups related to them assassinated community and labor leaders. One of the most devastating actions against the government was a succession of stoppages by trucking companies which caused fuel and food shortages across the country.

Nixon told his staff to "make the [Chilean] economy scream."[5] Government and business abided with a campaign to undermine the Allende regime and provide financial and logistical support to Chilean opposition groups. U.S. companies that supplied factory equipment and other goods waged an "invisible blockade" by accepting orders from Chile but failing to fulfill them. U.S. banks froze lending, and the Nixon administration blocked the Chilean government's access to loans from the World Bank and the Inter-American Development Bank. Beyond economic warfare, between 1970 and 1973, the CIA spent over $13 million in propaganda campaigns, payoffs, and in coordinating and supplying arms for possible coup attempts.

The effort by Chilean groups, U.S. businesses, and the U.S. government to sabotage the Chilean economy and strangle the Allende government had devastating results. The government's foreign currency reserves dwindled and its revenue – even with new income from the nationalized copper industry – failed to meet growing investments in new social policies, a commitment that in turn could barely keep up with rapidly rising public expectations. The tumultuous land reform along with price controls and resistance from business owners led to food shortages, followed by street protests by conservative women banging pot lids to symbolize their empty cupboards. Empty shelves combined with soaring inflation. By the eve of the coup, inflation exceeded 600%, the highest in Chilean history, though quite low in comparison to what Chileans would experience in the early years under Pinochet.

Between 1970 and 1973, life in Chile became chaotic and conflicted. Opposition to Allende intensified, but support for Allende and Popular Unity continued to increase. Allende won with barely a third of the popular vote in 1970, but in succeeding elections his party gained ground. It took nearly half of the vote in the 1971 municipal elections and 43% of the vote in the 1973 congressional elections. Despite financing from the United States, the opposition political coalition failed to gain the two-thirds majority it needed to impeach Allende, helping precipitate the coup later that year. Still, the economy was in disarray for a number of reasons. Allende's economic reforms shouldered much blame, as the failure of price controls and large public deficits propelled inflation, while land reform contributed to shortages. But the economic crisis was also the deliberate product of the campaign of sabotage carried out by Chilean business owners, U.S. companies, and the Nixon administration.

Allende's position was untenable. He had sought an incremental transformation of the Chilean economy, but was besieged by both his more radical leftist supporters and his even more radical right-wing opponents. He believed he could ease the antagonism of Chile's eco-

Figure 4.1   Communists celebrate victories in municipal elections, 1971.
Source: © Arquivo Nacional, Brazil.

Figure 4.2   Conservative women bang pots and pans in opposition to Allende, 1971.
Source: © Arquivo Nacional, Brazil.

nomic and political elite by waging scrupulously legal and gradual change. Just the opposite happened. In late 1971, Cuban leader Fidel Castro spent nearly a month touring Chile meeting with Allende's supporters and freely offering advice. His main diagnosis (which proved correct) was that by not attacking the country's conservative elites directly and divesting them of their property, and by not purging the senior officer corps (as Castro did in the Cuban revolution), Allende conceded to his opponents the resources they needed to oppose and defeat him. Allende rejected this assessment and persisted in his approach, though he did accept Castro's offer of help in training his bodyguards. During the coup, Chilean soldiers found a machine gun alongside Allende's body that was engraved with the dedication "From Fidel, With Love."

Why was Nixon so opposed to Allende? His election and his reform of the economy were backed by growing popular support. Their democratic legitimacy undermined the foundations of U.S. government's Cold War rhetoric: free people would not choose socialism. Initially, Nixon's task force on Chile campaigned unsuccessfully to prevent Allende from taking office. They began looking for military officers willing to stage a coup and secretly funneled weapons and cash to allies in the armed forces. Initially, the United States found it difficult to identify officers willing to depose the president, since the armed forces had a culture of divestment from politics and the commander in chief of the Army who succeeded the assassinated General Schneider, General Carlos Prats, was a defender of the constitutional order. But by 1973, as it became clear to Allende's foreign and domestic foes that there was no easy electoral path to defeating him, they redoubled their efforts to topple him. These erupted into the failed *tanquetazo* (a revolt with tanks), in June 1973, in which army officers sought to seize the La Moneda presidential palace and depose Allende. Army commander Prats suppressed the revolt, but the possibility of another coup attempt was palpable.

By August 1973, Allende and Popular Unity were politically isolated as Chile's other political parties closed ranks against them. Congress passed a resolution declaring Allende to be in violation of the constitution (though it still lacked the votes for impeachment). The same was true for General Prats, whose support within the military disintegrated, forcing his resignation and revealing the politicization of the armed forces, where opposition to Allende now outstripped traditional hierarchy. Even so, Allende became increasingly dependent on the armed forces, brought the commanders of the three branches into the cabinet, and appointed the seemingly apolitical General Augusto Pinochet as the new commander in chief of the armed forces.

On the surface, Pinochet had seemed a good choice. He was not complicit in the previous or ongoing attempts to depose Allende. To the contrary, the ranking conspirators in the three branches of the armed forces, including Admiral José Merino and Air Force commander General Gustavo Leigh, who were organizing a new military action against Allende, initially mistrusted Pinochet. Still, Pinochet counted on the support of the Army, which was the most powerful branch of the armed forces. Beginning with his late adherence to the conspiracy, he demonstrated a growing political acumen that placed him at the forefront of events.

The September 11 Coup

On September 11, 1973, the conspirators in the three military branches struck against Allende. Air Force jets bombed the Moneda presidential palace. Recognizing his fate, Allende broadcast a final radio message declaring "In this decisive moment, the last in which I will be able to speak to you, I want you to have the chance to learn what is happening: foreign capital, imperialism, and [Chilean] reactionaries have created a climate in which the Armed Forces have broken the tradition taught by General Schneider . . . [assassinated by] the same social sectors which with foreign assistance, are hoping today to re-conquer the power to defend their profits and their privileges."[6] Soldiers invaded the Moneda palace and overwhelmed the resistance from the Cuban-trained presidential bodyguards. Allende killed himself. Across the country, military forces quickly took control, overwhelming the sporadic and confused resistance of a handful of Allende supporters who lacked either the training or organization to repel a military action.

A military Junta replaced Allende. It was comprised by the commanders of the three branches of the armed forces and the commander of the national police, the *carabineros*. The members were General Pinochet (the most powerful because of the weight of the Army), Admiral José Merino, General Gustavo Leigh of the Air Force, and General César Mendoza of the Carabineros. The new regime was immediately recognized by the U.S. government, which released all the financial assistance that had been withheld from Allende.

As the Junta seized power, it declared a "state of siege in times of war" which gave it authority to conduct detention and summary execution, and through which it created a mindset among soldiers and police that was conducive to violent action against its perceived enemies. This first wave of repression took many forms. Soldiers executed individuals without arrest or trial. People such as UP municipal councilmen were asked to present themselves to the police for questioning. Many turned themselves in voluntarily, without realizing the jeopardy they faced: informally answering questions could and likely would result in detention, which could and sometimes did lead to death or disappearance.

The state of war was an abrupt and violent concept: suddenly people who had been involved in entirely legal practices were systematically hunted down as traitors. A person's participation in the Allende government, affiliation with UP, MIR, MAPU, the Communist party (PCC), or other parties on the left made them an automatic enemy of the state. So did activism in the labor movement, the student movement or land reform. The number of enemies was daunting, and the Junta arrayed massive resources and terrifying action against them. Scores of detention

Figure 4.3 The Moneda Palace in flames, September 11, 1973.
Source: © Arquivo Nacional, Brazil.

Figure 4.4 Workers detained for violating the curfew after the coup, November 1973.
Source: © Arquivo Nacional, Brazil.

Figure 4.5   Prisoners being taken to the Air Force Academy for execution, April 1974.
Source: © Arquivo Nacional, Brazil.

centers were set up across the country, including 20 alone in Santiago. The center of political activity, Santiago was also the center of repression – so many people were detained that the Junta used the National Stadium for months as an open air prison and torture center.

The conspirators intended the initial repression not only to sweep away Allende's core supporters but also to shock the public into accepting the new political order. A U.S. embassy official writing in the aftermath of the coup explained "The purpose of the executions is in part to discourage by example those who seek to organize armed opposition to the Junta ... Fear of civil war was an important factor in their decision to employ a heavy hand from the outset. Also present is a puritanical, crusading spirit – a determination to cleanse and rejuvenate Chile."[7] The American diplomat estimated the scale of the repression during the first two months under the Junta: 13,500 detained, nearly 7,000 exiled, and between 1,500 and 2,000 killed.

The conspirators also intended the violence to discipline the armed forces itself. In the weeks following the coup, Pinochet had confidant General Sergio Arellano travel to military installations across Chile and execute prisoners. Arellano's death squad traveled by helicopter from garrison to garrison, assassinating 75 people. As Pamela Constable and Arturo Valenzuela explain, the "state of internal war" declared by the Junta, and actions like the Caravan of Death, brought officers into

Figure 4.6   At a desk in front of the Ministry of Defense, a woman searches lists to see if her husband has been detained, 1973.
Source: © Arquivo Nacional, Brazil.

compliance with the Junta's directives and compelled them to "pursue subversives with ruthless dispatch."[8]

The new regime called on advice from Walter Rauff, a former SS officer who managed the logistics of concentration camps and mass executions in Nazi Germany but now lived in Chile. Rauff helped the regime develop a prison located on Dawson Island, in the frozen southern reaches of Chile. (When Rauff's whereabouts in Chile became public in 1984, the Pinochet regime refused to extradite him.) The Dawson camp held the main figures in Allende's government, including Foreign Minister Orlando Letelier and Defense Minister José Toha, whose health deteriorated from torture and hung himself, along with other ministers and senators, subjected to forced labor under extreme frozen conditions.

One detainee at the National Stadium, Brazilian exile José Serra, escaped through unusual circumstances, and his trajectory as a survivor of repression illustrates the costs of the violence inflicted under Pinochet. Serra had been the president of the National Student Union (UNE) in Brazil when the military seized power in 1964. As UNE president, Serra played a visible political role that included sharing the stage with João Goulart when he presented the program of Base Reforms before the 1964 coup. After the coup, Serra took refuge in the Bolivian embassy, which negotiated his exile. He settled in Chile where he studied and taught economics.

After the coup, Serra was detained and held at the National Stadium. The Brazilian regime had provided logistical support to the Chilean conspirators, recognized the Junta as the national government early in the coup, and trained the Junta's intelligence services. When Chilean officials notified Brazilian intelligence services that they had detained Serra, members of the Brazilian intelligence services expressed the wish that he be "dealt with."[9] Yet Serra was more fortunate than thousands of the other detainees. Serra was acquainted with the Swedish ambassador in Santiago. The ambassador contacted a Chilean army major whom he knew and who supervised prisoners in the stadium. The ambassador got the major to release Serra and some other detainees. The major was executed.

Serra's story could have ended at the stadium. Instead, after fleeing Chile, he completed his doctorate in economics at Cornell and taught at Princeton. Returning to Brazil, he became mayor and governor of São Paulo city and state, and ran for president. As Minister of Health in the 1990s, he was the linchpin of health reforms that changed the course of Brazil's experience with HIV and AIDS. The system he coordinated limited the impact of the disease to a level akin to that of the United States, making the Brazilian approach a model for the developing world. That Serra experienced this trajectory after walking out of the National Stadium in 1973 illustrates the cost of the executions and disappearances carried out by the military regimes in these countries.

Given the large number of people held there (up to 12,000 over the two months after the coup), many of the regime's disappeared were last seen there – historian Steve Stern estimates that 400 executions took place at the stadium.[10] Among those killed was folk singer Victor Jara (whose hands were smashed before he was killed so he could no longer play the guitar), and U.S. journalist Charles Horman, who was detained at his home in Santiago on September 12, tortured and killed at the stadium. His body disappeared (but was later recovered). Controversy ensued over the apparent cooperation of U.S. authorities with his detention – which became the subject of the 1982 Costa-Gavras film *Missing*. U.S. Embassy officials seemingly gave the Chilean military Horman's location. By some accounts, American officials were present at Horman's interrogation and torture. A Department of State investigation in 1976 concluded "U.S. intelligence may have played an unfortunate part in Horman's death. At best, it was limited to providing or confirming information that helped motivate his murder by the GOC [Government of Chile]. At worst, U.S. intelligence was aware that the GOC saw Horman in a rather serous light and U.S. officials did nothing to discourage the logical outcome of GOC paranoia."[11]

The Rettig Commission, established in 1990 (after Pinochet relinquished power) to investigate human rights violations under military rule, documented 3,196 assassinations and disappearances, while Stern estimates the total as well over 4,500.[12] The Rettig Commission prefaced its *Nunca Más en Chile* report explaining:

> First, it seems evident that the human rights violations committed by the Pinochet regime are by far the most severe and systematic of our national history. This is not only because of the great number of fatal victims it left behind, but also because it established a regime more repressive than any in the past: the closing of the National Congress; the banning of political parties; the destruction of the labor movement and, in general, of the array of organizations representing the middle and popular sectors of society; the imprisonment of hundreds of thousands of Chileans; the application of savage torture and mistreatment; political firings and mass exile; the establishment of a secret police which carried out state terrorism with impunity; censorship of all means of communication as well as cultural and artistic expression; intervention in all of the nation's universities; the night-time leveling of dozens of slums . . . the complete suppression of the freedom of assembly; the threat to all worker rights; and the over ten years of martial law are a few of the elements of what was one of the most

repressive dictatorships the world experienced in the second half of this century.[13]

Was Pinochet responsible for this? Was he just the face of the Junta? Both. The entity that claimed legal authority was the Junta consisting of the heads of the three branches of the armed forces and the commander of the carabineros (the national police). Under the rules they established, all Junta decisions had to be unanimous, and each Junta member retained authority over his military branch. As Commander in Chief of the Army, Pinochet asserted primacy from the outset: he was the face of the coup and the Junta appointed him chairman. A few months after the coup, the Junta named Pinochet "Supreme Chief of the Nation," and a year later named him president, though the title did not entail additional powers. To the contrary, what emerged was a stable balance of power: governing authority and administration of armed forces rested with the Junta, while Pinochet carved out the image as head of state and role of governing executive.

The dictatorship counted on ready support from the U.S. government. Secretary of State Henry Kissinger observed "however unpleasant they act, the [Pinochet] government is better for us than Allende was."[14] But public criticism of U.S. support for Pinochet as well as other covert action against democratic governments led to a congressional investigation that resulted in the (1975) Church Committee Report, named after the investigation committee chairman, Sen. Frank Church of Idaho. The Church Report documented the extent of U.S. government efforts and expense in undermining Allende, as well as the actions of businesses like telecommunications company ITT, and reported on ongoing clandestine support for Pinochet:

> The goal of covert action immediately following the coup was to assist the Junta in gaining a more positive image, both at home and abroad, and to maintain access to the command levels of the Chilean government ... Project files record that CIA collaborators were involved in preparing an initial overall economic plan which has served as the basis for the Junta's most important economic decisions ...
>
> Access to certain Chilean media outlets was retained in order to enable the CIA Station in Santiago to help build Chilean public support for the new government as well as to influence the direction of the government, through pressures exerted by the mass media. These media outlets

attempted to present the Junta in the most positive light for the Chilean public and to assist foreign journalists in Chile to obtain facts about the local situation. Further, two CIA collaborators assisted the Junta in preparing a White Book of the Change of Government in Chile. The White Book published by the Junta shortly after the coup, was written to justify the overthrow of Allende. It was distributed widely both in Washington and in other foreign capitals.[15]

Following the Church report, Congress suspended military aid to Chile. Under pressure, the Nixon and Ford administrations adopted a strategy of publicly criticizing the regime's human rights violations while privately supporting it. For instance, Kissinger qualified a speech he would give on human rights by telling Pinochet "I will say that the human rights issue has impaired relations between the United States and Chile. This is partly the result of Congressional actions . . . The speech is not aimed at Chile. I wanted to tell you about this. My evaluation is that you are a victim of all left-wing groups around the world and that your greatest sin was that you overthrew a government that was going Communist . . . We are not out to weaken your position."[16]

The regime created a security organization called the Directorate of National Intelligence (DINA). The DINA reported to Pinochet but included members of the separate intelligence services of the three branches of the armed forces. The DINA was led by General Manuel Contreras, who used its impunity and its network of agents and collaborators to conduct extortion, blackmail, and robbery. Contreras also was a "paid asset" of the CIA.[17] The DINA persecuted and assassinated former government officials and other opponents, and it concealed assassinations and human rights abuses (for instance, by arraying the bodies of its victims to make it seem they had killed each other in a shootout, or planting news reports in foreign newspapers and magazines to suggest victims of the regime were alive). It coordinated detention centers, including the Villa Grimaldi prison camp outside Santiago, where future president Michelle Bachelet (2006–10) was held and tortured along with her mother, after the death by torture of her father, General Alberto Bachelet, who had opposed the coup.

The DINA's activities reached over Chile's borders. In 1974 the DINA orchestrated the assassination of General Carlos Prats outside a Buenos Aires restaurant. Prats had been Allende's last Army commander before Pinochet. In 1976 the DINA detonated a bomb in the car of exiled former Foreign Minister Orlando Letelier in Washington, killing him and his secretary, Ronni Moffit. The DINA also masterminded Operation Condor, a kidnapping, assassination, and espionage ring which included the intelligence services of Chile, Brazil, Argentina, Uruguay, Paraguay, and Bolivia, with support from the United States. The DINA's ambitions, and its lack of restraint against the regime's real and imagined opponents, were not characteristic unique to the security apparatus. The economic and political projects implemented under Pinochet were equally unrestrained. Pinochet and the other members of the Junta were eager to remake Chile regardless of the cost.

A Laboratory for Free-market Reforms

The Chilean military had no experience with governance, but the intensity of the violence it inflicted upon taking power was indicative of a radical mindset: this was not an intervention to quickly depose a government and hand power to new civilian politicians. Instead, the Junta turned to two new sets of actors to chart its course: a cohort of ultra-conservative Catholic legal theorists called the Gremialistas, led by Jaime Guzmán; and a cohort of free-market economists called the "Chicago Boys." Both groups were from the Catholic University of Chile, a hotbed of conservative counterculture during the years leading up to the Allende regime. Both the Gremialistas and the Chicago Boys were ready to step into the void created by the coup.

The Chicago Boys were the product of a 1957 agreement between the University of Chicago and the Catholic University of Chile in Santiago that established an economics program that became a Chilean outpost of "Chicago School" free-market theory. Students from the Catholic University received scholarships to complete their doctoral studies in economics at the University of Chicago, and returned to Chile as disciples of University of Chicago economist Milton Friedman. The University of Chicago and U.S. government built the relationship with the Catholic University in Santiago in order to counteract the influence of ECLA, headquartered in Santiago, and its field of developmentalist studies.[18]

The Chicago Boys' free-market ideology derived from Friedrich von Hayek's "Austrian School" of economics. Hayek held that the market system is the primary source of information, so the price structure created by an unrestricted free market best communicates information to guide human action. Hayek rejected socialism: he believed state involvement in market systems was inefficient and that socialism robbed people of their freedoms, an idea he developed in *The Road to Serfdom* (1944). Milton Friedman's "Chicago School" built on this foundation. He went beyond Hayek's rejection of socialism to advocate the state's complete divestiture of influence over the market: other than defense, no activity could best be provided by the government. At the hands of the Chicago Boys, these ideas resulted in not just privatization of state businesses such as utilities, but also of traditional state functions such as education, healthcare, and pensions.

After the coup, the new regime adopted a conservative program to reverse the socialist reforms implemented under Allende. Though the regime returned nationalized businesses to previous owners or sold them off, it failed to arrest the economic crisis or control inflation, which, when it peaked at 3,376% between 1973 and 1975, was the highest in the world. It was in this context that the Chicago Boys gained Pinochet's ear. They arranged for Milton Friedman to travel to Chile in 1975 to give lectures on the free market. While in Chile, Friedman met with Pinochet and followed up with a letter promoting the virtues of privatization and deregulation for Chile's economy. Friedman insisted that what the Chilean economy needed, after decades of protectionism and developmentalist policies culminating in Allende's reforms, was nothing less than "shock treatment." Friedman and the Chicago Boys won over Pinochet.

Why did Friedman call his plan "shock treatment"? Because of the high levels of unemployment that resulted from reducing the monetary supply, slashing government spending, raising interest rates and devaluing the peso to stanch inflation, and lifting import barriers that had long protected domestic industry. For those who lived the consequences (as opposed to those like Friedman who comfortably theorized them), the impact was devastating. Over the first year of the reform, gross domestic product plunged 16% and unemployment soared to 28%. Those with jobs found their real wages fall to half their level in 1970. Living standards collapsed. Some 60% of Chileans could suddenly not afford enough protein and calories, and half of all children suffered malnutrition. This was not just "shock treatment," it was radical redistribution. If the top 5% of the population had received 25% of the nation's income in 1972, in 1975 that top 5% received 50% of the nation's income. Small businesses were ruined and domestic manufacturing crushed by the sudden flood of imports.

Friedman and Hayek lauded the Pinochet regime for applying their theories, regardless of the social cost, either in economic disruption or repressive violence. Hayek declared "My personal preference leans toward a liberal dictatorship rather than toward a democratic government devoid of liberalism."[19] In turn, Friedman remarked "Chile is not a politically free system, and I do not condone the political system. But the people there are freer than the people in Communist societies because the government plays a smaller role, because the free enterprise that has been emerging has been cutting down the fraction of the total income of the people spent by government."[20] The government's role did not seem so small to its many thousands of victims and their families.

As Friedman had promised, by 1977 the Chilean economy began to recover, and experienced a sharp expansion that peaked at 8% annual growth in GDP. This growth made the economy look very different than it had before 1975. Without restrictions on imports and capital flows, much of the growth was speculative investment and the growing world of high finance. Little of it came from industrial production. The boom created a new class of entrepreneurs that profited from the privatization of services and the deregulation of banking and finance. Privatization barons bought steeply discounted state enterprises and won uncompetitive contracts to provide services, building economically and politically powerful conglomerates. The Santiago district of Las Condes became the residential and commercial hub of this new wealth. As in Argentina and Brazil and Argentina at the peaks of their respective booms, this wealth was underwritten by extensive borrowing from Chilean banks that charged high interest to their domestic customers based on loans and investments drawn at lower rates abroad.

As the economy recovered from "shock treatment," the Chicago Boys restructured social policies. In 1980, Labor Minister José Piñera, designed and implemented the privatization of the state pension system. In place of a program like the U.S. Social Security system, Chilean workers now made contributions to one of six private Pension Fund Administrators (AFP). The AFP's would invest the contributions in the Chilean market, ostensibly stimulating the economy while providing a higher return for retirees at lower costs to the government. The AFPs fueled the second wave of privatizations carried by the regime during the 1980s, when the privately managed, for-profit funds invested the growing sums of pension contributions they collected. The AFPs gave the conglomerates that controlled them market influence far greater than any business group had seen before, while giving them a steady income from lightly regulated administrative fees. The AFPs were a boon for higher wage earners but challenging for workers at the economic margins: informal workers, or workers such as women taking time away from the labor force for child or elder care, who did not make the requisite minimal contributions, were excluded. In turn, the system never became self-supporting as it was designed to be, continuing to rely on government subsidies to provide a minimum threshold pension payment for poor workers whose contributions could not provide for their retirement.

The reformers brought the same model to healthcare. The Chilean healthcare system had been a mix of public and private resources. Wealthy Chileans saw private doctors as well as public and private hospitals. Poorer Chileans relied on the free clinics and hospitals of the National Health System, funded by salary withholding applied to all workers. In 1981, the Ministry of Health restructured this system, transferred the hospitals and clinics to local governments and created a private system of Institutional Health Providers (ISAPREs), akin to U.S. health management organizations (HMOs). Wealthier workers bought into these, applying their salary withholding to the private ISAPRE rather than the public system. The reform defunded public healthcare, creating a widening gap in quality between private ISAPREs that reached the wealthiest third of Chileans, and an increasingly threadbare network of locally administered public facilities available to the balance of the population.

The regime also privatized public education. The 1981 education reform shifted the nation's school system to local governments, and many of them handed administration of the schools to private businesses. The Ministry of Education introduced a voucher system by which school systems were paid by the number of students, and students could opt for private schools that would receive the public quotient for each student. The reform created a three-tiered system: affluent Chileans enrolled their children in private schools that did not accept vouchers, private voucher schools enrolled middle-class students, and largely poor students attended the remaining public schools, many under private management. The system reinforced inequalities in access to education: students attending public schools or private schools accepting vouchers were far less likely to pass university entrance exams than students attending private schools.

Despite the privatization of state enterprises and public services that had long been provided by the state, the most important element of Chile's economy remained in state hands. Pinochet did not reverse Allende's nationalization of the copper mining company, CODELCO. This was no small exception to the free-market reforms: CODELCO was the largest copper mining company in the world, and throughout its exports represented more than half of Chile's foreign trade during the Pinochet era. That a state-owned company provided such a large share of the country's foreign trade and its public revenue ultimately meant that Chile under Pinochet was really no more of a showcase for the free market than East Germany was a socialist paradise.

The Chicago Boys and Che Guevara

We can best understand the Chicago Boys' zeal as a system of beliefs, a moral framework – a *culture*. It entailed executing a revolutionary and utopian transformation of Chilean society far more ambitious than socialization sought by Allende. The best frame of comparison for ideology is not the Allende program it responded to, but the more ideologically ambitious ideas articulated by the godfather of Latin America's revolutionary left. The Chicago Boys were like Che Guevara in reverse.[21]

Guevara defined a "New Man" in the early years after the Cuban Revolution, when he worked as Minister of Industries. He synthesized his vision in a letter entitled "Socialism and Man in Cuba," which explained that the pursuit of profit resulted in exploitation of labor through domination and coercion. Guevara proposed to "liberate" people by freeing them from relationships based on the sale of labor and the ownership of property. The means to accomplish this were simple: workers should be freed from the yoke of material incentives, which produced subordination and dependency. Instead, workers who understood their labor was free could elevate their consciousness, realizing that by their liberated work in a socialist system, they contributed to the liberation of others. If they were motivated to help others through their work, they in turn motivated others to provide for them. These workers were unshackled from capitalists who could no longer coerce and constrain their freedom. Now, this "New Man" would be free to apply himself to transforming his society. Guevara declared:

In this way he will reach total consciousness of his social being, which is equivalent to his full realization as a human creature, once the chains of alienation are broken ... Man-as-commodity ceases to exist, and a system is installed that establishes a quota for the fulfillment of his social duty. The means of production belong to society, and the machine is merely the trench where his duty is fulfilled. Man ... starts to see himself reflected in his work and to understand his full stature as a human being through the object created, through the work accomplished. Work no longer entails surrendering a part of his being in the form of labor power to be sold, which no longer belongs to him, but represents and emanation of himself, a contribution to the common life in which he is reflected, the fulfillment of his social duty.[22]

These are lofty words that convey a romantic – yet wholly abstract – ideal.

At the other end of the spectrum, the "Chicago Boys," envisioned a different utopia. They saw the free market was not just a means to make money but as a way to organize society. They believed the market system was the fundamental human truth: the market alone, without state interference, provided the best social organization. Behind the spreadsheets and exchange rates, the Chicago Boys imagined a revolution, liberating the consciousness of Chileans much as Guevara had. Instead of socialism, Chileans would have the freedoms that come from unfettered ownership and consumption. Though they represented opposite ideological extremes, Guevara and the Chicago Boys shared ideological commitments that had much in common. They saw people through the lens of ideas, and their faith in these ideas blinded them to limitations and alternatives. Both mindsets were brutally simplistic: based on abstract definitions of an imaginary "man" to be "liberated" by their scheme, they did not see the complexity of their societies or the costs that their projects imposed.

For instance, both visions were gendered in ways that disadvantaged women, relegating them to roles that were hardly free or revolutionary, reflecting the bias of their advocates. Guevara only referred to workers and revolutionaries as "men," omitting the roles of women in the revolutionary struggle and the transition to socialism. In Chile, the correlation of workers to men resulted had pernicious consequences for women workers. These consequences reflected the dictatorship's patriarchal family laws that subordinated women's decision-making to their husbands and gave their husbands authority over their property. In the economic sphere, the privatized pensions disadvantaged women by reducing their retirement benefits for time spent raising children.[23] Both visions saw "work" in simplistic terms, failing to account for the experiences of workers who held multiple jobs, changed work frequently, or worked informally, a surprising omission given how significant these categories are in Chile as in all Latin America.

The "Quiet Revolution"

In 1987, one of the Chicago Boys, Joaquín Lavín, published a coffee table book that lauded the free-market utopia the regime had created. Amid photos of children lined up like regiments in front of Atari computers and happy workers picking grapes, *Chile: A Quiet Revolution* paints a landscape of consumer choice that was almost pornographic in its fetishization of a private marketplace that enveloped all areas of life from healthcare to groceries, to education and garbage collection.

Lavín's tone and the symbolic authority he brought to things that seem commonplace helps us understand how the Chicago Boys turned the free market into a system faith. The freedom of choice, and the marketplace delights this put within the grasp of (affluent) consumers belie the absence of political freedoms and human rights, as well as the inequalities that kept the majority of Chileans from reaching Lavín's dreams:

> During the last decade, Chile has undergone deep changes, transformations that are modifying the way in which new generations of Chileans live, think, study, work and rest.
>
> These transformations are the result of . . . a deliberate policy towards integration with the world, adopted as from 1975, which not only did away with commercial barriers, but broadened Chileans' horizons by providing them with access to information, technology and consumer goods . . . and all this in an atmosphere that has favored individual initiative, creativity, innovation, audacity and business capacity.
>
> This experiment . . . has produced an explosive compound: millions of Chileans making free decisions, with all the information available in a country that is part of a world which is advancing at supersonic speed, are bringing about a real revolution . . . a real "quiet revolution" is changing this country.[24]

Lavín presented a paradise of consumer choice, where private services always outperformed public ones. He was particularly interested in the experience of the generation of Chilean children growing up in the system he helped design:

> The "cartoon" and Atari generation – children and young people who spend several hours a day in front of a TV set or a computer – is several times more knowledgeable than their parents at the same age, a situation with unsuspected effects. In turn, children TV-watchers represent a new market in Chile, a market clearly in expansion, which is revolutionizing the world of advertising and consumer habits. In the last five years, the consumption of yoghurt has grown significantly, while youths drink more soda pops and less wine . . . A ten-year-old Chilean child has already spent about 7,300 hours of his life gathering information from his TV set . . .
>
> There is a new generation of children accustomed to choosing, who watch advertising and make their own little consumer decisions on the brand of ice cream or yoghurt they prefer.

Lavín's estimate translates to two hours of television, every day, since birth. As a parent, I concede my children watch a lot of television advertising, but I can't bring myself to think of this as a virtue. But children's experiences with the free market were not limited to shopping and television. Lavín lauded the privatization of the school system:

> The change in education, . . . is amazing. From December, 1986, when the process was completed, municipalities administrate 6,340 schools along the territory, most of them run by a corporation which is state-subsidized for each student attending classes every day . . .
>
> In a merciless competition to attract students – who may choose among the schools in their neighborhood, including those run by municipalities, and change if they wish to subsidized private schools have found themselves in the need to offer better services every day, even producing their own marketing campaigns. On Avenida Principal, in the Conchalí district, passers-by are amazed by a large mural advertising a school, showing a group of children operating a computer. The fact that their child would use microcomputers at school, could make parents prefer that one.

The freedom to consume and the delights it afforded, were not only for children. Lavín's adults were as much consumers in healthcare or pensions as they were in the grocery store:

The State is beating a retreat, and is being replaced by private companies in areas which, until a short time ago, seemed unassailable: private social security, private health and private education have already become an everyday fact, giving life to new industries which move thousands of millions of pesos . . .

Chileans are beginning to live in the midst of many more options than in the past . . . We can retire from the Pension Fund we choose, out of a selection of more than ten; we can entrust our health care to our favorite Health Insurance Fund . . .

[ISAPREs] have caused a deep change in the attitude of Chileans towards health: the formerly passive frame of mind developed under the state system, due to waiting and form-filling, has been replaced by an active position, where people feel free to demand better service since they know they are paying for it.

For Lavín this great marketplace of choice had its temple: grocery stores. And among these, the highest order were the supermarkets of Lavín's neighborhood, Las Condes, the trendy district for Chileans who made their fortunes under Pinochet:

Many of the clients of the new Unimarc or "Canta Gallo," in the Las Condes district of Santiago, are surprised when the cashier addresses them by their names . . . or congratulates them if it is their birthday, giving them a small present. The reason is quite simple: through a sophisticated computer program designed by Cenac, unique to Latin America, each client owns a card, which he must show to purchase something. The cash register, which is not just an ordinary register, but an Epson personal computer, reads the code of the card, displaying on the screen the client's name, birth date, and other information . . .

The zeal to improve client service is becoming incredibly sophisticated. In the Estoril Almac, also in the Las Condes district, a previously programmed device triggers a mechanism which, every certain amount of minutes, sprinkles a light shower of water on refrigerated vegetables, imitating the small dewdrops produced at dawn in the country-side . . .

Amid the artificial dewdrops in the produce aisle, Lavín could triumphantly declare: "Chile has become a leading country."[25]

Lavín's passion for mundane details is striking. There is simply nothing that the state can accomplish as well as the marketplace, be it garbage collection, education or pensions: all market outcomes are virtuous. Children benefit from television advertising; workers choose their favorite health plan; grocery shopping becomes family entertainment;

Ataris are an excellent educational tool. Public programs are a form of dependence, while market choices are freedom. Would the changes Lavín lauds not have taken place without a free-market revolution? Chile under Pinochet was different from Chile under Allende. But 1987 was also different from 1973.

Lavín's perspective can best be called a system of faith: he believed the free market was not only true, but absolute and capable of explaining everything. Naomi Klein suggests that "Like All fundamentalist faiths, Chicago School economics is, for its true believers, a closed loop. The starting premise is that the free market is a perfect scientific system, one in which individuals, acting on their own self-interested desires, create the maximum benefits for all. It follows ineluctably that if something is wrong within the free-market economy – high inflation or soaring unemployment – it has to be because the market is not truly free. There must be some interference, some distortion in the system. The Chicago solution is always the same: a stricter and more complete application of the fundamentals."[26]

Lavín's consumers were abstractions. He repeatedly evoked the experience of shopping in Las Condes. Perhaps all of its residents really lived the dream, but it was woefully distant from the experiences of the overwhelming majority of Chileans – even those who lived in Santiago. In Lavín's world, maids and housewives who bought the groceries came from imagined homes where affluence-rendered divisions of domestic labor and domestic service was ubiquitous. Many affluent Chileans benefited from the array of consumer choices in Chile under Pinochet, yet the "quiet revolution" was hardly typical.

Chile's reforms had a complex relationship with the United States. The ideas originated with Friedman and the Chicago School, which used Chile as a laboratory. In turn, Chile served as the showpiece of outcomes that inspired free-market reforms in the United States, including school voucher programs, charter schools, proposed replacement of Medicare with vouchers or tax credits, and proposals to privatize Social Security. When President George Bush proposed in 2005 to turn Social Security into private retirement accounts invested in the stock market, he acknowledged the Chilean inspiration of the reform, suggesting that the United States could "take some lessons from Chile, particularly when it comes to how to run our pension plans."[27] One advocate for the Bush plan was José Piñera, who as Secretary of Labor and Social Security

(1977–81) carried out Chile's pension privatization and in 1994 became a fellow at the Cato Institute, a libertarian think tank in Washington, DC.

Rapid Growth and Economic Crisis, 1978–82

Amid the of privatizations of social services, Chile experienced a speculative bubble, soaring indebtedness among businesses and the wealthy, and overvaluation of the peso, which combined to trigger a new economic crisis. The global recession of the early 1980s, triggered by the second oil shock of 1979 and rising U.S. interest rates, caused a crisis of liquidity which threatened Chile's banking system. The Chicago Boys proposed a free-market response: allow debtors to go bankrupt and banks to fail. But in place of a national banking collapse, the Chilean Central Bank assumed the debts and nationalized many the country's banks, in turning private loans into public debt, which again spurred inflation. The collapse of credit, the debt crisis, and a drop in exports, along with the government's response to these crises that entailed a series of steep currency devaluations, caused another devastating recession. Unemployment surpassed 30% and real wages dropped by a fifth. The GDP shrank 14% in 1982 and 5% in 1983.

What became clear in the boom and bust cycle that followed Chile's free-market reforms since 1975 is that the reforms created a national economy that was especially vulnerable to international conditions. Chile's economy was relatively small – in 1980 the country's entire population was 11 million – fewer than the number of inhabitants of the metropolitan area of São Paulo. Consequently, it had weak internal markets and relied heavily on exports. Before 1975, trade barriers, price supports, and public development projects provided some protection from international market conditions. The free-market reforms stripped these away. At moments of global economic expansion, demand grew for Chilean exports, foreign capital and speculative investment flooded in, and the economy grew at above average rates. But at moments of global contraction, the reverse was true: investment fled, demand for exports diminished, and the government no longer had the economic presence to mitigate the toll.

Even Lavín acknowledged this in his *Quiet Revolution*, though naturally he presented it as a virtue of the free market: "The imperative need for efficiency, increased by the experience of passing from a closed economic policy to one which is open to the world, from recession to boom, and again back to recession, to end in a new recovery, has deeply influenced attitudes ... It has brought about modernization and the capacity to compete, on equal terms, with large international corporations in the conquest of world markets."[28] While the economic cycle made companies more competitive, this efficiency came at dire social costs. The system's rewards concentrated in the hands of finance conglomerates which thrived by purchasing privatized businesses at low rates and profited by providing privatized services amid weakened regulations.

The Chilean Road to Socialism had given way to the Quiet Revolution.

Notes

1   Robert Barros, *Constitutionalism and Dictatorship in Chile: Pinochet, the Junta and the 1980 Constitution* (Cambridge University Press, 2002); Carlos Huneeus, *The Pinochet Regime* (Lynne Rienner, 2007).

2   Marcos Novaro and Vicente Palermo, *La dictadura militar, 1976/1983: Del golpe de estado a la restauración democrática* (Paidós, 2001), 41.

3   Peter Kornbluh, *The Pinochet File: A Declassified Dossier on Atrocity and Accountability* (New Press, 2004), 28.

4   Robert Jervis, "Identity and the Cold War," in Melvyn Leffler and Odd Arne Westad (eds.), *Cambridge History of the Cold War*, vol. 2 (Cambridge University Press, 2012), 33 (22–43).

5   CIA Director Richard Helms, "Notes on Nixon's plan for Chile, September 15, 1970," www.gwu.edu/~nsarchiv/NSAEBB/NSAEBB8/ch26-01.htm, accessed October 14, 2012.

6   His broadcast can be heard at www.youtube.com/watch?v=NYGxGeLAMBE, accessed October 14, 2012.

7   www.gwu.edu/~nsarchiv/NSAEBB/NSAEBB212/19731127%20Chilean%20 Executions.pdf, accessed October 14, 2012.

8   Pamela Constable and Arturo Valenzuela, *A Nation of Enemies* (Norton, 1991), 54.

9   Elio Gaspari, *A ditadura derrotada*, 356, in the series *A Ditadura Envergonhada, A Ditadura Escancarada, A Ditadura Derrotada, and A Ditadura Ecurralada* (Companhia das Letras, 2002–4).

10   Steve J. Stern, *Remembering Pinochet's Chile: On the Eve of London, 1998* (Duke University Press, 2006), 158.

11 Department of State Memorandum "Charles Horman Case," August 25, 1975, www.gwu.edu/~nsarchiv/news/19991008/01-04.htm, accessed October 14, 2012.

12 Stern, *Remembering Pinochet's Chile*, 159.

13 Comisión Chilena de Derechos Humanos, *Nunca Más en Chile: Sintesis Corregida y Actualizada del Informe Rettig* (LOM, 1999), 6.

14 U.S. Department of State, "Summary of Secretary's Staff Meeting," October 1, 1973, www.gwu.edu/~nsarchiv/NSAEBB/NSAEBB110/chile03. pdf, accessed October 14, 2012.

15 The entire Church Committee Report is published online by the Department of State, http://foia.state.gov/Reports/ChurchReport.asp, accessed October 14, 2012.

16 Peter Kornbluh, "Kissinger and Pinochet," *The Nation*, March 29, 1999, www.whale.to/b/kornbluh.html, accessed October 14, 2012.

17 www.gwu.edu/~nsarchiv/news/20000919/index.html, accessed October 14, 2012; Patrice McSherry, *Predatory States: Operation Condor and Covert War in Latin America* (Rowman & Littlefield, 2005).

18 Juan Gabriel Valdez, *Pinochet's Economists: The Chicago School of Economics in Chile* (Cambridge University Press, 1995), 49; Naomi Klein, *The Shock Doctrine: The Rise of Disaster Capitalism* (Picador, 2007), 74.

19 Cited in Greg Grandin, *Empire's Workshop: Latin America, the United States, and the Rise of the New Imperialism* (Owl, 2006), 172–3.

20 Milton Friedman, *Free to Choose, Vol. 1: The Power of the Market*, http://miltonfriedman.blogspot.com/, accessed October 14, 2012.

21 Valdez, *Pinochet's Economists*, 7–8.

22 Che Guevara, *Socialism and Man in Cuba* (Pathfinder, 1989), 9.

23 Alberto Arenas de Mesa and Verónica Montecinos, "The Privatization of Social Security and Women's Welfare: Gender Effects of the Chilean Reform," *Latin American Research Review*, 34:3 (1999), 7.

24 Joaquín Lavín, *Chile: A Quiet Revolution* (Zig-Zag, 1987).

25 Lavín, *Chile*, 150.

26 Naomi Klein, *The Shock Doctrine*, 51.

27 Larry Rohter, "Chile's Retirees Find Shortfall in Private Plan," *The New York Times*, January 27, 2005, www.nytimes.com/2005/01/27/business/world business/27pension.html?pagewanted=1&sq=chile%20pension%20bush% 20reform&st=cse&scp=4, accessed October 14, 2012.

28 Lavín, *Chile*, 85.

5

Argentina
The Terrorist State

On March 24, 1976, a Junta comprised of the heads of the three
branches of the armed forces detained Isabelita Perón and took
power. Tanks rolled into central Buenos Aires as trucks swarmed around
major cities, deploying troops at strategic and symbolic locations. Television and radio alternated between broadcasting military communiqués
and a national soccer team match against Poland transmitted from
Warsaw. Media was subject to strict censorship. *The New York Times*
described footage that Navy censors kept an Argentine television station
from transmitting by satellite to NBC in the United States: "the scene
that was cut short showed troops firing automatic weapons into the
entrance of a Communist Party office and then manhandling someone
who came out of the building with his hands above his head."[1] The new
Junta, Argentina's third military government since 1955, announced a
Process of National Reorganization, the Proceso. The new military dictatorship held power for nearly eight years.

The harshness of Proceso was clear from the outset. The Junta dismissed the president, the cabinet, the congress, judges, governors and
major city mayors. Government posts at all levels were distributed among
officers from the three branches of the armed services. Coincidentally it
was payroll day at the Argentine Congress. That morning, legislators
slipped into the building to pick up what they knew were their last pay-
checks. Rights to assembly and protest were suspended and union leadership and bargaining rights were removed. The constitutional right of
Argentines to freely leave or enter the country was blocked.

Dictatorship in South America, First Edition. Jerry Dávila.
© 2013 Jerry Dávila. Published 2013 by Blackwell Publishing Ltd.

Many Argentines greeted the Proceso with relief. Perhaps this was be a new beginning. Perhaps the epidemic of political violence would end. Even if its methods against subversives were violent, was it not necessary to break some eggs to make an omelet? The major political parties all expressed support for the coup and the work of the Junta. In anticipation, stocks in the Argentine market soared on March 23. The senior Catholic clergy met to bless the armed forces and their forthcoming act.[2] As was the case in Brazil in 1964 and Chile in 1973, the U.S. government quickly recognized the Junta. Even among the radical left there was enthusiasm for the coup: finally the regime would be exposed for what it is, giving Argentines a real choice. For the leadership of the Montoneros, this seemed like a step toward swift victory, through a now open war against the forces of repression.

More fittingly, wealthy Argentines saw this as their victory. *The New York Times* correspondent Jonathan Kandell reported on the tone of a dinner party held at a wealthy Buenos Aires home a few days after the coup:

This was the first weekend after the military coup, and the collapse of the three-year-old Peronist government gave a special glow to the sumptuous dinner parties that still make upper class Argentines the social lions of Latin America.

The guests began to arrive only around 11 last night at Mario's 10-room apartment in the Palermo district . . . There was the usual mix of estancieros – wealthy farmers – middle-aged businessmen, artistic personalities, fashion models and idle rich.

"My husband is so happy over the coup that he's going to pay taxes for the first time ever," said the wife of an agricultural-machinery contractor.

"That's right," her husband said. "All of my friends are saying the same thing. We really want to see this Government succeed. If these military fellows are as serious as they look, we'll get serious also.

Tax evasion is widespread in Argentina . . . the gap between government revenues and expenditures – partly as a result of tax evasion – has been bridged by the printing of huge amounts of paper money . . .

It was almost 1am before the guests sat down for dinner . . . Six waiters, dressed in tuxedos and white gloves, served the four-course meal – fish mousse, beef broth, filet mignon with embedded raisins and potato soufflé, and a cream meringue cake, along with red and white wines.

The host graciously acknowledged the flow of compliments and treated his guests to carefully rolled joints of Colombian marijuana.

He then led the way back into the living room for coffee, cognac and dance music. Inevitably the conversation drifted back to politics and the armed forces.

"It was such a quick, dull coup," said Mario with ironic lament. "Such precision, you would have thought they were Germans, not Argentines."[3]

Only the wealthiest Argentines had the means to benefit from the chaos that preceded the coup, and only the wealthiest Argentines would benefit from the chaos that ensued.

The Junta intended the Proceso to end the violence and instability that had reigned since 1973, or even since the Cordobazo of 1969. Under the Junta's logic, only a patriotic institution like the armed forces could cleanse the nation. The reality was different: the armed forces were hardly apolitical, after all they had held direct national power for roughly half of the years since they overthrew Juan Perón in 1955, and had constrained politics during much of the remaining years. They had been responsible for most of the violence of preceding years through the campaign to "annihilate" subversives in Tucumán and elsewhere.

The latest Argentine dictatorship succeeded with one set of aims, but it was a colossal failure at achieving its subsequent goals. The regime quickly achieved its first objective: it destroyed the old political order, drove the Peronists from power, and wiped out not just the armed left committed to revolution, but much of the political left as well. But having wiped the slate clean, the military regime was utterly unable to establish a new political and economic order. Though the military regime promised a new beginning for Argentina, it proved more able to destroy than to create. It relied on a flatly incorrect premise that it was possible to build a new society by suppressing all social and political participation.[4]

The members of the Junta were influenced by the Brazilian and Chilean experiences, of which they had long and detailed knowledge. Looking at Chile, they drew lessons from both Allende and from Pinochet. Some of the armed forces and business groups were inspired by the Chilean model. They believed that applying the laws of the free market would achieve desired economic and political outcomes: the Chilean model of free-market reforms would not just stabilize and revive the economy, it would also tame the unions and drain the political and social conflicts at the core of what Novaro and Palermo call the democratic industrial model.[5] They hoped repression and reform would wipe their opponents off the board the same way Pinochet had after 1973. For the Argentine Junta, Pinochet's success was to be repeated with a campaign to quickly wipe out the left. Other members of the armed forces drew different lessons from the Brazilian experience. They saw the seeming success of the Brazilian armed forces in creating economic growth fueled by accelerating industrialization, along with stability that seemingly allowed the regime to dictate the country's future political order.

The Junta also drew lessons from the previous experience with military rule at home: the Argentine Revolution (1966-73) had also promised to put the country on sounder foundations. The officers who came to power in 1976 believed the earlier military regime had not been sufficiently thorough. That regime jailed political opponents, and the members of this opposition were released from prison by the Hector Cámpora government that succeeded it in 1973 – indeed many of those imprisoned were members of Montoneros, ERP, FAR and other armed leftist groups which returned to the fight and targeted the armed forces. To avoid a repeat of this experience, the Junta of 1976 resolved simply to kill its foes.

As was the case in Brazil and Chile, what the armed forces proposed, and the language they used, was as radical as any dreams of liberation and transformation conceived by the left. The difference was that the armed forces could place themselves in the position to carry out their project. The Junta's leaders, especially President Jorge Videla, described Argentina's left as a "cancer" and described their action as "radical surgery." Military leaders coined the term "Dirty War" to describe a form of combat in which their opponent was not a traditional military foe but an enemy that could only be defeated through elimination.[6] These metaphors aptly described the carnage that the military and police inflicted on a scale out of proportion to the violence of neighboring dictatorships. Though the Junta spoke of a war waged by the left, the reality was that the regime applied force that was well out of proportion to anything done by the left. If the term genocide is applicable to the state terrorism of South American dictatorships, it was here.

The Junta believed it was fighting the Third World War. It subscribed to a theory that international Communism, led by the Soviet Union, was using new and radical means to overthrow free societies and impose Marxism. According to this doctrine, armed revolutionaries were not the only – or even the main – threat. The real threat was cultural, or more precisely, counter-cultural. The threat included rock musicians and their fans, youth with long hair (student culture in general), as well as professionals like journalists and psychiatrists, who ostensibly threatened the traditional pillars of western society. Anyone who advocated for social justice – the rights of women, minorities, landless rural workers, etc. – was a subversive. The regime judged even those who did not engage in armed resistance to be a subversive social threat, simply for their way of being. This was the mindset which conjured "major surgery" as an appropriate action to inflict on its own population, and which saw Dirty War as the only path to victory.

By this notion of a Third World War, traditional powers like Western Europe and the United States failed to recognize the threat in time and were now weakened. French colonial forces in Indochina and Algeria, and U.S. forces in Vietnam, had learned too late how to win wars of subversion. The Junta believed that lessons from those conflicts could be applied now in Argentina. The senior officers of the military regime studied French counterinsurgency methods, including torture, and they received counterinsurgency training from the U.S. military – training that included lessons on the application of torture. These officers studied the means employed by the British government to combat the Irish Republican Army, including torture techniques that did not leave visible marks on the victims. Argentine torturers called the room where they subjected detainees to noise, light and temperature extremes the "English Room." As Hugo Vezzetti observes, there was a basic difference between the U.S., French or British perpetrators of these acts and their Argentine counterparts: Argentine soldiers and policemen were the only ones to employ these techniques on their own citizens, and on such an enormous scale.[7]

The Junta exported its crusade, helping topple the government in neighboring Bolivia, carrying out assassinations abroad in coordination with Chilean and Brazilian intelligence services as part of Operation Condor, providing military training to right-wing regimes in Central America, and waging war to capture the Falkland Islands from Britain. Like the Brazilian and Chilean dictatorships, the Argentine Junta justified its existence on three planes: moral and Christian; economic; and constitutional. The Junta described its mission as a struggle to save western civilization by waging a holy war. It also created a roadmap of free-market reforms. Finally, by the legal standard it asserted, the very existence of the Junta supplanted the constitution, and the Junta's actions, by their existence, were the constitutional order. The regime recognized no limits to its power, and tolerated no dissent.

The dictatorship began with four main actors. Army Commander Jorge Videla chaired the Junta and served as president. Navy Commander Admiral Emilio Massera, was the next most influential member of the Junta, followed by Air Force Brigadier Orlando Agosti. They gave extensive power to one of the few civilian members of the cabinet, Finance Minister José Martinez de Hoz (1976-81). The Junta presented Hoz with two contradictory goals: remake the economy in the mold of Chile's experiment, but without diminishing employment, so that the Junta could surf a crest of popularity that would give it space to remake the political system, as the Brazilian regime appeared to do. These objectives were not just contradictory: they were incompatible and rendered economic policy incoherent.

The contradictory economic goals reflected political divisions within the armed forces and the Junta that were more serious than in Brazil or Chile. The Junta held sole authority over political and economic decisions, but lacked the cohesion to make them. Instead, the service branches avariciously divided federal and local government, public institutions, and state-owned businesses into fiefdoms. The Army gained the lion's share of cabinet positions and provincial governorships. The Navy and Air Force assumed the government of provinces where their installations were located. The result was a feudal system in which central political authority and coordination of policy were almost nonexistent. Officers in command of local government or state businesses served and obeyed the hierarchy of their respective branch rather than the government or even the Junta.

The system was inherently corrupt. Officers knew there was little oversight of their actions, either as managers of state enterprises or as government administrators. Consequently, as the armed forces divided the spoils of government, the branches competed to seize potentially lucrative assets. For instance, as the country prepared to host the 1978 Soccer World Cup, Admiral Massera fought for control of the event and its planning (whose construction and logistics had a massive but gauzily managed budget) as part of his dominion. Before the coup, preparations for the Cup had been in the hands of an Army officer. As Massera took control of the event, the officer was assassinated in an action blamed on the Montoneros.

Horacio Verbitsky relates an anecdote that captures this climate. It concerned a powerful rancher and retired general who felt inconvenienced by a state inspector. He visited the military security chief for the region, seeking to use his wealth and standing to get the Army colonel (who he outranked, even in retirement) to reel in the cattle inspector. The rancher presented his case to the security chief over breakfast in his home. The colonel responded by saying that he could not withdraw the inspector because he was under a different jurisdiction. "But, if you wait until I dress, we can grab the truck and disappear him."[8]

The rancher balked at this option, but the police and the armed forces generally did not. They cast a wide net against "subversives." Though this was ostensibly a war against both the violent left and the violent right, the reality was different: members of the right-wing AAA were absorbed into military and police task forces involved in disappearances. Within months of the coup, the armed forces and police had virtually wiped out ERP and Montonero organizations in Tucumán and Córdoba. Over the course of 1976, the rate of violence (ever more the monopoly of the armed forces and the police) rose to an assassination every 5 hours, a bombing every 3, and 15 kidnappings per day. Calveiro estimates by the end of 1976, 2,000 Montoneros had been killed, and over 5,000 detained, facing torture and disappearance.[9]

The most intense repression took place in the first year, at the hands of task forces of the Army, Navy, and Air Force, as well as city, provincial and federal police. Each waged its own war, with its own targets, detention facilities, and practices of torture and disappearance. There were hundreds of detention centers, mostly concentrated in cities like Buenos Aires and Córdoba. The decentralization of repression in no way diminished its intensity – to the contrary, it multiplied the chances that an Argentine be a target. Despite the decentralization, the patterns of action were similar. Drawing on both her own experience and the accounts of others, Calveiro synthesizes the process, explaining how the systems of repression were compartmentalized and relied on euphemisms to carry out their violent work: an estimated 15,000 to 20,000 Argentines were "sucked into" detention. There, the interrogators "danced" with the detainee. For 90% of them, this concluded with the fatal word that they were being "transferred."[10]

The Junta's armed services built a bureaucracy of detention, torture, and disappearance. Calveiro explains that this bureaucracy shielded perpetrators of violence from the full meaning of their acts by breaking them down into small steps, each one seemingly manageable or even inconsequential, and masking them in euphemisms. When an order for detention was given, a task force called a *patota*(slang for gang) apprehended a victim, though that was the limit to their responsibility. The *patota* was entitled to the spoils of the person or family captured. They seized cars and looted homes, even taking the furnishings. Detainees described military garrison attics and basements filled like warehouses with items taken from the homes of victims. Survivors relate seeing their captors wearing clothing or watches that had belonged to them.[11]

The victims were deliberately dehumanized. The commander of the Buenos Aires provincial police, General Ramón Camps, who claimed he was responsible for over 5,000 deaths, rationalized that "people didn't disappear, subversives disappeared."[12] The construction is telling: the general employed a semantic trick to describe the violence as being directed at an abstract problem rather than at concrete people. What is more, he used the passive voice so that the events seemingly happened on their own rather than being committed by members of the armed forces. In turn, torturers justified their actions by believing that their victims made them torture by withholding information: the responsibility belonged to the victim for being a victim.

The clandestine detention centers were sites where every form of degradation imaginable was carried out. Rape was systematic. Ethnic minorities were harassed with slurs. Jewish newspaper editor Jacobo Timerman recalled constant anti-semitic and nazi-phillic abuse when he was in detention. Once the torturers no longer deemed their victims useful, they usually marked for death and "transferred" them. As victims changed hands, their executioners dehumanized them by calling them "packages," which made it psychologically easier to carry out the final acts of murder and disappearance.[13] The physical act of disappearance of so many thousands in such a short time was itself logistically daunting. Many were buried in mass graves. Many others, sedated but still alive, were loaded onto military cargo planes and dumped in the open ocean.[14]

The sheer number of people detained contributed to a particularly complex and tragic legacy. One-third of the disappeared listed in the CONADEP report *Nunca Más* were women, some of whom were pregnant. Pregnant detainees were held until they gave birth, often at the Campo de Mayo military hospital, and then disappeared. Military and police families or their friends adopted the children, who never knew their origins or their parents' fate. *Nunca Más* documented 174 such cases, while the Grandmothers of the Plaza de Mayo, an association of relatives of the disappeared mothers, estimated the number of these children at over 500.[15]

The Navy pursued the Dirty War with particular zeal. The torture and detention center at the Naval Mechanics School (ESMA) became the most notorious of site of repression. Located in central Buenos Aires, at least 5,000 detainees passed through it. Though an estimated 90% of the victims held there were disappeared, some were kept for work on Navy projects. The Navy ran the Foreign Ministry and the 1978 World Cup, so it contended with the negative image abroad created by the regime's violence. ESMA detainees with public relations or journalism experience were kept alive to write articles and press releases aimed at improving Argentina's image. Detainees at other centers similarly survived as forced laborers. Since many of the detention centers were located in cities, survivors related the surreal experience of living a world of horror that was just a wall away from streets of oblivious passers-by.

Who was detained? By 1976, the armed forces and the police had long lists of suspected subversives, be they Montonero or ERP fighters, or simple sympathizers of these movements, or people linked to the left. In detention, they were tortured to give up the names of others, who in turn were "sucked" and interrogated, generating longer lists of suspects. A victim's address book became a list of people to detain. *Patotas* raided homes and workplaces, or grabbed victims off the street or out of their cars. Calveiro notes that nearly all the survivors relate having been "sucked up" in the presence of other bystanders, who were powerless to intervene.[16] Roadblocks became ubiquitous. At times, soldiers shut down major roads, such as 14-lane-wide Av. 9 de Julio in central Buenos Aires, during rush hour by blocking off its side streets. The soldiers went from car to car, matching the identification cards of the thousands of trapped motorists to their lists. It was easy to be "sucked up" mistakenly, or for witnessing an act by a *patota*.

Imagine the reach of this fear as violence spread. If you were a student at the University of Buenos Aires, you were in an environment under intense scrutiny by the security forces. This was an important recruiting ground for the Montoneros and the ERP. After March 1976, you were aware of people who had gone missing – students, a professor or your regular bus driver. You dismiss these more distant cases – they could be gone for any reason and they might be anywhere – but you are aware of their absence. But the disappearances inch closer and a friend goes missing. His shaken sister tells you that men took him away in a green Ford Falcon, the ubiquitous car of the *patota*. Now your mind is ablaze. Why is this happening? That meeting? The petition we signed? What if you are next? What would happen to you, to your family? The connections in your life terrify you. Almost without thinking, you pull your address book out of your bag and throw it in the garbage can you pass on the street corner. You look back at it over your shoulder. Is that man reaching into the garbage can? You hear a car brake sharply next to you and its doors open. Moments like this spread like the flu through Argentine universities, factories, and neighborhoods. Tortured detainees gave up more names. The hum of typewriters accompanied the growing piles of reports, which in turn, were typed into new lists of victims.

The CONADEP report *Nunca Más* has scores of survivors' accounts of the climate of fear generated by disappearances. A striking set of accounts comes from workers at a Ford automotive plant. Shortly after the coup, supervisors called a meeting of union delegates. They explained that Ford no longer recognized them as representatives of the workers, and that the workers should now just "devote themselves to their jobs and forget their claims." One of the union delegates asked about ongoing wage negotiations and received the cold response "you'll be giving my regards to a friend of mine, [General Ramón] Camps," the notorious chief of the Buenos Aires provincial police. In the coming days, the union delegates were taken away, "two or three a day." The detainees survived and were released months to a year later. Still, the message to the remaining workers from their supervisors at Ford could not have been clearer.[17]

A Dirty War with Clean Hands? The Human Rights Struggle

How did the Argentine Catholic Church respond to the Dirty War? It was divided. Some clergy adhered to precepts of liberation theology, opposed the dictatorship and were sometimes victims of the repression. This was the case of French nuns Alice Domon and Leonine Duquet, apprehended, tortured at the ESMA, and killed in 1977. Opposition did not reach the Church hierarchy. The Argentine Council of Bishops gave early and ongoing support to the Junta, which it defended as the nation's safeguard against communism. The link between conservative Catholicism and the military's anti-communist culture kept them bound together. The Argentine Church denied that disappearances or other human rights violations took place, even when members of the clergy were the victims.

Pilar Calveiro reflects on the faith of General Videla, who attended mass every day: "After taking communion on Sunday, would it be Monday that General Videla would give the orders to assassinate the prisoners? Or perhaps he had done it on Friday and confessed Saturday? . . . Just as one could be both a bureaucrat and an assassin, mediocre and cruel, one can be a good head of the family, Christian, a moralizer, and also a disappearer."[18] Members of the Junta and their subordinates did not see themselves as conducting violence despite their faith, but in consonance with their faith. The allegiance of the senior clergy to the regime morally eased the ties between their political convictions and their violent acts.

Though the regime counted on moral support from the Church and eradicated opposition from the left, it faced a formidable new challenge: non-violent protest. This kind of protest began barely a year after the coup, when Church officials refused to meet with mothers seeking help for finding information about their disappeared children. Rebuffed, the mothers began circling the Plaza de Mayo in Buenos Aires, in front of the Interior Ministry, holding photos of their children and signs asking *¿donde está?* (where is s/he?). Their Thursday marches drew international attention to the violence of the dictatorship. They became an organization, the Mothers of the Plaza de Mayo, which collected information on the disappeared and pressed the regime on their fate. Another group joined them: the Grandmothers of the Plaza de Mayo, who sought information about the fate of the children of pregnant women who had been disappeared.

The Mothers and the Grandmothers presented an image that was difficult for the military regime to suppress: they were not young radicals, instead they reflected the concept of family the regime purported to protect from Marxism. They did not criticize the regime or propose political alternatives: instead, they acted in their most traditional roles – caring for children and grandchildren. Their quiet march around the plaza did not violate of the regime's injunctions against protests or political meetings. On its face, the Mothers were not political at all, though in reality they mounted the most direct political challenge the regime could face.[19] The regime struggled to find a response. Occasionally, police would disperse the Mothers (when this happened, the cathedral on the plaza would shut its doors to prevent the Mothers from taking refuge inside). The regime even disappeared several of the group's organizers as well as supporters such as the murdered French nuns.

The Mothers of the Plaza de Mayo helped innovate a new kind of political challenge: defense of human rights. This was different from the kinds of political language employed before in Argentina and a clear break from the long antagonism between left and right. Human rights advocacy presented a blistering criticism of the military regime. The Junta had a record of carnage with few parallels (none of them flattering). The ongoing visibility of the Mother's protest kept this violence in view, helping define the regime by that violence rather than by its discourse of renewal. It also placed Church leaders in a bind. They continued to support the regime even amid accusations of human rights violations. The Argentine Council of Bishops faced pressure from the Vatican to change its course.

The Mothers were part of a growing human rights movement both within Argentina and abroad. The Permanent Assembly for Human Rights (APDH) drew support from members of the political parties that had supported the coup, including Raúl Alfonsín of the Civic Radical Union Party, who would become the first civilian president elected after military rule (1983-1989). Adolfo Pérez Esquivel, leader of the human rights group Service for Peace and Justice, was detained in 1977, just as the Mother's protest started. He was held for over a year and tortured. In a sign of the growing gap between the Argentine Church and the Vatican, while Esquivel was imprisoned, he received a papal commendation. In 1980, Esquivel received the Nobel Peace Prize – an act that intensified international pressure on the Junta, which in turn prevented Argentine media from reporting on Esquivel's address when he accepted the prize.

When Esquivel received the Nobel Prize, the question of human rights was at the forefront of Argentine politics. With the armed left eliminated, the regime's leaders began to contemplate the nature of a transition to civilian rule like the one underway in Brazil. They envisioned a gradual process that would result in a civilian presidency perhaps by 1985. But could they avoid prosecution by those they handed power to? They believed their actions were the legitimate costs of war, and that their cause was just, but they understood the challenge to their legitimacy that human rights advocacy presented. Civilian political leaders pursuing a dialogue with military leaders about a transition to civilian rule were equally hamstrung by the question of human rights. It was well known that the military regime had been responsible for murder on an unimaginable scale, despite the murderer's attempts to disappear the victims and the crimes. Even though the major political parties supported the 1976 coup, their leaders balked at reaching an agreement re-establishing civilian rule but abjuring the dictatorship's responsibility for this violence. Would absolving the dictatorship's crimes make political leaders into accomplices?

Human rights discourse shifted the political terrain away from longstanding antagonisms between leftist populism and anti-communist conservatism. The dictatorship destroyed the legitimacy of institutions and the political process, but only after it had been frayed by years of political violence. Human rights were a new framework for defining the legitimate functions of public institutions and political parties. Where the major parties had once defended the coup and supported violent solutions to political problems, now these parties found new legitimacy through defense of human rights. The Junta promised a new beginning, yet only produced violence. The human rights movement repudiated violence to produce a new beginning.

Reorganization: A Victory in the World Cup

The Argentine military regime was equal parts ambitious and chaotic. Under Videla, it pursued bold measures to transform the economy and cultivate patriotic sentiments. The success of these efforts was fleeting and their consequences were for the most part disastrous. The regime's clearest success came in its orchestration of the 1978 Soccer World Cup – the first (and only) played on Argentine soil, and the first (of two) won by Argentina. Its most consequential failure came from its attempt to reorganize Argentina's economy. Together these efforts capture the regime's vision of transforming Argentina beyond the scope of its Dirty War.

By any measure, the World Cup was a milestone. Soccer in Argentina is as popular as every U.S. professional sport combined, and the country has produced many of the world's best players, though by 1978 it had neither hosted nor won the sport's signal championship. After the decision to host the World Cup in Argentina was made at the beginning of the decade, the Cup experienced a life as convoluted as any other in

Argentina. The organizing commission created the logo for the event just as Perón returned to Argentina: a soccer ball, flanked by two bands in the sky blue of the national flag, evoking the silhouette of Juan Perón addressing the workers from the presidential palace balcony. After the 1976 coup, planning for the Cup was taken over by Admiral Massera, who was stuck with the logo invoking Perón.

The World Cup reflected the dictatorship, right down to the rumors of mass graves under the stadium in Córdoba. Exiles and human rights groups attempted to organize a boycott, though no country adhered to it. Admiral Massera's Navy responded to the boycott by coercing ESMA detainees to produce favorable news stories. At the Argentina matches, the members of the Junta sat together, sternly, amid multitudes waving Argentine flags, as the national team won its first title. After the matches, crowds of young men took to the streets cheering, singing soccer and Argentine hymns and waving the national flag, a striking contrast to the protest marches of a few years earlier. The image of an ordered and triumphant nation was broadcast across Argentina and the world. Argentines saw this mostly in black and white. Color television was introduced by the regime to coincide with the World Cup, but few households had a color television set.

For Argentines prisoners in the hundreds of detention centers, the Cup offered surreal experiences. Both torturers and victims were Argentines, but how could a detainee share in the pleasure their tormentor found in an Argentine goal? Sometimes, detainees were allowed to watch the games on television. Others strained to hear what their guards were watching. Some detainees recalled even being dragged out of their cells by their captors and loaded into cars to cruise around their cities amid the celebration of victories, before being returned to their confinement and torment. The most perverse of these experiences was at the ESMA: it was practically in the shadow of the stadium where most of the Argentine games were played, so prisoners could hear the roar of the crowds at the match, palpably close yet impossibly far away.

An unusual victory by the Argentine team spurred rumors of a fix by the dictatorship. After a draw and a loss in the first round, the Argentine team needed to win its game against Peru by a huge margin in order to advance. The two teams were well matched and a blowout win seemed impossible. During halftime, Videla's guest at the game Henry Kissinger, visited the Peruvian team in its locker room. In the second half of the game, the Peruvian team collapsed, giving Argentina the 6-0 win to advance. A few months later, the Argentine government donated a large shipment of grain to Peru. Whether the game was fixed or not, the rumor reflects a basic element of life in a dictatorship: since the actions of those in power were shielded from public view, events were interpreted through fragments of information – the odd visit by Kissinger, an unusual gift, the weird and abrupt collapse of a well-performing team.

Argentina beat the Netherlands in the final, taking its first title. That the Argentine coach and the members of the Dutch team refused to shake Videla's hands did not diminish the national triumph. This was a new Argentina: strong, successful, with social conflict disappearing beneath blue and white banners and exuberant expressions of national pride. The win was like a sugar high – intense but short-lived. This success shaped a pattern of governance that was increasingly devastating: as the Junta came to rely on these kinds of patriotic appeals to cultivate public support and legitimate actions, it became trapped in a cycle of feeding fleeting expectations through erratic and ill-conceived schemes – chief among them being the invasion of the Falkland Islands.

Reorganization: A Failure in the Economy

Among these schemes was the economic plan implemented by Finance Minister Martínez de Hoz. Martínez de Hoz sought a free-market reform similar to that implemented in Chile, though he pursued it in a very different political context than Chile's. His plan reduced trade barriers to make the economy globally competitive, and lifted restrictions on the flow of capital so that Argentine businesses could attract investment and seek foreign credit. He also sought to dampen the 335% inflation rate inherited by the Junta.

As in Brazil and Chile, the Junta gave its finance minister a free hand to implement economic policy by shielding his actions from public pressure, while staking much of its success on the outcomes of economic reform. Since these regimes governed with impunity and through force, its legitimacy did not rest on popular consent exercised through democratic participation in governance, nor from its adherence to established institutional and political conventions (that it was dismembering). The legitimacy of the regime depended not on process but on outcomes. The 1978 World Cup win was one. The radical transformation of the economy would be another. Videla bet the success of his regime on

Martinez de Hoz' economic project more than on any other of the government's initiatives.

Initially, the air of stability created by the dictatorship, U.S. government support, and the actions taken by Martinez de Hoz, created a climate that attracted foreign investment. In turn, the regime's repression of unions gave Martinez de Hoz flexibility to suppress wages to stifle inflation, as Roberto Campos had done in Brazil after 1964. The early results of Martinez de Hoz's program created a surge in the Argentine stock market and a flood of new credit that spurred an economic boom for affluent Argentines. They traveled abroad, consumed more and, as the saying went, learned to say "I'll take two" in many languages. For the affluent, these were the days of "plata dulce" – sweet money. At the same time, reducing import barriers brought cheap imports into the Argentine market, even if these remained well out of reach of the working class whose wages were continually eroded by persistent inflation.

The Junta was not unified behind Martinez de Hoz's economic plan. He had the support of Videla. The other members of the Junta each cultivated their own base of political support, and promoted the interests of the business groups they lined up behind them. Each branch also controlled a share of the country's many state-owned enterprises, each with its own market interests that often ran contrary to Martinez de Hoz' goals. As a result, behind the veneer of Martinez de Hoz' economic program lay competing and often contradictory goals that made a consistent economic program impossible. Paradoxically, one of the few areas of consensus within the Junta interfered with Martinez de Hoz's reforms: maintaining full employment.

At first, military leaders believed unemployment would feed the ranks of "subversives" they were working to defeat, so they were adamant that public spending and the business sector were positioned to avoid mass layoffs. Later, they wanted high employment and economic prosperity, regardless of the costs, in order to ease the political transition. These goals undermined Martinez de Hoz's plans. His aim of making industry more globally competitive by reducing tariff barriers meant that Argentine consumers would buy cheaper, often better-made imported goods, depressing demand for Argentine manufactured goods. This drove smaller companies into bankruptcy and compelled larger companies to make layoffs as they suffered declining sales. Under strict free-market rules, the Argentine government would not intervene in the unemployment resulting from liberalization of trade, but for the Junta this outcome was untenable. As a result, the finance ministry was compelled to help large companies (which were often politically connected to the armed forces) by facilitating their access to foreign loans, while pressuring the companies to inefficiently retain their workers. At the same time, spending on public works projects and enormous expenditures by the armed forces to modernize its hardware helped push the government into further debt.

The results were the opposite of what Martinez de Hoz intended: manufacturing became more dependent on the government, public spending continued to increase, and inflation persisted. Worker wages decreased substantially during the dictatorship, as inflation wiped away buying power while the regime restricted unions. But this was not enough to offset the inflationary pressure generated by full employment policies and government spending. The results were worker misery and persistent inflation. Martinez de Hoz found himself compelled to adopt a version of Brazil's "crawling peg indexation." The *tablita* was a schedule of peso devaluations that coincided with the rate of inflation, according to which wages were adjusted, interest rates set on loans and deposits, and contract values set months in advance.

The economic plan seemed successful for the quick infusion of foreign investment it generated, but it soon became clear that Martinez de Hoz' formula, and its political context, were unsustainable. Foreign investments were largely speculative, taking advantage of the rapid rise of the Argentine stock market and the high interest rates charged by banks. A larger inflow of money came in the form of borrowing by the government and businesses. By 1980, the country's banks strained under the weight of foreign loans, and large companies that had become heavily indebted were in increasingly dire straits. The finance ministry stepped in to guarantee or absorb bank and business debt. This kept the economy afloat in the short term, but placed soaring debt in the hands of a government that increasingly lacked the means to pay it.

Martinez de Hoz could not balance the Junta's conflicting goals. The foreign debt reached $25 billion by 1981, much of it negotiated at high interest rates and short payment terms. The finance ministry and central bank underwrote large amounts of corporate debt. Inflation remained uncontrollable. In March 1980, a string of banks collapsed, unable to balance speculative investment and high indebtedness. These bank failures triggered a run on accounts by both domestic and international investors, an exodus the Martinez de Hoz tried to arrest by steep devaluation of the peso, which further burdened Argentine businesses indebted in dollars.

The transformation of the economy was meant to be Videla's showpiece. Its failure epitomized the limitations of governance by the Junta. Martinez de Hoz was undermined by military spending as well as the autonomous actions of senior officers, many of whom directed state enterprises the armed forces had divided among themselves. The other members of the Junta under Videla, as well as ranking Army officers, built their own business and political alliances, challenged Martinez de Hoz's program and jockeyed to replace Videla as President. These ambitions further eroded the Junta's limited cohesion. The two other members of the Junta, Admiral Massera and Brigadier Agosti curbed Videla's authority by compelling him to resign as commander-in-chief of the Army to serve only as president. He was able to secure the appointment of his main ally, Roberto Viola, as chief of the Army, though this only emboldened Viola to seek the presidency for himself.

Reorganizing the Reorganization

When Videla's 5-year term determined by the Junta ended in March 1981, Roberto Viola became president and a second Junta comprised of the new chiefs of the armed forces took the reins. President Viola struggled to manage the economic crisis triggered by the bank failures, devaluation, and spiraling indebtedness. He replaced Martínez de Hoz, but his new financial team, led by economist Domingo Cavallo, could not arrest the crisis or create a sense of stability amid the accelerating flight of both foreign and Argentine capital. David Rock lays out the bleak scenario: "throughout 1981, the peso depreciated by over 600 percent of its value, the gross domestic product fell by 11.4 percent, manufacturing output by 22.9 percent and real wages by 19.2 percent."[20] Viola was overwhelmed by the crisis, and his replacement as Army Chief of Staff, Leopoldo Galtieri, forced him from power at the end of 1981.

General Galtieri, a Patton-like figure who had headed one of the Army's few combat-ready divisions, counted on the support of officers of the three branches of the armed forces who believed that Videla and Viola had acted with too weak a hand and had given up too much in dialogue with civilian politicians in search of a gradual transition from military rule. These hardliners believed that Argentina's problems –

economic and political – could be solved with a firm assertion of military power and a return to the zeal with which the armed forces had conducted the Dirty War in 1976 and 1977 – notwithstanding the fact that the regime by now liquidated almost all of its enemies and faced economic and political problems of its own making.

Galtieri channeled a strain of military thought which held that under military rule, Argentina had emerged as a crucial defender of freedom against a global communist menace, and its political and economic difficulties were the product of opposition to that historic role. In other words, rather than acting out of desperation, Galtieri's regime acted out of a delusional sense of grandeur fueled by the success of the Dirty War and the military's campaign to export it. The Argentine dictatorship had meddled in the politics of neighboring Bolivia, helping topple its president in 1980 and training its security forces in the kinds of methods it employed against Argentines in the Dirty War. It had skirmished with the Pinochet regime over control of the several remote islands along the Beagle Channel in Tierra del Fuego, a conflict that was now being mediated by the Vatican.

The Junta also involved itself in the civil wars in Central America, believing these were part of a communist struggle to take control of the Americas. Ariel Armony and Horacio Verbitsky detail the presence between 1977 and 1984 of Argentine military advisors drawn from units active in the Dirty War, who provided training and logistical support to the Contra faction fighting against the Sandinista government in Nicaragua, helped train death squads in Honduras, and provided equipment and interrogation training to government forces in Guatemala and El Salvador.[21] When Ronald Reagan took office in 1981, Carter's human rights advocacy yielded again to Cold War contention. Though the Junta believed it had found common cause with Reagan, it overestimated the influence their involvement in Central America would bring them in the U.S. government.

By early 1982, Argentina was at the edge of a precipice of the regime's own making. Its economy was in crisis, with a collapsing peso, unfettered inflation, capital flight, and indebtedness. A new hard-line regime under Galtieri was foreclosing the political opening envisioned by Videla and Viola (and complicated by the question of human rights). Instead, Galtieri envisioned a different kind of transition in which, within some years, he would, himself, be elected President as Pinochet had engineered in Chile. To get there, rather than focusing on the country's political challenges and economic crisis, Galtieri conceived what he saw as the Proceso's boldest stroke yet – one which would seize Argentina's historical destiny by, at last, wresting control of the Falkland Islands from Britain. This scheme, conceived by delusional hubris rather than perhaps justifiable desperation, would not just turn the page of Argentine history, but would give shape to a new moment in South American history that would drive the re-democratization of Argentina, Brazil, and finally Chile.

The Falkland Islands (Islas Malvinas) War

The idea to retake the Falkland and South Georgia Islands was a lasting Argentine aspiration. The desolate, remote islands had been claimed by Argentina until Great Britain took possession of them in 1833. The claim focused Argentine nationalism, defining national identity against the depredations of an imperialist foe. For generations, schoolchildren were taught that "las Malvinas son y siempre seran Argentinas" ("the Falklands are and always will be Argentine"). Now the Navy quietly drew up plans to seize the islands and presented them to Galtieri.

For General Galtieri, the invasion of the Falklands seemed a natural step: it built on the experience the armed forces had acquired at home in the Dirty War, in Bolivia, and in Central America. It drew from a deep well of nationalism and would recreate the kind of enthusiasm kindled by the 1978 World Cup win, distracting the people from the mounting problems with debt, inflation and unemployment the country was facing. Galtieri would use this enthusiasm to define a transition to democracy on the triumphant military's terms, in which Galtieri would stand as a civilian candidate for president, to be elected on the heels of victory against Britain.

The invasion of the Falklands did not turn out that way: to the contrary, the invasion was based on bad assumptions. First, the armed forces believed Britain was decadent and had neither the will nor the means to fight for the islands (consequently, the armed forces stationed inexperienced conscripts on the island who would be incapable of repelling a British invasion). Second, the armed forces believed the real threat they faced was from Chile, against which the Argentine Junta had contested dominion over the Beagle Channel: their more seasoned troops were deployed on alert against Chile. Third, they wrongly believed they had

U.S. support. In view of the assistance Argentina gave its proxies in Central America and believing that the U.S. Monroe Doctrine compelled the United States to defend Argentina against Britain. Fourth, they thought the invasion would ease Argentina's growing economic anxieties (instead, it worsened the country's debt crisis as international lenders cut off credit to the belligerent regime). The Junta's presumptions all proved catastrophically unfounded.

At the beginning of April 1982, the Argentine armed forces occupied the Falkland Islands (a few days later, they had occupied the even more remote South Georgia Islands, which had once held a few whaling stations). They met little resistance from the small number of the islands' inhabitants, English citizens who had long resisted annexation by Argentina. They now found themselves subordinated to a military Junta that had waged war on its own citizens, and compelled them to exchange their British pounds for pesos that quickly lost value due to inflation. Argentine diplomats pressed Britain to negotiate sovereignty of islands now in Argentine possession. The occupation seemed to be the end of the operation and a breathtaking victory for the Junta. Ecstatic crowds swarmed the centers of cities and towns in Argentina celebrating the occupation of the islands. Believing the operation to be complete, the Argentine Air Force spent much of its limited capacity for airlifting supplies to the islands carrying firewood for celebratory *asados* – barbecues by the victorious soldiers.

Though British diplomats met with Argentine negotiators, they simply played for time while Prime Minister Margaret Thatcher prepared the military re-conquest of the islands. If occupying the islands was a means to bolster public support for the Junta, it provided the same opportunity in Britain. Thatcher faced economic recession and public dissatisfaction with the free-market reforms her government implemented (inspired by her friend Pinochet's reforms in Chile). Though the Falkland Island war did save a government, it just wasn't the Junta.

Once its naval task force reached the islands, British diplomats suspended negotiations. A British nuclear submarine fired three torpedoes at an Argentine cruiser, the *Belgrano*, which was returning to the mainland after patrolling the islands. It sank, killing 323 sailors. The Argentine Navy, which had made the plans and pressed the case for the invasion, recalled its ships to port. It had played the key role in triggering a war that it would now sit out. This left two branches of the armed forces in the conflict. Of them, the Air Force played the main role. It had begun to purchase French Exocet missiles but had not received the training to arm their guidance systems. Air Force pilots innovated, flying their planes at sea level to avoid detection and dropping their missiles onto ships, a tactic that caused the majority of British casualties.

The leaders of the Argentine Junta faced the military crisis they had unleashed with a combination of disbelief and powerlessness. They had not prepared for the possibility that Britain would respond with force. Though they believed Chile would take advantage of the conflict to assert supremacy over the Beagle Channel, they were also not prepared strategically for the fact that Chilean military radar and listening posts gave Britain ongoing and detailed information about Argentine mobilization – the British Navy learned from Chilean Naval Intelligence about each sortie of Argentine fighter planes that took off. U.S. Secretary of State Alexander Haig had worked vigorously to prevent the conflict, but once the war began, the United States threw its full support behind Britain. Britain quickly retook the islands.

The Junta was just as unprepared to absorb bad news from the front as it was unready to hold the islands: the invasion was not intended as an international military action but as a domestic political action. And it had unleashed frenzied public support. How could the Junta now offer bad news? It simply didn't: newspapers were lined with stories based on ministry reports that bore no relation to reality. They reported heavily on the courage of Naval Captain Alfredo Astiz and his band of hard-core commandos who occupied a post on the South Georgia islands, repelling repeated British attempts to retake the islands – long after he and his band surrendered without firing a shot. Astiz perhaps singularly reflected his regime: years before, he had gone undercover and infiltrated the Mothers of the Plaza de Mayo, orchestrating the operation that resulted in the torture and disappearance of the French nuns.[22] He was part of the Naval task force that ran the torture center at the ESMA. And now he became the face of Argentine defiance in the Falklands long after his ignominious surrender. Amid the country's dire economic crisis and punishing defeat in the Falklands, it became manifestly clear that the Argentine Junta's only military capability was killing its own citizens.

The Army and Marines had little ability to hold the islands. The troops were untrained. Their commander, General Mario Menéndez, was like Astiz: a dirty warrior who had participated in the campaign against the ERP in Tucumán and had under his command the infamous La Perla detention center. When British forces landed on the Falklands, Menéndez defied Galtieri's orders and surrendered his forces rather than place them in a battle they were unprepared for. Menéndez sought two conditions from British Commander Jeremy Moore: that the Argentine soldiers remain under the command of the Argentine officers, and that the Argentine officers be allowed to retain their sidearms: he worried the soldiers would turn against their officers.[23] The war ended June 14, 1982, with 255 British and 649 Argentine casualties. Four days later, Galtieri and the other members of the Junta resigned. Over the coming year, a final Junta headed by General Reynaldo Bignone made a hasty transition to civilian rule. The last Junta legalized political parties, restored press freedoms and held elections. The opposition rallied around Raul Alfonsín, a leader of the Civic Radical Union (UCR) who had been an outspoken critic of the regime. He was elected in October and took office in December 1983, facing daunting political and economic challenges.

During the Falkland Islands war, one of the hardest tasks fell to Foreign Minister Nicanor Costa Méndez. A veteran diplomat, Costa Méndez was not deluded by the fantasies that governed the Junta. Instead, he traveled furiously seeking to avoid war, and once it began, to reduce Argentina's isolation and preserve its access to credit. By the end of the war, he had made the desperate move of traveling to Cuba to plead for support against Britain. The emissary of a dictatorship that existed to wage war on Argentines who were Marxists, believed it was fighting the Third World War, and export its war to Central America, played its last card.

Coda

As Costa Méndez traveled abroad to salvage Argentina's position during the war, he frequently passed through Brasília to meet with Brazilian Foreign Minister Ramiro Saraiva Guerreiro. Of Argentina's two major neighbors, Chile had sided with Britain and Brazil had skirted involvement. Privately, however, the Brazilian government had tried to induce the United States to remain neutral in the conflict – pressure that reached the point of President Figueiredo delaying a state visit to the United States. Saraiva Guerreiro lent Costa Méndez an ear and offered advice, hoping to mitigate the impact of the unfolding catastrophe in Argentina. Historically, Brazil and Argentina had been rivals. Each country was at that moment engaged in a race to develop atomic bombs whose presumptive target would be the other.

Yet behind closed doors, Brazil's generals and diplomats fretted at what was unfolding in the South Atlantic. They feared that a humiliating defeat might have devastating consequences for their neighbor: the government might lash out violently in another direction or possibly collapse. A humiliated Junta could fail to muster the governing capacity to manage elections. Brazilian leaders were keenly aware too that the war had a ruinous toll on Argentina's finances: intractable economic problems were being magnified not only by the cost of the war but the lack of credit (Britain, a center of international finance, discretely ensured that its foe would have no access to capital). The deepening Argentine economic crisis directly affected Brazil, as well as other Latin American countries like Mexico and Chile, because it increased risk assessment made by foreign lenders and the costs they charged for those countries' intense borrowing. Two months after the end of the war, Mexico declared a moratorium on paying its debt and the ensuing crisis engulfed Brazil, Chile, and Argentina.

The Falkland Islands war turned out to be one of the major factors in the transition to democracy in all three countries. It was a watershed that immediately destroyed the viability of the Argentine Junta, but it resulted in economic pressures that sped the pace and set the terms of Brazil's transition. Chile felt the effects in multiple ways: the 1982 economic crisis tempered the regime's free-market fanaticism and helped shape the political strategies pursued by Pinochet's opposition. But the war and its aftermath also changed the climate: Argentina had been an ally of the United States in Central America and sough to trade on its anti-communist posture. This logic failed to resonate. And once Argentina and then Brazil began to re-democratize, the Pinochet regime found itself isolated. Even as the Reagan administration in the United States funneled aid and training to anti-communist factions in caustic civil wars in Central America, it distanced itself from the Pinochet regime.

The year 1982 would be the high water mark of dictatorship in South America.

Notes

1   "New Junta Imposes Prior Censorship on Nation's Papers," *The New York Times*, March 25, 1976.
2   Marcos Novaro and Vicente Palermo, *La dictadura militar, 1976/1983: Del golpe de estado a la restauración democrática* (Paidós, 2003), 24.

3   Jonathan Kandell, "At an Argentine Party after the Coup," *The New York Times*, March 28, 1976, 1.

4   Novaro and Palermo, *La dictadura militar, 1976/1983*, 19.

5   Novaro and Palermo, *La dictadura militar, 1976/1983*, 41.

6   This language is the subject of Marguerite Feitlowitz, *A Lexicon of Terror: Argentina and the Legacies of Torture* (Oxford University Press, 1999).

7   Hugo Vezzetti, *Pasado y presente: Guerra, dictadura y sociedad en la Argentina* (Siglo XXI, 2003), 74.

8   Horacio Verbitsky, *Malvinas: La última batalla de la Tercera Guerra Mundial* (Sudamericano, 2002), 42.

9   Pilar Calveiro, *Política y/o violencia* (Norma, 2005), 140.

10 Calveiro, *Política y/o violencia*, 92; Pilar Calveiro, *Poder y desaparición* (Colihue, 2006), 29.

11 Calveiro, *Poder y desaparición*, 144.

12 Calveiro, *Poder y desaparición*, 37; Marguerite Feitlowitz, *A Lexicon of Terror* (Oxford University Press, 1999), 13.

13 Calveiro, *Poder y desaparición*, 37, 71; Feitlowitz, *A Lexicon of Terror*, 59–69.

14 A process detailed in Horacio Verbitsky's, *Confesssions of an Argentine Dirty Warrior* (New Press, 2005).

15 www.abuelas.org.ar/english/history.htm, accessed October 14, 2012.

16 Calveiro, *Política y desaparición*, 149.

17 *Nunca más: The Report of the Argentine National Commission on the Disappeared* (Farrar, Strauss, Giroux, 1986), 373–6; Vezzetti, *Pasado y presente*, 81.

18 Calveiro, *Poder y desaparición*, 142.

19 See Marguerite Bouvard, *Revolutionizing Motherhood: The Mothers of the Plaza de Mayo* (Rowman & Littlefield, 2002).

20 David Rock, *Argentina, 1586-1987: From Spanish Colonization to Alfonsín* (University of California Press, 1987), 375.

21 Verbitsky, *Malvinas*; Ariel Armony, *Argentina, the United States, and the Anti-Communist Crusade in Central America* (Ohio University Press, 1997).

22 Verbitsky, *Malvinas*, 154.

23 Verbitsky, *Malvinas*.

6

Brazil
The Long Road Back

On March 15, 1974, a decade after the armed forces seized power, Brazil's fourth consecutive military president took office. General Ernesto Geisel's inauguration came amid economic expansion and a growing record of detentions, torture, and disappearance. Neighboring dictators like General Pinochet attended the inauguration in dress uniforms that clashed with the sober dark suit worn by Geisel. Brazil's military presidents almost always wore civilian clothes, unlike the generals in Chile, Argentina, Bolivia, Paraguay, and Peru. They thought the dress uniforms of neighboring dictators were tasteless. Brazil's generals did not want to be thought of as dictators at all. They presented themselves as protecting democracy, even as they ruled by decree, violently stifled dissent, and held power for more than two decades.

Geisel's inauguration reflected two peculiar aspects of Brazil's dictatorship. First, it took pains to present itself as legal, constitutional, and democratic. The National News Agency's broadcast of the inauguration made repeated references to Geisel's election by Brazil's Electoral College, comprised of members of Congress and a handful of delegates from state assemblies. The armed forces presented their single choice for president, and the Electoral College ratified it. Geisel was "elected" without Brazilians voting. Second, the inauguration of a fourth out of five military presidents holding fixed terms made Brazil's dictatorship different from Chile's, where Pinochet prevailed for nearly 18 years, or from Argentina's, where four military presidents over 7 years reflected the disarray of the armed forces. Instead, the Brazilian presidency changed hands through

Dictatorship in South America, First Edition. Jerry Dávila.
© 2013 Jerry Dávila. Published 2013 by Blackwell Publishing Ltd.

what the armed forces decided was a constitutional term, via what the armed forces decided was an election. Why? The presidential succession reflected the armed forces imagination of a political project to repair the damage purportedly caused by populists, who they compared disdainfully to the *caudillos* (strong-men) they believed made Spanish America less civilized than Brazil. General Pinochet, in his uniform, drew an emblematic contrast.

Geisel took the helm of a regime characterized by excess. The dictatorship was shaped by successive military hardliner victories. These extended from compelling Castelo Branco to institutionalize the regime, to erecting the legal and bureaucratic edifice of repression that included AI-5, networks of intelligence services, detention centers, and competing squads of secret police. The generals had also fulfilled longstanding national security goals through aggressive development and national integration. And they wrapped the dictatorship in an imaginary about Brazil's emergence as a world power, adeptly employing economic growth and achievements such as the 1970 World Cup victory as signs of the country's emerging stature.

Geisel set out to moderate the regime's course. He defined a gradual process of political opening (*abertura*) and decompression (*distensão*) of the regime's authoritarian restrictions, leading to a slow transition to democracy. Elio Gaspari suggests that Geisel's embrace of a process of transition did not indicate that Geisel had democratic leanings. Instead, Geisel was guided by a professional's distaste for the politicization of the armed forces in government and the indiscipline that the hard line and its machinery of repression brought to the armed forces.[1]

By defining the process for a transition to democracy, Geisel curbed the hardliners. By initiating the transition, Geisel hoped to control its outcomes and shape the future democracy, as Pinochet would in Chile. But as in Chile, the interaction between economic and political factors defined the transition. Geisel set the framework, but the opposition learned to use it. He spurred economic growth to smooth the transition, but his policies culminated in a debt crisis which eroded the credibility of the regime, facilitated an alliance between business and opposition groups, and created profound challenges for the civilian government that took office in 1985.

In carrying out *abertura*, Geisel depended on economic performance as his predecessors had. Castelo Branco defined stabilization as a rationale for institutionalizing the dictatorship. Médici turned the miracle into a symbol of military rule. Geisel inherited an overheated economy. Before taking office, Geisel was president of Petrobras, so he understood the consequences of the oil crisis. As president he worked to moderate the country's economic course much as he sought to moderate its political trajectory. His approach for doing so meant increased state planning and borrowing to support an array of projects intended to maintain growth while reducing the country's dependence on imported oil.

Geisel replaced Médici's economic team, displacing the public face of the miracle, Delfim Neto. Following the precedent set under Médici, Geisel's new minister of planning, João Reis Velloso, set bold goals for industrialization and infrastructure development. Energy independence would be achieved through colossal investments in hydroelectric and geothermal power, the development of nuclear power plants (preferably ones that would sustain a weapons program), and oil exploration. The regime implemented a project to turn sugarcane into fuel. The program PRO-ALCOOL mandated production of cars that ran on pure ethanol, financed the construction of ethanol refineries, and developed a national distribution system for ethanol.

The Geisel government fell short of its economic objectives though it succeeded in creating stratospheric levels of foreign debt. The curious thing about this indebtedness was its source: petrodollars. After oil prices peaked in 1973, they stabilized at a much higher level than they had been before the embargo. Oil prices spiked again in the aftermath of the 1979 Iranian Revolution. The higher prices Brazilians and other consumers spent on oil resulted in huge profits for oil exporting countries. These profits were deposited with large international banks, which in turn issued loans with it. To break its dependence on oil imports, the Brazilian government took out loans that were financed by the profits oil exporters made from the oil Brazilians consumed. This cycle proved ruinous.

Brazil and the Third World: An Emerging Power?

In November 1975, the Geisel government took two steps in its foreign policy that demonstrated the unusual combination of international pressures and national ambitions that characterized the military regime's circumstances. Over the vehement objections of the United States, the Brazilian government voted in favor of UN Resolution 3379, which defined "Zionism is a form of racism and racial discrimination." The next day, the Geisel regime made Brazil the only western nation to recognize the Marxist MPLA liberation movement as the government of Angola, as it emerged from Portuguese colonial rule.

Geisel's decision to recognize the MPLA government in Angola seemed ironic – how could an anti-communist dictatorship develop diplomatic relations with a regime whose revolutionary Marxism was suppressed by violence at home? This act served two purposes: first, it allowed the Brazilian government to make up for lost time in pursuing African markets for its exports, after having supported Portugal in its wars to retain its colonies since 1964. Second, the act helped signal Brazil's growing autonomy. Geisel believed that "we were too hitched to the United States ... we needed to have a bit more sovereignty and independence, not be subservient. We had to live and deal with the United States, whenever possible, as equals."[2]

If Brazil's actions in Angola indicated independence in international relations, the decision to vote in favor of the UN resolution on Zionism was an even more visible assertion of Brazilian autonomy from the United States and its alignment with Third World countries. Through the resolution, Arab countries equated Israel's practices with regard to Palestine to South African apartheid, and drew scrutiny to Israel's close relations with South Africa. It was sponsored by Muslim nations and Cuba, and it garnered support from the Soviet Bloc countries, China, most of Africa, Southeast, and South Asia. In Latin America, besides Cuba it was supported only by Brazil, Mexico, and Marxist Guyana. Curiously, both of Geisel's actions shared common cause with revolutionary Cuba, which had sponsored the UN resolution and which sent troops to defend the MPLA government against invasions from South Africa and Zaire.

Geisel's actions were part of a foreign policy which entailed greater distance from traditional alliances with the United States, Portugal, and Israel; stronger relations in Africa and the Middle East, particularly Iraq and Libya; and restoring relations with China. By aligning with Arab countries, Geisel hoped to avoid the risk of a future oil embargo while opening markets that eased Brazil's trade imbalance. The Brazilian government also pursued a nuclear energy program with West Germany that was intended to both reduce its future reliance on oil imports while providing energy to its expanding urban and industrial base. As the regime realigned its international relations, Foreign Minister Antônio

Azeredo da Silveira told Henry Kissinger, "if you could supply us with a million barrels of oil a day, perhaps this shift would not be so abrupt."[3]

While the new foreign policy was shaped by a strategic quest for energy resources for a large and import-dependent nation, it was also guided by the perception of emerging Brazilian "grandeur," and the seeming decline of the United States in the wake of the Vietnam war, Watergate, and the Oil Embargo. As Azeredo da Silveira presented the picture:

> In 1960, Brazil was a country with 60 million inhabitants, and only 45% of its population lived in cities. The gross national product was $14 billion and per capita income was almost $200. The electricity generating capacity was 5,000 megawatts, our steel mills produced 2.5 million tons of steel ingots and our nascent shipyards delivered ships with a total capacity of 25,000 gross tons. The production of vehicles in our newly created automobile industry was 130,000 units. In 1960, Brazilian exports were worth less than $3 billion, 90% of which were primary commodities, while manufactured exports were no more than 5% of the total.
>
> Today we are 115 million people, 60% of which are urban residents. The GNP is $160 billion and per capita income is almost $1,500. The electrical generating capacity is 23,000 megawatts, and the steel industry produces 11 million tons of steel ingots. Our shipyards deliver ships with a total capacity of 500,000 gross tons and the annual vehicle production is on the verge of reaching the million-unit mark. Our exports total $24 billion and manufactured goods are a third of that. By its dimensions, the Brazilian economy is today already the ninth in the world in GNP.

These numbers sufficed for Silveira to proclaim Brazil a "radically new country" which existed in a world "that has undergone profound transformation."[4]

Silveira's data were one facet of an imagined "radically new" Brazil. Over the course of the 1970s, state participation in the economy expanded dramatically, with state companies even competing with private enterprise. Geisel explained: "If Brazil wants to become a modern country, without hunger and a host of other ills we suffer from, we have to develop. The main instrument for that is the federal government. The nation won't just develop spontaneously. It is necessary to have someone who can guide and propel, and that role falls to the government. This is an old idea that I hold, long espoused by the Army War College."[5] By the end of 1975, the federal government owned 49.5% of the capital invested in the largest 1,069 companies in Brazil, and had outright ownership or a stake in 74.4% of the largest 100 companies.[6]

If the economic data quantified emerging Brazil's emerging greatness, it is equally important to qualify it, and this perception can partly be qualified by locating it. It could be located most broadly in the Southern Hemisphere, seemingly ascendant over the decadent North. In a narrower sense, it could be located in Brasília, less than 20 years old and still incomplete. Brasília was the capital of a future that was just beginning to come into focus: a city so planned and sterile that the noise of political opposition and the ferment generated in busy cities like Rio de Janeiro and São Paulo, by students, workers, activists for racial and ethnic minority rights, or the womens' movement, could seemingly be made inaudible.

Two Deaths and the Rebirth of Opposition

In March 1973, geology student and activist Alexandre Vannucchi Leme "fled from police and committed suicide by jumping in front of a bus," according to an official account. A different official account claimed he had cut his own throat with a razor blade while in detention. Other than the fact that Leme was dead, both stories were fictions sustained only by the authorities' insistence, and by the fact that the authorities buried the body themselves, without an autopsy, rather than returning it to the family. He had been detained by Army intelligence service (DOI-CODI) agents and tortured to death. The problem was that other students and Leme's family knew about his detention, so his death under torture elicited a cover-up.

Leme's death, and the regime's implausible explanations met with criticism from the Catholic Church. Though a political activist, Leme had not been involved in violence against the regime. The bishop of Leme's home city accused his captors of "torturing and killing the victim." The Archbishop of São Paulo, Cardinal Evaristo Arns, celebrated a memorial mass attended by 3,000 at the most prominent civic space in São Paulo, the downtown Sé Cathedral. Arns condemned Leme's captors as worse than the Romans who had crucified Christ (at least they had the decency to return his body to his family). Historian Ken Serbin defines Leme's death as a turning point for the Church and opposition to the dictatorship. Members of the clergy, particularly Archbishop

Helder Câmara, had spoken out against the regime's violence since 1964, and the Pastoral Commission for Peace and Justice had challenged the extrajudicial detention of opponents to the regime since 1967, building the most comprehensive archive of detentions, torture, and disappearance by the regime. But the Church's response to Leme's death was the first time it led a public protest criticizing the regime for its violation of human rights.[7]

Since 1968, the war against subversion had resulted in a growing rate of arrests, tortures, and disappearances that generated a climate of fear that muted responses to state violence. Elio Gaspari suggests this climate of fear "encapsulated" death, torture, and disappearance: victims of torture were typically silent about what happened to them; families buried their dead privately; torture and disappearance were not reported. To do otherwise risked further repression.[8] Memorializing Leme and denouncing torture, Church leaders began to break the silence that had been one of the most important accomplishments of the dictatorship's system of repression.

In October 1975, opponents of the dictatorship drew on their experience with Leme's death to challenge the circumstances of the death of São Paulo journalist Vladimir Herzog. Though Herzog was once a member of the Communist Party, he now stuck to his job as news director for a São Paulo public television station. When DOI-CODI agents summoned him for questioning he went voluntarily and was taken into custody. Other detainees heard his screams under torture. Soon after, DOI-CODI agents informed his wife that he committed suicide by hanging himself with the belt of his prison uniform (the uniforms did not have belts). There was nothing new to his torture and murder, but there was to the reaction.

The president of the Israelite Congregation of São Paulo, Rabbi Henry Sobel, challenged the regime's account of his death by arranging his burial at the main part of the Jewish cemetery, rather than in a separate plot (the custom for suicides). Sobel's action implied that the DOI-CODI murdered Herzog. This act framed a month of protests over Herzog's death that defined a new approach for opposition to the regime. The groups that responded to Herzog's death worked closely together and innovated a powerful strategy. Herzog's journalists' union sought a public memorial service. Cardinal Arns, who attended the vigil before Herzog's burial, offered to hold an ecumenical service at the Sé Cathedral. Simultaneously, students at the University of São Paulo, where

Herzog had studied, went on strike. The protest spread to other campuses and within days over 30,000 students went on strike.

The journalists' union coordinated carefully with religious leaders like Sobel, Arns, and Presbyterian Pastor James Wright, as well groups like the Brazilian Association of Lawyers, and student leaders to raise the profile of the memorial service but avoid actions that would invite a crackdown. Their tactic: silence. Initially, striking students planned a noisy march to the cathedral. This approach would play into the regime's hand and the police and armed forces, who were well prepared for this kind of action. They blocked traffic across the city, harassing drivers with "safety checks," effectively shutting down the routes for a march and, according to Gaspari, creating the worst traffic jam in the history of São Paulo (a prodigious feat). The authorities worked feverishly to compel the journalists' union and Cardinal Arns to desist. The governor of São Paulo told Arns that he should not attend the service because there might be shootouts, and that 500 police would be in the cathedral plaza waiting for orders to fire.[9]

Religious leaders, the journalists' union and the striking students avoided creating the pretense for repression by not holding a march. Instead they appeared in silence at the cathedral, filling its plaza. Though there were no banners, songs or shouts provoking the authorities, their presence defied and condemned the regime. During the memorial service, Cardinal Arns spoke to the crime: "Those who stain their hands with blood are damned." Like Sobel's challenge to the regime in not burying Herzog as a suicide, Arns' address, made in the face of threats of violence levied by the governor, was a daring act. Five years later, Archbishop of El Salvador Óscar Romero was assassinated while holding mass because he similarly denounced the human rights abuses perpetrated by his regime. During Romero's funeral, gunmen opened fire on mourners gathered at the national cathedral, killing dozens.

Censors forbade the media from mentioning the memorial service until a military inquiry into his death concluded (naturally) that he had committed suicide in order to avoid giving the names of supposed conspirators. Still, another channel for the dissemination of information remained open. The Diocese of São Paulo issued a document to be read from the Church's pulpits, stating "it is not lawful during interrogation of suspects to use methods of physical, psychological or moral torture, above all when taken to the limits of mutilation and even to death, as has been happening." Priests reading the document declared "We are witnessing acts of flagrant disrespect of the human person characterized by arbitrary imprisonments, which generally take the form of veritable kidnappings."[10] The Church's actions culminated with a call for a day of fasting in defense of human rights.

A new kind of opposition to military rule was born. Unlike earlier generations of dissent that drew on strategies such as protest marches or guerrilla actions, this approach defined the regime as arbitrary and illegal, and defined the opposition as defenders of the rule of law. The approach subverted the regime's governing rationale that it represented the preservation of order, and it claimed the moral high ground of defending human rights rather than a radical political ideology. In doing so, the opponents of the regime built a framework upon which civil society groups ranging from professional associations to the Church, unions and students could collaborate. Increasingly, they defined the logic and the language of political change.

The opposition asserted that the regime must be subject to the rule of law: that it could not govern with impunity, that its violations of human rights were subject to sanction, and most important, that citizens should be able to exercise political choice, even if they chose to end the dictatorship. There were two concepts at the center of this assertion of the rule of law: first, the defense of human rights, which already galvanized domestic and international opposition; and second, "liberalization," the defense of freedoms constrained by authoritarian rule. In immediate terms, it meant lifting AI-5, freeing the press from censorship, allowing political organization, and restoring the right of detainees to face their charges and to be tried in civilian courts.

By changing its approach, the opposition helped build a coalition that began to count on the support of business groups. They saw liberalization in economic rather than political terms: as means of generating greater transparency and accountability in economic policymaking. In this area, the government's unwillingness to listen to market signals amid growing public indebtedness and rising inflation was becoming a recurrent concern for business. It also meant freeing private enterprise from the expansion of state economic planning and business ventures. Since liberalization did not imply a (potentially radical) political ideology, it was now easier for groups that had supported the regime and been its beneficiaries to join the opposition.

If Herzog's death marked a new chapter for the opposition, it also set off a chain reaction within the regime. For Geisel, the death of Herzog looked like indiscipline. The military command in São Paulo had become an increasingly autonomous political body whose hardline leadership thrived in the war against subversion. The death of Herzog suggested that São Paulo military commander General Ednardo D'Ávila would neither surrender the glory of waging this war even when they had to invent enemies, nor acknowledge the president's authority over him. Herzog's death prefigured a test to Geisel's authority.

Was Geisel the president, and therefore the commander of the armed forces? Or was Geisel the representative of the Revolution of 1964 who occupied the presidency? This was the crux of the tension between moderates and hardliners since the coup. Castelo Branco had deferred this question by preempting hardliners with increasingly authoritarian measures, and seeking to bind them with the 1967 constitution. But as Gaspari explains, the hardliners believed "there was a revolutionary regime, the armed forces were its constitutional body, and the president of the republic was their delegate."[11] Geisel responded to Herzog's death less out of respect for human rights than as a means of asserting presidential authority over the hardliners. He warned General D'Ávila against allowing further detainee deaths. Three months later, a metalworker detained by DOI-CODI "committed suicide," by allegedly hanging himself with his socks.[12] Geisel sacked D'Ávila, but it became dangerously clear that the president and military hardliners were pursuing conflicting agendas.

The hardliners would not yield easily and coalesced around a critic of Geisel, Army Minister Sylvio Frota. When Geisel extended diplomatic recognition to Angola's MPLA, Frota, accused him of violating the spirit of the 1964 Revolution. In doing so, he asserted the power of the "Revolution" over the president. Frota told Geisel "we do not understand how our revolutionary government, founded on anti-communism, could have been the first to recognize [Angolan MPLA leader] Agostinho Neto, propped up by Cuban troops."[13] It was true that there was an inconsistency: the same regime that murdered Herzog for supposed ties to Marxists at home forged ties with revolutionary Marxist regimes abroad. The irony was not lost on the *Estado de S. Paulo* newspaper, which editorialized that any Brazilian journalist or private citizen who had done what Geisel's foreign ministry had just done "would wind up having problems with the DOPS."[14] What the *Estado de S. Paulo* could not see was that there were really two regimes working at cross-purposes: one pursued communists and asserted the primacy of the Revolution, the other (Geisel's) pursued *abertura* and asserted the primacy of the presidency.

To stop *abertura*, General Frota began campaigning for president within armed forces, aiming to make Geisel a lame duck well in advance of the 1978 indirect elections. Geisel fired him, but this was no simple task. Frota resisted his dismissal by calling a meeting of senior officers from around Brazil to draft an ultimatum to Geisel. This approach had succeeded against Castelo Branco, but this time Geisel had prepared by giving those officers notice that Frota would be dismissed. Outmaneuvered, Frota issued a call to arms denouncing Geisel's "criminal complacency in the face of communist infiltration and leftist propaganda." The officers did not respond, Geisel prevailed, and Frota retired. Gaspari defines the turning point: "Geisel reestablished the constitutional authority of the Presidency over the Armed forces."[15] After almost a century of the armed forces playing the role of political moderator, Geisel seized this authority for the presidency.

A sign of this success is evident in a failure. Hardliners had repeatedly used a real or imagined threat of leftist extremism to control the political process and justify the repression that they used to silence their opponents. They attempted this again in 1981 by planting a bomb at a concert at the Rio de Janeiro Riocentro convention center. The bombing would be blamed on radical leftists in order to disrupt the transition to democracy. The plot failed because a military intelligence officer and an army sergeant blew themselves up in their car while trying to arm the bomb. By 1981, this kind of tactic seemed as out of place as it was incompetent.

The Transition Accelerates

Though Geisel established the authority of the presidency and set the terms of *abertura*, this did not mean he intended to yield power easily. He sought to control the transition and its outcomes by manipulating electoral rules to maintain control over congress, while continuing to purge and persecute elements of the opposition he saw as threatening. Still, *abertura* increased the space for opponents of the regime to press a political project that differed substantially from the generals' vision. Geisel had tamed the hardliners when he outmaneuvered Frota. The opposition from the left was more daunting.

When congressional elections in 1976 doubled the opposition MDB's representation in congress and in state legislatures, Geisel risked losing control of the two-thirds majority needed to pass constitutional amendments through congress. His transition to democracy made recourse to the now common practice of changing the political rules on order to game the outcomes. In early 1977, Geisel recessed Congress, which gave him authority to amend the constitution. He issued a set of amendments called the April Package, that made gubernatorial elections indirect, extended the gubernatorial electoral colleges to include municipal councilmen (restoring an electoral majority to ARENA and control over the governorships to Geisel), and reduced the threshold for constitutional amendments to a Congressional majority vote.

After the April Package, Geisel returned to *abertura*. He repealed AI-5 in 1978, which restored basic civil rights such as due process for those arrested, and ended presidential power to recess congress. He returned some autonomy to the judiciary and reduced the number of crimes subject to national security law. In 1979, a blanket amnesty released political prisoners and allowed exiles to return. The amnesty also shielded soldiers and police from prosecution for their acts of repression. The contradictory reforms, which employed arbitrary power to manipulate elections but restored long suppressed civil liberties, reflected the cautious nature of *abertura* and Geisel's effort to keep control. The question of Geisel's successor was critical to *abertura*. Seeking a general he could trust to continue the process, he chose the director of the SNI intelligence service, João Baptista Figueiredo, a laconic figure who lacked an independent political base and any presidential ambitions. The choice was perfect: President Figueiredo (1979–85) departed little from the parameters defined by Geisel.

Geisel's belief that the transition could be commanded from above was met by resurgent political activism among industrial workers. Workers had little formal recourse for the erosion of their wages through inflation, since unions were tightly controlled by the regime. The 1968 relaxation of this control had unleashed strikes that drove a year of mounting political dissent. AI-5 and the growing security apparatus dealt harshly with labor activists after 1968.

A decade later, with AI-5 still in force, workers in São Paulo's ABC region of industrial suburbs (Santo André, São Bernardo, and São Caetano) began organizing independently of their unions. In May 1978, automotive workers in São Bernardo staged an illegal sit-down strike coordinated by local union leader Luiz Inácio da Silva, known as "Lula" (who became president of Brazil from 2002 to 2010). Soon, 500,000 workers joined the stoppage. They won an 11% wage increase. This gain was small, given the rate of inflation. But they forged a "new unionism" by which workers would retake their unions from their co-opted leadership and organize across cities and industries. Lula became the face of new unionism.

Building on the groundwork set in 1978, the São Bernardo metalworkers' union staged strikes a year later intended to coincide with the inauguration of President Figueiredo. This time, the metalworkers drew the statewide union into their action. Though the strike took place after the end of AI-5, the labor code allowed the government to remove Lula from the presidency of his union, and the national security law allowed the regime to jail 200 strike leaders. The strike again ended with small wage gains, but it drew wider social groups into solidarity with the workers and sparked similar strikes nationwide. In particular, the workers forged a link with Catholic clergy who adhered to liberation theology.

Metalworkers again struck in April 1980. This time, the regime purged union leaders and carried out waves of arrests – including Lula, who was jailed for a month. DOPS and DOI-CODI detachments broke up demonstrations. The strike failed and the workers' demands went unmet. Still, the strikes signaled a changing climate. On one hand, the government shied away from direct repression, realizing that path would be hard to arrest and that a broad cross-section of society was now ambivalent about the regime. On the other hand, workers built an independent labor movement that became a beacon for the opposition. There was a palpable sense that a tipping point had been reached.

When the restrictions on independent political parties were lifted in 1979, Lula and other new unionist leaders, along with Catholic activists identified with liberation theology and human rights converged to form the Workers' Party (PT). The PT reflected the changing political culture of opposition: the decision to create a new party rather than join the long suppressed Communist Party or the reconstituted PTB, Brazilian Labor Party, headed by returning exile Leonel Brizola reflected changed alliances and tactics. The PT represented a broad coalition of groups ranging from the feminist and gay rights movements, movements for the rights of black and indigenous Brazilians, and the land reform movement. By converging under a new party structure, they eschewed the legacies of hardened opposition that traditional parties had experienced in the years leading to AI-5. The PT embraced socialist ideas about development and ameliorating social inequalities – two of its early ideologues were liberation theologian Leonardo Boff and educator Paulo Freire, who pioneered approaches to education that were intended to help marginalized peoples recognize the causes of their oppression. But what most characterized the PT was the manner in which it integrated the discourse about human rights, the rule of law, and government transparency that constituted a common front against military rule over the course of the 1970s.

The wave of strikes had peaked by 1980. The deepening recession triggered by the second oil shock and the debt crisis debilitated Brazilian industry in ways that undermined worker wage demands. But the military regime now faced a more complex environment of organized and effective public dissent as well as a rapidly deteriorating economy.

The Debt Crisis Defines the Shape of Re-Democratization

The second oil shock, triggered by the Iranian Revolution in 1979 was a blow that could not be absorbed like the 1973 crisis had been. Figueiredo's response was to bring back Delfim Neto, architect of the "miracle." Neto at first sought to repeat the process of debt-led growth, hoping to outrun the 1979 crisis as he had in 1973. The immediate result was inflation that reached 100% by 1980. But the actions since 1973, particularly the heavy borrowing, eroded the government's capacity to respond to the second shock. Debt, the cost of oil, and an economy which worked at the limits of its productive capacity became too much to brook.

International conditions deepened the crisis. Rising oil prices choked economies around the world, suppressing markets for Brazil's exports. Meanwhile, oil prices provoked rapid inflation in the United States. The Federal Reserve responded by raising its interest rates to over 17%, stifling lending and triggering a recession that curbed U.S. inflation. This was a double blow to Brazil: its largest export market was in recession, and its largest creditor was raising its rates. Loans held by the Brazilian government and state agencies became much more expensive to service, and new loans came with terms that were difficult to digest.

The Mexican government, which had financed development projects on estimates of future oil revenues, found itself fiscally overextended. As global recession triggered by rising oil prices and rising interest rates in the United States suppressed demand for oil, the Mexican government found itself without the oil export revenue needed to meet its debt obligations. The Mexican government imposed a steep devaluation of the peso and a moratorium on its debt payments. The consequences were devastating for the over-indebted dictatorships of Brazil, Argentina, and Chile. Banks panicked and either stopped lending to these countries or did so at enormous premiums and for short terms. The risk of default loomed over each of the countries. Fidel Castro suggested that the nations band together and cease payments, forcing lenders in developed countries to renegotiate the terms of debts in developing countries.

Neto reversed course: rather than seeking to accelerate growth through borrowing, he now slashed expenditures and conducted the first of a series of currency devaluations. These efforts were dwarfed by the crisis. When the first oil shock hit in 1973, Brazil's foreign debt reached $12 billion, an amount so large that it had become self-sustaining (the government had to borrow in order to make payments on the debt). As the regime pursued economic growth and created an alternative energy sector, financing development with borrowed petrodollars, the rate of indebtedness climbed to $43.5 billion in 1978. The economic costs of the second oil shock, recession, rising interest rates, and risk premiums resulting from Mexico's moratorium and the Argentine economic and political crisis following the Falklands War, drove Brazil's debt to record levels – $83 billion by the end of 1982. Interest payments alone cost more than half the value of Brazil's total exports.

Brazil now held the largest debt in the developing world and a deepening recession. Between 1978 and 1980, Brazil's trade deficit nearly tripled to $2.8 billion. In 1981, the country returned to a trade surplus which grew over the decade, but this surplus revealed the depth of the problem: Brazil's capacity to import was now less than the capacity of other countries to buy Brazilian goods. In 1983, the value of Brazil's imports was 40% of their peak in 1976. The value of imports in 1980 would not be matched again until 1993.[16]

The debt crisis produced a "lost decade." During the 1980s, the economy shrank by 0.05%, punctuated by declines of 4.5% in 1981 and 3.5% in 1983. This crisis defined the end of military rule. As historian Thomas Skidmore explains, "all the Brazilian economic policymakers were now discredited in the eyes of the public, notwithstanding the fact that uncontrollable external forces had played a large role. After all, Delfim [Neto] and his team had never hesitated to claim credit for the 'miracle.' Why should they now be denied credit for the disaster?"[17] The regime's discredit strengthened the hands of its opponents, who won

59% of the vote in the 1982 state and congressional elections. Since the regime had gamed the electoral process, the opposition's majority of the vote did not produce a congressional majority. The Electoral College that would choose the new civilian president was still dominated by the regime's political allies.

The economic crisis discredited the dictatorship in is final years and hobbled the civilian government after 1985. Arbitrary rule and economic crisis had eroded the legitimacy of public institutions and faith in the capacity of the new government to solve the country's problems. After all, the military justified seizing power partly on its diagnosis of the inability of civilian politicians to solve a crisis defined by an 88% inflation rate and a debt of $3.2 billion. The military left behind an inflation rate of 235% and $95 billion in debt. In 1964 the debt was just over twice the value of the country's exports. After two decades of accelerated growth, industrialization and efforts to boost exports, Brazil's debt in 1985 was almost four times the value of its exports. The costs of growth outweighed the growth itself.

An Incomplete Transition

As the handover to civilian rule approached, protests nationwide demanded *Direitas Já!* – direct elections – rather than the indirect vote by the Electoral College by which the regime intended to control the handover to civilian rule. In the early months of 1983, rallies in major cities drew millions to the streets in support of direct elections. Rio de Janeiro experienced the largest rally in the country's history – 500,000 people. The rallies were festively defiant, featuring performances by well-known musicians. Though television newscasters were prohibited from reporting on the rallies, they did so anyway.

The regime did not relent, but the rallies focused the opposition and seized the political and cultural mainstream. What remained now was for political parties to negotiate the presidential ticket to submit to the electoral college. The military's candidate was São Paulo politician Paulo Maluf. The congressional opposition built a coalition with some pro-regime politicians and agreed on a split ticket that garnered broad support. For president, they chose Tancredo Neves, a leader of the opposition MDB. A longtime leader of the pro-regime ARENA party, José Sarney was selected as the vice-president. Neves was a popular advocate of re-democratization and his ticket sailed through the Electoral College vote on January 15, 1985. As the Electoral College voted, a music festival called Rock in Rio was staged in Rio de Janeiro. Between performances by bands like AC/DC and the Scorpions, festivalgoers kept track of the vote and cheered "Eu, eu, eu! Maluf se fodeu!" (politely, Maluf, the defeated military candidate, "got screwed").[18]

In the weeks before the March 1985 inauguration, Neves took ill and underwent a series of failed surgeries. As his health deteriorated, he and those around him feared the regime would use his illness as a pretense to hold power. Argentine President Raúl Alfonsín, leader of the only country so far to free itself from military rule, sat at Neves' bedside and wept. The course of re-democratization in South America seemed to teeter on Neves' failing health. Neves died. In this context, Sarney's inauguration reflected a victory for re-democratization. But the first civilian president in 21 years had not even been indirectly elected to the office. He faced daunting challenges. The most pressing, and the most evocative of the political limits of the new democracy was inflation.

In the year after taking office, Sarney's economic team developed a stabilization plan called the Cruzado Plan, introduced in February 1986. The plan created a new currency, and froze the rate of exchange, prices, and wages. The Cruzado Plan reflected difficult political realities: Sarney felt his mandate was too weak to carry out a reform that induced economic hardship. The price and wage controls were meant to break the inflationary momentum of the long held expectations that prices rise, but the rates of exchange between the old and new currencies boosted consumer spending power. This was politically expedient but it strained prices, as did the government spending that resulted from newly unleashed political demands. The plan survived less than a year. When the price and wage controls collapsed, inflation returned with a vengeance, reaching 1,700% by 1989.

Rebuilding democracy meant more than replacing generals with civilians. A new basis for political and institutional legitimacy had yet to be created. In this context, the drafting of a new democratic constitution, ratified in 1988, loomed large. Opponents of military rule grew demoralized by political and economic continuities that were the legacy of military rule. Judges, the ranks of local politicians and national legislators, the police and police culture, and the entire federal bureaucracy were all remnants of the dictatorship. So too were inflation and the debt crisis, which precluded the many avenues for reform.

The most effective place to begin the process of change, then, was drafting a new charter that reflected the aspirations for re-democratization and set the terms for redefining the nature of the state. To this end, a striking element of the 1988 constitution is its regard for minority rights. Among the "fundamental objectives of the Republic" defined by the constitution are "eradicate poverty, marginalization, and social and regional inequality . . . [and] promote the wellbeing of all, without prejudice based on origin, race, gender, color, age or any other form of discrimination." Defense of human rights and a focus on inequality and discrimination framed Brazilian re-democratization. The constitution defined civil rights, the labor code, and specific rights for indigenous communities and communities of descendants of runaway slaves. The constitution guaranteed access to healthcare and education. Yet these rights reflected aspirations rather than realities, and Brazilians would struggle to exercise the rights they held on paper. The end of the cycle of military rule in Brazil left two challenges: addressing the burdens of debt and inflation, while bringing substance to the human rights defended by the new constitution.

Notes

1   Elio Gaspari, *A Ditadura Encurralada*, in the series *A Ditadura Envergonhada, A Ditadura Escancarada, A Ditadura Derrotada, and A Ditadura Ecurralada* (Companhia das Letras, 2002–4).

2   *Ernesto Geisel*, ed. Maria Celina D'Araujo and Celso Castro (FGV, 1997), 336.

3   *Jornal do Brasil*, march 14, 1976, www.webartigos.com/artigos/artigo-o-presidente-ernesto-geisel-e-o-estabelecimento-do-retorno-a-democracia-ao-brasil-pos-regime-militar-de-1964/51497/, accessed October 14, 2012.

4   "Conferência pronunciada pelo Ministro de Estado das Relações Exteriores, Embaixador Antônio F. Azeredo da Silveira, na Escola Nacional de Informações, ESNI, Brasília," June 12, 1978. Azeredo da Silveira Archive, AAS mre/ag 1974.05.27, *FGV/CPDOC*.

5   *Ernesto Geisel*, ed. Maria Celina D'Araujo and Celso Castro, 287.

6   "A palavra que falta," *O Estado de S. Paulo*, November 14, 1975, 3.

7   Kenneth Serbin, *Secret Dialogues: Church–State Relations, Torture, and Social Justice in Authoritarian Brazil* (University of Pittsburgh Press, 2000).

8   Gaspari, *A Ditadura Encurralada*, 214.

9   Gaspari, *A Ditadura Encurralada*, 198.

10 "Issue of Torture Growing in Brazil," *The New York Times*, November 16, 1975; "Brazilian Bishops Accuse Authorities of Murder," *The New York Times*, November 12, 1975.

11 Gaspari, *A Ditadura Encurralada*, 227.

12 Gaspari, *A Ditadura Encurralada*, 214.

13 Sylvio Frota, *Ideais traídos: Brasil acima de tudo* (Zahar, 2006), 190.

14 "Dize-me com quem andas e …," *O Estado de S. Paulo*, November 13, 1975, 3.

15 Gaspari, *A Ditadura Encurralada*, 479–81.

16 Baer, *The Brazilian Economy*, 6th edn. (Rienner, 2006), 409; *Dicionário Histórico-Biografico Brasileiro*, vol. 2, 2nd edn. (FGV, 2001), 1887–8.

17 Thomas Skidmore, *The Politics of Military Rule* (Oxford University Press, 1990), 237.

18 My thanks to Alexandra Lemos Zagonel for sharing this account, from "Brazilian Rock and Redemocratization in Brazil," MA thesis, University of North Carolina at Charlotte, 2012.

7

Chile

A "Protected Democracy"?

In 1975, Augusto Pinochet declared there "will be no elections in Chile during my lifetime nor the lifetime of my successor."[1] A more absolutist remark is hard to imagine: a leader ascribing to himself power over a country's decision-making that extended beyond the grave.

But behind this bravado, complicated questions swirled. What was the nature of authority in the new Chile? Were the new rules simply the arbitrarily will of the Junta? Of Pinochet? Were there any limits to their power? Did authority rest on institutions or individuals? Amid these questions the distinction between the power of Pinochet and the authority of the Junta became significant. The competition between them drove a process of institution building and rulemaking that consolidated their power, culminating in a constitution ratified in 1980. This question of authority and the constitution it produced created the framework around which political opposition coalesced, guiding the transition to democracy. As it happened, there would be four more presidential elections in Chile during Pinochet's lifetime.

What became clear when the Junta seized power was that by invoking the "state of siege" powers of the 1925 constitution and governing through them, the Junta's actions voided all of the other elements of that constitution. The Junta held unlimited legislative and executive power that was not subject to judicial review. Essentially, the Junta became its own constitution. Its rule that its decisions be unanimous served as the final arbiter, constraining Pinochet's executive authority. In turn, Pinochet applied his political and administrative acumen to building a general

Dictatorship in South America, First Edition. Jerry Dávila.
© 2013 Jerry Dávila. Published 2013 by Blackwell Publishing Ltd.

staff of senior Army officers as well as loyal teams of legal and economic advisors who helped him expand his influence while avoiding conflict with the other members of the Junta.

Though Pinochet was the Junta's front-man, its members shared authority and they distributed national and local governance among the service branches. For each area of administration, a council was created which reported to a Junta member. These councils had both administrative and legislative authority, though their legislation was subject to unanimous approval by the Junta. The Junta members guarded their authority by controlling promotions and retirements in their respective branches. This control, along with the unanimity rule, created an effective separation of powers, even if this separation was entirely within the armed forces.

Pinochet and the other members of the Junta were keen to institutionalize and extend their rule, and wary that ceding power could make them subject to retribution for their actions. Soon after the coup, they created a Constitutional Commission charged with drafting a new document which would create a "protected democracy" by the constitutional order would prevent future actions like those implemented under Allende. Constitutional scholar Robert Barros called this "binding the future out of fear of the past."[2] For Barros the production of the new constitution reflected enduring divisions within the Junta and the competition for power between Junta members and Pinochet, conflicts that stretched the drafting and ratification process from 1973 to 1980, while both consolidating and limiting Pinochet's authority.

The architect of the Chile's new legal framework was Jaime Guzmán, leader of the Gremialista movement. Guzmán was a Catholic ultraconservative who advocated a system of government called corporatism, a concept that emerged from fascist Italy. It was implemented in Spain under Francisco Franco (1939–75) and in Portugal under Antonio Salazar (1932–68). Corporatism also influenced Brazil's authoritarian 1937 and 1967 constitutions, drafted by Guzmán's ideological counterpart Francisco Campos. Corporatism shunned representative democracy in favor of a strong state that directed social, political, and economic decision-making. Though corporatism's authoritarianism and political language was similar to that of fascism, corporatist states did not rely on an official political party.

For Guzmán, the comparison between Pinochet and Franco was instructive. Franco seized power in a civil war against a socialist republican government. He violently repressed his opponents and ruled for decades over a dogmatically Catholic, socially conservative and orderly (if staid) country. But if Franco's dictatorship inspired Guzmán, it also offered a warning. After Franco's death in 1975, the King of Spain, Juan Carlos II, whose monarchy was restored as part of the political transition envisioned by Franco, did not turn out to be the corporatist protégé Franco expected. To the contrary, Juan Carlos II oversaw a transition to democracy in which the newly reconstituted Socialist Party won office and carried out reforms that turned Spain into a bustling social democracy. Guzmán envisioned a constitution that would enshrine the regime's political and social vision, preventing the election of another Allende. As Jaime Guzmán wrote in a memorandum to the Junta shortly after the coup: "the Junta takes on the mission of creating a *new* stage in the country's history, planning its action through a regime that for a long time will perpetuate the philosophy, the spirit and the style of the armed forces."[3]

The Letelier Assassination and Mounting Pressure against Pinochet

Pinochet and the Junta faced withering international criticism over its violence, criticism that culminated in September of each year when the United Nations General Assembly convened and served as a forum for denunciation of the regime. In response, Pinochet presented a token measure each year timed to placate that criticism: the promise of restoring legal rule through the enactment of a constitution (which was always years away); military orders requiring respect for human rights (which were intended to be ignored); an amnesty releasing some political prisoners (and legally exempting the armed forces from scrutiny for their acts); agreeing to receive delegates from the United Nations Commission on Human Rights (but abruptly withdrawing the invitation at the last minute). Each of these steps was a cynical ruse intended to defuse international pressure rather than to change the course of the regime.

Still, one event rattled the regime and compelled more substantive reform. In 1976, former Foreign Minister Orlando Letelier and his assistant, Ronni Moffit, were killed in Washington, DC, when a bomb detonated in their car. Cuban exiles working for the Chilean Directorate of National Intelligence (DINA) planted the bomb. The U.S. FBI requested the extradition of several DINA agents. Pinochet refused, but former CIA agent Michael Townley, who worked for the DINA and planned the assassination, was convicted. Townley was also implicated in assassinations of exiled Chileans for the DINA in Europe and South America.

International pressure over the Letelier case, especially condemnation by the U.S. government, opened divisions between the Junta and Pinochet. For the Junta, the repercussions highlighted the need for a defined path toward a new constitution and re-democratization. But Pinochet sought to continue in power. The way he did so reflected his political style: Pinochet reluctantly dissolved the DINA and retired its director, General Contreras; he pursued a spurious referendum on his rule; and he usurped the Junta's constitutional debate. These steps displayed Pinochet's understanding of the severity of the crisis and his reluctance to relinquish power. Though Contreras was cast aside and the DINA dismantled, he replaced it with a National Intelligence Service (SNI) with many of the same powers.

In 1977, Pinochet seized on the questions of constitutionalism and re-democratization in a speech delivered on National Youth Day. In a spectacle choreographed by the Gremialista movement, thousands of right-wing students gathered in Chacarillas, in the outskirts of Santiago, for a nocturnal ceremony, holding torches and singing nationalist hymns. Pinochet delivered an address written by Jaime Guzmán, invoking the "mission that God and history have placed on our shoulders," and took credit for saving Chile from "the imminent threat of communist totalitarianism." He suggested that the success of the economic program meant that the country could turn its attention to giving "shape to a new democracy that will be authoritarian, protected, integrational, technical, and having authentic social participation."[4] In other words, an order in which policies like Allende's could not take root, and in which future political leaders would be bound by constraints envisioned by the dictatorship. Under Pinochet's proposal, the government would gradually impose constitutional articles, and when the process was complete – he estimated 8 years (1985) – direct elections could again be held.

The Chacarillas speech was typical of Pinochet's style. It characterized the public political persona he cultivated since taking power, presenting his role in messianic terms: acting, through sacrifice, to carry out the will of God and save Chile. Humberto Lagos analyzes this discourse: "it was 'divine providence' that brought him to the role of Commander in Chief of the Army; he 'draws his strength from God;' Chile has been blessed because 'God himself gave him faith in Chile's destiny'; anyone who opposes the divinity represented in the 'chosen one,' the 'messiah' faces the 'wrath of God.'" [5] Beyond the stagecraft lay smart politics: Pinochet framed a constitutional process which was more gradual and controlled than the Junta sought. From this starting point, he would accommodate the Junta's preferences over the process of drafting the constitution, while prolonging his grip on power.

While appropriating the constitutional debate, he again defied the Junta's wishes by proposing a referendum on his presidency. Gremialistas posed the idea, but Junta members resented it as an attempt by Pinochet to sideline the Junta. Pinochet cast the referendum differently: as a means of defying criticism that the regime was a dictatorship by demonstrating that the public backed him. Pinochet announced the referendum in response to a UN vote condemning the regime's human rights violations, and he framed it as a patriotic choice between supporting the nation or its foreign enemies. The January 1978 referendum was shamelessly manipulated. There was no voter registration against which to validate votes (or against which a high rate of abstention could signal rejection of Pinochet). A publicity campaign blanketing television and radio called on voters to "Say Yes to Chile!" Pro-Pinochet rallies were organized across the country, with supporters bearing signs with slogans like "I shit on the UN!"[6]

Opposition marchers faced arrest. Censors prohibited criticism of the referendum or of Pinochet. The only concession was a brief local television interview in Santiago with former Christian Democratic President Eduardo Frei (1964–70). Frei, the main tolerated critic of the regime, declared that he "rejected the national referendum in form and in content."[7] Other members of the now unofficial Christian Democratic Party, including a former congressman, were arrested for distributing flyers critical of the referendum and asking Chileans to vote "No."

When voters went to the polls they were presented with a ballot with a question reading: "Faced with international aggression unleashed against our Fatherland, I support President Pinochet in his defense of the dignity of Chile and reaffirm the legitimacy of the government of the Republic."[8] Voters could mark the box "Yes," which appeared alongside the Chilean flag, or "No" which appeared alongside a black flag. The effective choice was voting for or against "Chile" rather than Pinochet or the regime. On referendum day, huge banners hung from buildings reading "Chile votes for Chile" and "Chile says yes." The referendum favored Pinochet with 75% of the vote.

Pinochet's decision to hold the referendum deepened divisions within the government. Héctor Humeres, the official was responsible for orchestrating national elections, called the referendum illegal. He used the logic of the regime to object: it did not have the unanimous consent of the Junta. Pinochet immediately replaced him with Gremialista Sergio Fernández, who had been Minister of Labor. Pinochet argued that the referendum was a prerogative of his executive power, but Humeres' objection reflected a significant division: neither Junta members Admiral Merino nor General Leigh supported it. Both Merino and Leigh voiced their objections to Pinochet, and Leigh made his criticisms public: a copy of the letter made its way to *The Washington Post*, drawing international attention to the disagreement within the government and to what Leigh saw as Pinochet's overreach. Leigh's dissidence mounted. He publicly called for a return to democracy within five years – well short of Pinochet's stated goals, and he threatened to withdraw the support of the Air Force from the Junta over mounting evidence in the FBI investigation about DINA director General Contreras' role in the Letelier assassination.

A year after the Chacarillas speech and six months after the referendum, Pinochet pressed Junta members Merino and Mendoza to remove Leigh from command of the Air Force and expel him from the Junta. Pinochet's ability to remove a member of the Junta showed the growth of his political authority after the Chacarillas speech and the referendum. But it also reflected the desperate political straits Pinochet found himself in over the Letelier case. Brazilian news magazine *Veja* journalist Paulo Sotero presented Pinochet's predicament provocatively: it was like Watergate, but with dead bodies rather than a hotel break-in.[9] Sotero suggested that as Nixon had done, Pinochet distanced himself from responsibility for an act that would not likely have occurred without his consent. Instead he heaped responsibility on Contreras and suggested that the assassination was a "simple settling of scores between exiled groups."[10]

Pinochet faced additional pressures from the Letelier case domestically and even within the armed forces, the police and intelligence service. Soldiers and police who worried they might face prosecution became reluctance to commit violence, threatening one of the pillars of Pinochet's rule. He responded by appointing Sergio Fernández, the Gremialista who had overseen the referendum, as the regime's first civilian Minister of the Interior. Fernández drafted and Pinochet promulgated the 1978 Amnesty decree which shielded soldiers and other state agents from legal jeopardy for any acts committed anywhere in Chile.

Pinochet's removal of Leigh reflected not impunity but desperation: he rid himself of an internal critic as he fought off external criticism. Barros also suggests that the willingness of Merino and Mendoza to agree to remove Leigh did not indicate weakness relative to Pinochet, but rather their growing disagreement with Leigh over economic policymaking. Leigh was not convinced by the free-market reforms and resisted some privatization measures.[11] Pinochet weathered the crisis, though the new Junta member, Air Force General Fernando Matthei, echoed his predecessor's independence and the Junta continued to control the drafting of the constitution, producing a more complete and binding document than the one sought by Pinochet.

The 1980 Constitution

On September 11, 1980, Chileans cast ballots again to ratify the new constitution drafted by Gremialista jurists. It provided two legal frameworks: one for a future democracy, and one for the temporary continuation of the dictatorship. The Pinochet regime would not be subject to the permanent clauses of the new constitution: instead, its framework came in the form of a series of "Temporary Dispositions" (TDs) that would last a decade. The TDs gave Pinochet and the Junta much of the same power they already had, and kept Pinochet in power until at least 1990 – perhaps until 1997. The TDs scheduled a plebiscite in 1988 by which the military would nominate a single candidate (Pinochet) for ratification.

The new constitution bore Jaime Guzmán's imprint. It established a "protected democracy" through several mechanisms intended to prevent the return of socialism, regardless of the preferences of voters. The measures included a category of appointed (rather than elected) senators, comprised of former presidents (who became senators-for-life), and a dozen senators appointed by branches of government and the armed forces. In addition, the constitution adopted a "binomial" system for distributing votes: the two parties that received the most votes, regardless of the margin, received almost the same number of congressional seats. By design, in the years following re-democratization, this gave conservative parties nearly as many seats in Congress as the center-left coalition, which had much stronger electoral support.

The constitution included a Constitutional Tribunal to mediate conflicts between branches of government. It also gave the armed forces both autonomy from and authority within the political system. For instance, the president could only appoint heads of the branches of the armed forces from a list provided by each branch, and the president could not remove them once named. But the armed forces were empowered to "guarantee the institutional order of the Republic." The president was given additional powers, such as the ability to close congress, declare a state of siege, suspend civil liberties, and dissolve the Chamber of Deputies.

The 1980 constitution reflected the philosophy and language of corporatism, which differs considerably from the language that characterizes liberal constitutions. It promoted "the harmonious integration of all the sectors of the Nation" and defined "the family is the basic core of society." The constitution banned political parties "intended to propagate doctrines attacking the family, or which advocate violence or a concept of society . . . based on class warfare," making it the only constitution in the world to ban Marxist political parties. Anyone guilty of violating that clause was barred from elected office, public service, acting as university president, school principal, teacher or professor, or involvement in the media, nor could they lead political associations, unions, or student groups. The constitution also defined "terrorism" as a crime, making it exempt from amnesty laws. By this clause, the 1978 amnesty applied to the armed forces, but not members of the opposition. The constitution outlawed abortion, in reflection of Guzman's conservative Catholicism.

The 1980 constitutional plebiscite was much like the 1978 referendum. The government mobilized supporters and the media for a short campaign in favor of the constitution. As in 1978, the plebiscite took place at a moment of economic expansion between recessions, and the country's economic performance cast the regime favorably. The regime continued to silence opposition or dissent, so debate about the nature and merits of the constitution were impossible. Political action against the proposed constitution resulted in arrest and internal exile.[12]

Former president Frei spoke for the opposition to the constitution and urged Chileans to vote against it. Prior to the referendum he gave an interview in Brazil, where the regime had eased restrictions on the press. He explained "This is nothing more than a fiction allowing the government to perpetuate its power for at least another nine years . . . I don't recognize the referendum as valid." After he cast his ballot, he declared "I feel ashamed and humiliated for having to participate in this fraud."[13] Even Conservative former president Arturo Alessandri, who had supported the regime and served on its symbolic Council of State, complained the constitution incorporated none of the Council's suggestions. Alessandri's objection highlighted the reality that regardless of the outcome of the vote, the 1980 constitution was an undemocratic document: it was prepared behind closed doors, without debate or inclusion of voices other than those of Pinochet, the Junta and their advisors. It was submitted for ratification without the public having the right to freely debate the document that would govern them.

The plebiscite orchestrated by Interior Minister Sergio Fernández, resulted in a 67% vote in favor of ratification. The constitution became effective in March 1981, but it placed all of the protections of civil and political rights out of reach by the Temporary Dispositions (TDs). The TDs preserved the structure and practices of the dictatorship, gave Pinochet a new 8-year term, and set a 1989 referendum on his continuing for another 8 years (instead of an open election). constitutional president for the first time, Pinochet moved into the Moneda palace, which had been restored after the 1973 bombing but was unoccupied. There was one modification to the design: the side door through which Allende's body was carried out was walled over. (In 2003, for the 30th anniversary of the coup, president Ricardo Lagos, a Socialist, had the door restored.)

Opposing Pinochet

Opposition to the dictatorship began with the onset of the coup, as handfuls of Allende's supporters futilely fought the soldiers encroaching on their neighborhoods, workplaces, or the Moneda. The intensity of the Junta's violence was intended to shock Allende's supporters into paralysis. Still, many of the thousands of Chileans at home and abroad formed organizations and networks that brought international awareness to the violence of arbitrary rule under Pinochet.

The main armed challenge to the regime came from the MIR. Its leadership had been reluctant supporters of Allende, believing Popular Unity to be too moderate. Now the MIR waged a guerrilla war against the dictatorship, relying on the doctrine of "no exile": remaining and fighting. The MIR's decision to remain in Chile made it fodder for the DINA, which soon liquidated most MIR members. The MIR's presence as a revolutionary organization avowedly fighting the regime served as a pretense for Pinochet, who justified the regime's excesses as a response to this threat. MIR militants who did seek exile organized a new campaign against the dictatorship in the late 1970s called "Operation Return," and in 1980 sought to organize a rural Guevarist *foco* in the southern mountain region of Neltume. The MIR received some funds the Cuban regime disbursed from the Montoneros' Born ransom. With the exception of the MIR's assassination of the commander of the Army Intelligence School, these efforts resulted in the deaths of the majority of its militants while enabling the Pinochet regime's "state of war."

Members of the Chilean Communist Party, who had shunned violence and participated in the Popular Unity coalition, were among the Junta's principal targets in 1973. While many were jailed or assassinated, several thousand thousand found exile in East Germany, Mexico, Cuba, and the Soviet Union. Their experience with exile reshaped the opposition. Socialists in East Germany became disillusioned with its political and economic system, and when they returned to Chile after amnesty, they brought moderated ideas about social reform. The Communist Party moved in the opposite direction. Its leaders reflected on their failure as a legal party and on the illegal nature of the dictatorship they confronted. They embraced a new strategy called Popular Revolutionary Struggle, which considered legitimate all means of overthrowing the dictatorship.

The Manuel Rodriguez Patriotic Front (FPMR), a guerrilla group that emerged from the Popular Revolutionary Struggle, waged actions through the 1980s, including an assassination attempt against Pinochet in 1986. FPMR guerrillas ambushed his motorcade, en route to the dictator's country retreat, and fired upon it with rocket-propelled grenades. Pinochet escaped unharmed. After the crackdown that followed, what remained of the FPMR broke from the Communist Party and continued armed actions well into the transition to democracy, though these had the character of acts of retribution, rather than attempts to overthrow the regime. In 1989, members of the FPMR attempted to kill retired General Gustavo Leigh, shooting him five times (he lost use of an eye but recovered). In 1991, the FPMR assassinated then senator Jaime Guzmán at the entrance to the Catholic University.

Armed action against the regime thrived in an environment where peaceful dissent was violently suppressed. By virtue of his stature, former president Eduardo Frei was one of the few people who could voice opposition. His Christian Democratic Party initially supported the coup but was quickly repelled by the military's methods and desire to retain power. Still, even Frei lived in fear and understood that his telephones were tapped and his ability to organize, debate, and criticize was curtailed. Former politicians resorted to keeping radios turned up in their homes in order to block the eavesdropping they suspected they were subject to.

Among Chileans who lacked the privileges and protections enjoyed by Frei, the ability to peaceably organize or debate was even more restricted. These restrictions were especially harsh on women. The regime restored the archaic Catholic principal of *potestad marital*, giving husbands authority over families and wives' property. Though the regime imagined women would return to family duties at home, the hardships of economic reform drove more women into the labor force.[14] If the patriarchal vision of the regime placed pressure on women, economic conditions undermined the patriarchal authority the *potestad marital* was intended to reinforce. Historian Heidi Tinsman offers the example of rural laborers undergoing the transition from communal or small plot farming created under the Frei and Allende reforms, to incorporation as day laborers in the large export farms that coalesced under military rule. Tinsman suggests that as women turned to farm labor, men faced a loss of authority as farmers and breadwinners through their loss of the right to organize and through the pressure of declining wages.[15]

As in Brazil and Argentina, the military leaders' archaic ideas about women pressured them in the political sphere and often in the workplace. Yet these biases also created spaces of political opposition. Women, acting as mothers, faced less risk when they made demands about the whereabouts of disappeared children, and formed organizations like Families of the Detained and Disappeared, which coordinated with Catholic Church organizations to document the toll inflicted by the regime. A hallmark of this mobilization were the *arpilleristas*, women who gathered, typically in churches, to embroider *arpilleras* – quilts – rendering images of missing relatives and other experiences of repression and hardship under Pinochet.

The *arpilleras* were a creative response to the limits to protest imposed by he regime. The *arpilleras* were seemingly apolitical: a traditional women's craft, conducted in silence within the confines of a Church. The quilting exercise helped organize communities of opposition to Pinochet, offered a spiritual and emotional outlet by which women could confront the loss and violence they experienced. The Church arranged for exhibits of the *arpilleras*, which were shown around the world to dramatize the violence of the Pinochet regime.

With political parties banned and public critics persecuted, one of the few entities in Chile capable of challenging the regime and its abuses was the Catholic Church. Many clergy supported the regime, and many leaders of the Gremialista movement were members of the Catholic order Opus Dei. But if the Church had one branch that was guided by traditional notions of morality and aversion to communism, another brought Catholic humanism into an embrace of humanitarianism and human rights. This group included Cardinal of Santiago, Raúl Silva, who brought the moral authority of the Church to bear against the regime.

Religious groups' activities began in the weeks after the coup, in response to the demands on parishes by Chileans seeking asylum, help leaving the country or finding detained or disappeared relatives. Soon after the coup, Lutheran Bishop Helmut Frenz, Presbyterian Pastor Ben Harper, and Cardinal Raúl Silva created the Ecumenical Committee for Peace (COPACHI), an organization that included Methodist, Pentecostal, Greek Orthodox, and Jewish groups.[16] COPACHI gave legal and financial assistance, as well as counseling for victims and their relatives. It became the only organization in Chile capable of challenging detentions, turning to the courts for information on a growing list of missing persons. The regime was reluctant to directly challenge COPACHI, but it harassed participants, barred Bishop Frenz from the country and exiled the committee's director.

Ultimately, COPACHI brought 2,342 cases seeking information on missing persons to court. It employed the limited latitude it had under the protection of church authorities, avoided criticizing the regime directly and presented itself as a non-political entity concerned with specific legal questions regarding the whereabouts of individuals. COPACHI incubated other human rights organizations such as the Association of Family Members of the Disappeared, and the Association of Family Members of Political Prisoners. The courts ignored the Committee's requests. To the contrary, the regime concealed the disappearance of the individuals sought by COPACHI. Newspapers of the pro-Pinochet *El Mercurio* group (which received millions from the CIA and American businesses) claimed COPACHI acted in bad faith and quoted invented foreign newspaper stories claiming that the disappeared had "exterminated [each other] like rats."[17] In 1975, Pinochet demanded that Cardinal Silva dissolve COPACHI after members sheltered MIR militants wounded in a shootout with DINA agents.

Though Cardinal Silva complied with Pinochet, he now set upon direct opposition. He formed a new organization, the Vicariate of Solidarity, which unlike the inter-faith COPACHI, rested completely under Catholic Church administration, which shielded it from pressure from Pinochet. Vicariate of Solidarity became the cornerstone of the Chilean human rights movement, serving as the repository of documentation on human right abuses, the champion of human rights in the judicial system, and supporting victims and their relatives. It was the Vicariate that organized the *arpilleristas* and disseminated their work abroad. It also continued COPACHI's legal challenges to detentions and disappearances, eventually registering more than 45,000 denunciations of detained or disappeared persons and bringing over 10,000 legal actions in favor of detained or tortured victims.[18]

In 1978, the Vicariate of Solidarity uncovered the first evidence of mass murder by the regime. An informant revealed the location of 15 bodies of indigenous farmworkers who disappeared after being detained by the police shortly after the coup. The bodies were found in an abandoned lime kiln in Lonquén, outside Santiago. A bishop took journalists to the site where their remains of the victims were found, with bullet wounds to their heads. Steve Stern describes the Lonquén discovery as a watershed that not only substantiated the alleged disappearances but also to the anguish of survivors of the disappeared, who until then had no acknowledgement of or recourse over the loss of their relatives.[19] The discovery began a new phase in the work of the Vicariate, which received and investigated tips on a growing number of locations of human remains of the disappeared, which in turn served as evidence of crimes that could be brought to court. Lonquen became the subject of *Of Love and Shadows*, a novel by Isabel Allende.

In the years after the coup, the Chilean judiciary system proved deaf to challenges by the opposition or claims of violence by the regime. But Lonquen and Yumbal created a public record of crimes. Accompanied by the ratification of the 1980 constitution (still shackled by the Temporary Dispositions), the discovery of the mass graves created an atmosphere in which some judges were willing to review accusations about detentions and disappearances, if the killings were protected by the 1978 amnesty law.

The 1982 Economic Crisis Shapes Democratization

Pinochet claimed that Chile was no longer a dictatorship because the 1980 constitution had been ratified in a plebiscite that elected him president. On the surface nothing had changed. The Temporary Dispositions kept the dictatorship in place and gave it a free hand. The judiciary remained largely unwilling to investigate the regime. There was no Congress. Laws were still imposed by decree. Censorship remained and opponents continued to be arrested, tortured, or disappeared, even if no longer with the intensity of the early years. Still, the new constitution established a clear set of rules for the first time, creating conditions akin to what opposition groups in Brazil found: the opposition learned to use the emerging legal framework as its fulcrum to wrest Pinochet from power. Though this was an authoritarian constitution tailored to preserve Pinochet a as president armed with Temporary Dispositions preserving his arbitrary powers, "even custom shoes bind," in the expression used by Junta member Matthei.[20]

As in Brazil, the Chilean economic miracle had boosted the dictatorship's fortunes, helping Pinochet weather the Letelier case and push through the 1978 referendum and the 1980 plebiscite. But as in Brazil, the transition to democracy was shaped by the 1982 economic crisis that was triggered by the second oil shock, the rise in interest rates in the United States, and the threat of default by Mexico, Brazil, and Argentina, and global recession.

Because of the Chicago Boys' policies, Chile was especially vulnerable. The Chilean "miracle" of rapid economic expansion from 1977 to 1981 brought a wave of foreign investment to Chilean banks which fueled a bubble of speculative investment and borrowing by businesses struggling to remain competitive in their open market environment, as well as by the affluent Chilean beneficiaries of the free-market reforms. Foreign investment overvalued the peso, causing a balance of payments deficit because exports had become uncompetitive and wealthy Chileans bought growing amounts of inexpensive imports on easy credit. The economic crisis caused a run on Chile's loosely regulated and over-leveraged banks (circumstances that resembled the 2008–9 U.S. banking crisis). The banking system was on the verge of collapse, resulting in the nationalization of half of Chile's banks and the government absorbing their private debts.

Because free-market reforms removed limits on imports and currency flows, the crisis caused a recession far deeper than those experienced by the other Latin American countries beset by the debt crisis. By 1983, nearly one-third of Chilean workers were unemployed, while those employed saw their wages decline on average by 20% over the course of the year. After growing at up to 8.7% per year during the preceding boom, the GDP declined by 14% in 1982, and another 5% in 1983. Chile's privatized economy had little cushion to absorb the blow. Businessmen endured the 1975 recession triggered by the Chicago Boys' "shock therapy" on the promise that it would result in lasting prosperity, not an intensified boom and bust cycle. They confronted Friedman's acolytes, who saw the crisis as evidence of the need for even greater liberalization and who had even advocated for allowing the nation's banks to collapse.

Pinochet was compelled to moderate the economic course. He reshuffled the cabinet, replaced Finance Minister Sérgio de Castro and cast about for a fiscal manager who could balance the demands of businessmen seeking protection, Chicago Boys pushing for even fewer controls on the economy, and the need to arrest the deepening recession. Though Sérgio de Castro had been finance minister for five years, between 1982 and 1985 Chile had six finance ministers who eased the extreme policies implemented by de Castro. Defying free-market doctrine, the finance ministers Carlos Cáceres Contreras (1983–4) and Luis Escobar Cerda (1984–5) stimulated the economy though spending in areas like public housing, devalued the currency, imposed import barriers and controls on capital flows, and created loan guarantees and subsidies for business. The high-stakes table at the casino was closed.

As Chile's economy stabilized, Pinochet turned again to one of the Chicago Boys, Hernán Büchi, who had been involved in the privatization of pensions, to head the Finance Ministry. Under Büchi (1985–9), the Finance Ministry restored many of the reforms reversed during the crisis, but without the puritanical zeal of the preceding years. The costs of the boom and bust cycle proved too high even for Pinochet to absorb. Under pressure from businessmen seeking greater protections from Chile's unfiltered integration into the global marketplace, he replaced many of the Chicago Boys in government with moderate figures tied to business. Though this moderation did not resemble the developmentalist policies that prevailed before 1973, it provided a more stable platform for business by creating protected classes of loans, restricting speculative investment, and waging a succession of currency devaluations to protect exports and discourage imports. The rhetoric of the free market persisted after the 1982 crisis, even as the economic policies were quietly tempered.

The regime's departure from free-market orthodoxy reflected the depth of the debt crisis but also a changing political reality. Business groups began to criticize the regime's policies. In October 1982, a business coalition issued the Valdivia Proclamation, declaring "We hold economic policymakers responsible for the breakdown of the national productive apparatus and for the transfer of resources from the productive sector to the financial system."[21] A decade of reform had produced inconsistent results at often unacceptable costs, and the Allende years were long gone. Chilean businessmen began to consider re-democratization an attractive alternative: might capitalism survive without the old man? Could the "protected democracy" of the 1980 constitution provide businessmen the influence over economic policy that eluded them under the Chicago Boys? That the dictatorship began to accommodate business interests to such a greater extent after 1982 revealed its recognition of this possibility.

Unseating Pinochet and Defining a Path to Democracy

The 1982 crisis created the foundations for renewed opposition to the regime. The rules created by the 1980 constitution and its TDs set in motion both a slow transition and a lengthy continuation of Pinochet's presidency. He would be president until 1989. In a 1988 plebiscite, Pinochet would appear unopposed on the ballot, presumably win the up-or-down vote, and have a second term that would last until 1997. If he did not prevail in the 1988 plebiscite, competitive elections would be held the following year. The constitution was engineered specifically to keep Pinochet in power. The political opposition that coalesced after 1982 would prevent that.

The hardships wrought by 30% unemployment and the collapse of wages spurred a wave of protests from 1983 to 1986. The labor movement had been dismantled after 1973, but now workers organized again and found an unexpected ally in business groups seeking limits to the free-market reforms. Inhabitants of the *poblaciones*, shantytowns around cities like Santiago, were among the hardest hit by unemployment and staged protests as well. Students reconstituted political organizations on university campuses. Other social groups challenged the regime as well: the Catholic Church advocated for human rights and for investigation of disappearances. Groups like the Association of Family Members of the Disappeared, and the Association of Family Members of Political Prisoners, comprised predominantly of women, as well as groups mobilized against the regime's patriarchal suppression of women's rights, created a broad grassroots challenge to the regime. Each group had its own concerns – wages, jobs, human rights, women's rights – but these concerns converged in demands for an end to the Pinochet regime and a substantive transition to democracy.

Within this changing environment, two coalitions of opposition political parties emerged. The Democratic Alliance (AD), which included the Christian Democratic Party and moderate Socialists, issued a Democratic Manifesto calling for Pinochet's resignation, a new constitutional convention, and direct elections. In November 1983, AD staged the first political protest rally held since 1973, drawing hundreds of thousands of supporters to the main park in Santiago. The Communist Party and radical Socialists formed an organization focused on protest against the regime, the Popular Democratic Movement (MDP). The government invoked the anti-Marxist clause of the constitution and disbanded it. The Communist Party's continued support for armed action against the regime helped reinforce its political marginalization.

The regime responded to the opposition in two ways. In 1983, Pinochet appointed Sergio Onofre Jarpa as Minister of the Interior – one of the first significant cabinet appointments of a civilian who had been politically active before 1973. Jarpa's charge was to sustain dialogue with legal opposition groups like the AD in order to prevent radicalization of the opposition and to preserve the legal framework of the 1980 constitution. At the same time, the regime continued to arrest, torture or kill protestors in order to intimidate the opposition. This violence, rendered increasingly visible amid growing public protests helped sustain international attention on the regime and its human rights record. By this time Argentina's Junta had collapsed and Brazil's transition to democracy was well underway, making the Pinochet regime an awkward standout subject to growing foreign pressure, even from the Reagan administration.

Though opposition groups denounced the 1980 constitution as a tool of the dictatorship (it was), they began to see it as providing an opening for challenging Pinochet. The means to pursue it were organized by the successor to Cardinal Raúl Silva. Juan Francisco Fresno, named Cardinal in May 1985, proposed a political framework called the National Accord for Transition to Full Democracy. The Accord called for open elections, restoration of civil rights by lifting the state of emergency, and an end to political banishment and exile. In addition, the Accord established a set of political principles, including respect for both the constitutional order and the free market. The Accord cultivated support from business groups weary of Pinochet, by easing fears that re-democratization would threaten the Chilean economic system.

The parties affiliated with AD signed on to the National Accord, while Pinochet and the far left rejected it. Together, the positions assumed by Pinochet, AD, and the Communist Party shaped a new political landscape: the National Accord and its supporters emerged as the country's political center, seeking to gain space against two factions inflicting (disproportionate) violence upon each other and threatening a peaceful transition to democracy. Within this environment, supporters of the National Accord used the 1980 constitution and the forthcoming 1988 plebiscite as the tools to forge Chile's transition to democracy.

Since the 1988 plebiscite took place under rules defined by the constitution, its conduct would was less arbitrary than in 1978 or 1980. An independent Electoral Tribunal oversaw the vote, which for the first time was based on voter registration (this increased the transparency of vote counting, as the number of votes cast had to be proportionate to the number of voters registered in a precinct). The constitution also provided a framework for registering political parties, which gave the Christian Democrats and other supporters of the Accord room for political and electoral activity. The parties supporting the National Accord saw a chance to remove Pinochet, using tools that had eluded them since 1973: political organization, relative freedom to organize, a political platform (the Accord), an election in which the opposition was allowed to campaign, and an electoral system overseen by an independent authority. Finally, by this time Argentina and Brazil had established democratic regimes, making the endurance of the Pinochet regime seem out of place, and making a democratic alternative seem more concrete.

The NO

As the January 1988 plebiscite neared, Chileans organized around two words: Yes and No. Yes, renew Pinochet's mandate until 1997; No renewal, the end of Pinochet's rule and direct national elections. The political opposition organized a Coalition of Parties for the "No" (the *Concertación*). It included not just the members of the Democratic Alliance and backers of the National Accord, but even drew in factions of the MIR and the Communist Party. Pinochet also arrayed considerable support, mobilizing not just affluent Chileans who had benefited from his policies, but also many poorer Chileans whose support he gained by turning public housing construction projects, and other aid programs instituted during the economic crisis into an electoral propaganda machine.

For the first time since 1973, the opposition could campaign, and the campaign organized around the "NO" became a milestone: for a generation of artists, television producers, and others who had lived the past 14 years under a heavy blanket of censorship and the constant threat of violence, the creative space provided by the "NO" campaign opened the gates to a flood of artistic expression. This energy contrasted with a colossal campaign with predictably patriotic themes organized by National Renewal, the coalition of right-wing parties led by the Independent Democratic Union (UDI), which supported Pinochet.

Members of the Concertación threw themselves into the campaign for the "NO" with trepidation. Would the election be fair? Would Pinochet and the Junta accept a loss? Or would they simply change the rules of the game? If the "NO" won, would the businessmen and bankers who had become unimaginably powerful in neoliberal Chile respect a transition to democracy? Would the military truly yield power? Would the pursuit of investigations into human rights abuses prove an impediment to the military's respect for the transition? How much of the undemocratic "protected democracy" clauses of the constitution could they reverse?

Concertación hedged considerably because of these questions. Its platform maintained the free-market reforms to placate conservative Chileans who, though they may not vote "NO" would hopefully be more likely to accept the results. To protect against fraud, they established a network of polling monitors and a parallel system for tabulating the results alongside the official count. And the Concertación helped maintain unity among opposition parties and social groups by providing an overall framework and political platform, while allowing parties to maintain their own distinct organization, preventing the fragmentation and weakening of the opposition.

On January 2, 1988, 56% of Chilean voters cast their ballots for "NO," rejecting the dictator's pursuit of a new term in office. Pinochet himself seemed dumbfounded by the results. On the night of the tabulation, he tried to deploy the army to the streets, ostensibly to preserve order, but the Junta overrode him. The Junta compelled him to accept the results. To settle the outcome, Junta member General Matthei (Gustavo Leigh's successor) publicly announced Pinochet's defeat. In his concession speech, Pinochet reminded Chileans that he would remain president for another year. Still, the end was in view.

With its victory, Concertación had shown the success of its strategy of using the dictatorship's own rules against it – success which brought the more radical leftist parties into the fold, though a splinter group of the Communist Party would continue to carry out acts of retribution, such as the assassination of Jaime Guzmán in 1991. After the plebiscite, the Concertación of Parties for the No became the Concertación of Parties for Democracy, a durable political coalition that fielded single candidates for president and established consensus candidates for congress and for local office. Meanwhile, a coalition of conservative politicians, some still loyal to Pinochet, others seeking to build a political movement independent of the dictator and his regime, formed Democracy and Progress, the opposition to Concertación. Parallel to the presidential campaign, Concertación, the political right and the regime carried out a complicated negotiation about a package of reforms to the 1980 constitution that reflected the rapidly changing political landscape and reinforced political rights. This marked the first step in an ongoing process of revision and renegotiation of the constitution that resulted in successive modifications of the document over the course of the re-democratization process. The 1989 revision of the constitution was approved by plebiscite. In the presidential election Concertación's candidate, Christian Democrat Patricio Aylwin, won over the candidate of National Renewal, former Finance Minister Hernan Büchi.

Justice Done but a Long Road Ahead

In March, 1990, Augusto Pinochet handed the presidential sash to Patricio Aylwin, completing the first step in Chile's transition to democracy.

In a clear sign of the limits to this step, Pinochet remained Commander-in-Chief of the Army, a position protected from presidential interference by the terms of the 1980 constitution. When he retired from the Army in 1998, he assumed the position of Senator for life, with considerable legal protections, also provided by the constitution. The National Security Council, on which Pinochet had a powerful voice, remained a check on civilian authority. The 1979 amnesty remained in effect, shielding all members of the police and armed forces from prosecution for human rights violations committed in Chile during the military regime.

Concertación proved adept in overcoming these constraints. Beginning with Aylwin, it won four consecutive presidential elections, which included the presidencies of Eduardo Frei-Tagle (1994–2000), son of former Christian Democratic president Eduardo Frei, who had spoken out against Pinochet; Ricardo Lagos (2000–6), Chile's first Socialist president, and Michelle Bachelet (2006–10), a victim of torture under Pinochet and whose father, an Army General who opposed the coup, died in detention from medical problems caused by torture.

Despite the amnesty law, in 1991 the Chilean congress created a Truth and Reconciliation Commission, which investigated human rights violations during the dictatorship and published the Rettig Report (named after commission chair Raul Rettig). Though all of Chile's judges during the early years of re-democratization had been appointed under Pinochet, some began accepting and trying cases that explored the boundaries of the amnesty. Among these was the conviction of former DINA director Manuel Contreras for assassinations committed outside of Chilean national territory – like the Letelier bombing – since these were not covered by the amnesty law. When Contreras resisted sentencing by taking refuge in an army base, he triggered the first test of the willingness of the armed forces to respect the process of re-democratization even when it resulted in the punishment of crimes committed by men in uniform. Pinochet, still Commander-in-Chief of the Army, supported Contreras and sought to keep him out of prison. But the commander of the garrison where Contreras had sought refuge surrendered him after President Frei agreed to several concessions, including the construction of a special prison for Contreras, a pay raise for the armed forces, and limits on future trials over human rights abuses.

Unlike in Argentina, where the Junta collapsed amid economic crisis and humiliation in the Falklands War, the Chilean dictatorship had taken advantage of a moment of economic growth to prepare the framework for an eventual transition to democracy, in a manner similar to what Geisel had accomplished in Brazil. The transition to a civilian government in Chile, as in Brazil, took place according to the rules of the dictatorship. But the Chilean transition differed from the Brazilian one in two key respects: first, the Gremialista framers of the 1980 constitution went further than the Brazilian military regime had in binding the future regime. And second, where the Brazilian opposition focused its energies in the transition toward drafting the 1989 constitution, Chile's political opposition found itself compelled to retain, in large measure, the 1980 constitution and the economic formula that were Pinochet's legacy.

Notes

1 U.S. Congress, "Church Report: Covert Action in Chile, 1963–1973" (U.S. Government Printing Office, 1975), http://foia.state.gov/Reports/ChurchReport.asp, accessed October 14, 2012.

2 Robert Barros, *Constitutionalism and Dictatorship: Pinochet, the Junta and the 1980 Constitution* (Cambridge University Press, 2002), 226.

3 Cited in Carlos Huneeus, *The Pinochet Regime* (Lynne Rienner, 2007), 141.

4 The speech is available at: "Discurso del general Augusto Pinochet en cerro Chacrillas con ocasión del día de la juventud el 9 de julio de 1977," http://es.wikisource.org/wiki/Discurso_de_Chacarillas, accessed October 14, 2012, and excerpts can be found on You Tube.

5 Humberto Lagos Schuffeneger, *El general Pinochet y el mesianismo político* (LOM, 2001), 32.

6 "Agora, o poder pessoal?," *Veja*, January 11, 1978, 60.

7 "Agora, o poder pessoal?," *Veja*, January 11, 1978, 63.

8 Pamela Constable and Arturo Valenzuela, *A Nation of Enemies* (Norton, 1991), 68.

9 Paulo Sotero, "Começa a explosão," *Veja*, August 9, 1978, 33.

10 Ibid.

11 Barros, *Constitutionalism and Dictatorship*, 214.

12 Huneeus, *The Pinochet Regime*, 88.

13 "A democracia incomoda," *Veja*, August 20, 1980, 41; "O soberano do Chile," *Veja*, September 17, 1980, 39.

14 Maria Elena Valenzuela, "The Evolving Roles of Women under Military Rule," in Paul Drake and Ivan Jasic (eds.), *The Struggle for Democracy in Chile, 1982–1990* (Nebraska University Press, 1991), 162–3.

15 Heidi Tinsman, "Reviving Feminist Materialism: Gender and Neoliberalism in Pinochet's Chile," *Signs*, 26:1 (2000), 145–88, 159.

16   Pamela Lowden, "The Ecumenical Committee for Peace in Chile (1973–1975): The Foundation of Moral Opposition to Authoritarian Rule in Chile," *Bulletin of Latin American Research*, 12:2 (1993), 193.

17   Lowden, "The Ecumenical Committee for Peace in Chile," 195–8.

18   Lowden, "The Ecumenical Committee for Peace in Chile," 201; www.vicariadelasolidaridad.cl, accessed October 14, 2012.

19   Steve J. Stern, *Remembering Pinochet's Chile* (Duke University Press, 2006), 59.

20   Barros, *Constitutionalism and Dictatorship*, 255.

21   Guillermo Campero, "Entrepreneurs under the Military Regime," in Paul Drake and Ivan Jasic (eds.), *The Struggle for Democracy in Chile, 1982–1990* (University of Nebraska Press, 1991), 136.

Conclusion

As General Benito Bignone, the last president of Argentina's Junta, regarded the country's military rout, its economic crisis, and the brutal violence perpetrated by his regime against its own citizens, he understandably sought to diffuse responsibility. He declared "never did a general wake up in the morning and say 'let's topple a government.' Coups are something different, something that come from society, that go from society to the Army, and the Army never did more than meet this request."[1] In other words, society made us do it. As a means of evading responsibility, the statement is completely untrue: the decisions and actions of the Junta, of the police and armed forces under it, of its finance ministers, were their own. What is more, they were made in an environment in which the Junta used both the law and extralegal violence to suppress any possible criticism of its actions.

Yet in another sense Bignone was right: his dictatorship, like those in Brazil and Chile, relied upon varying degrees of public support, in particular the extensive support of wealthy, conservative and more powerful members of their societies. At the critical initial moments, the regimes counted on the support of major political parties, banks, businesses, the mainstream media, sectors of the Church, and – crucially – the United States and multinational corporations. Without it, they would have been unable to consolidate their rule. Though by the end of the military rule large parts of each of these groups had turned against the dictatorships, and even disavowed past support, these sectors had been essential for creating the environment in which the dictatorships, and their excesses,

Dictatorship in South America, First Edition. Jerry Dávila.
© 2013 Jerry Dávila. Published 2013 by Blackwell Publishing Ltd.

were not only possible but regarded as necessary and even normal. As Marguerite Feitlowitz asks: "The Dirty War happened because, in some measure, every part of Argentine society allowed it to. How does a country confront – let alone punish – *that*?"[2]

But decisions by allies of military rule to shift their support to opposition movements were essential to re-democratization. The emergence of a "new left" in each country that foreswore revolution or radical social transformation, was a crucial step. The nonviolent legalism of the new left was more attractive than the violence of arbitrary regimes. The left's evolution was not met by evolution by the military regimes: they were largely unable to evolve from their early radicalism, and were increasingly confined to the unfortunate consequences of their policymaking.

It is tempting for former participants in these regimes to take credit for the character of re-democratization: that they "tamed" the left and created conditions for democracy to flourish. Yet the reverse is true: it was the left that tamed the dictatorships by learning to frame a critique that was impossible for the dictators to respond to. The left's use of force against the regimes justified the regime's violence. In contrast, it was the left's embrace of legalism and human rights de-legitimated the dictatorships and their methods. The new left learned to build bridges with the dictatorships' allies, and to sidestep the asymmetrical confrontation it had sustained with the dictatorships. In doing so, it offered the clearer long-term path for each of the three countries.

The left's acquiescence to the free-market principles advocated under military rule was critical to these transitions. Transition governments of the left and center-left in Argentina, Brazil, and Chile turned out to be better followers of the free market, and more cautious managers of economic and development projects than the generals had been. In part, this was a necessity forced by the debt crisis of the 1980s. But in part it was the product of a historical moment: the transitions to democracy coincided with the collapse of the Soviet Union and its model of state socialism in Eastern Europe. In this regard, there are interesting comparisons to be made between the transitions to democracy and economic reform in Latin America and Eastern Europe.[3]

In Chile, this political formula took the form of the center-left coalition Concertación's acceptance of the 1980 constitution and the free-market policies implemented under Pinochet, which made it impossible for Pinochet to challenge the results of the referendum against him and the subsequent election. Later, the decisions by Concertación

Presidents Eduardo Frei and Ricardo Lagos to pursue Pinochet's release from arrest in Britain consolidated the political legitimacy of the Chilean left among sectors of society which had once been willing to wage war upon it. This legitimacy provided the basis for challenging some of the less democratic elements of the 1980 constitution, such as the powers of the National Security Council and the office of senator-for-life, as well as the amnesty that shielded members of the dictatorship from prosecution for their acts of violence. Though Pinochet was freed from arrest in London, his last years were spent under investigation and indictment for corruption and human rights violations.

Concertación won four consecutive presidential elections, including the election of Michele Bachelet, Chile's first woman head-of-state. Bachelet's trajectory epitomized Chile's history of dictatorship and democratization. Her father was a general who was jailed and died after torture for remaining loyal to Allende. Bachelet and her mother were also tortured before being exiled. In the years after Pinochet's arrest, Bachelet was named Minister of Defense, a striking appointment both given her past abuse under military rule, and the possible reluctance of members of the armed forces to be placed under the authority of a woman. Bachelet overcame this apprehension as an effective advocate for the armed forces within government, and in 2005 was elected president. In 2010, conservative Sebastián Piñera succeeded Bachelet, marking the first political transition from a party in power to an opposition party in post-dictatorship Chile, and reflecting the emergence of a political right in Chile no longer tethered to Pinochet, who died in 2006. Still, the past remained present: Piñera's government included ideologues from the Pinochet regime, among them Joaquin Lavín, author of the *Silent Revolution*, appointed minister of education (his tenure in this position was short-lived: Lavín was dismissed in 2011 for his failure to resolve a national student strikes over the accessibility and cost of university study).

In Argentina, these questions were addressed through the role Peronism continued to hold in the nation's political life. UCR President Raul Alfonsín (1983–9) struggled to rebuild democracy in the aftermath of the Dirty War while contending with the debt crisis. In 1985 and 1986, the members of the three Juntas that governed from 1976 to 1983 were put on trial, as were hundreds of military and police officers responsible for disappearances. Videla and Massera were sentenced to life in prison. General Ramón Camps, who had claimed that "people didn't disappear, subversives disappeared," was convicted of 600 counts of homicide and sentenced to 25 years in prison.[4] The Trials of the Juntas resulted in revolts by soldiers who applied camouflage to their faces – the *caras pintadas*. The military unrest compelled Alfonsín to end the prosecutions through a Ley del Punto Final (1986, which ended prosecution for human rights abuses) and the Ley de Obediencia Debida (1987, which determined that members of the military and police were immune to prosecution because they were following orders).

Alfonsín's effort to control inflation, the Austral Plan collapsed in 1989, resulting in inflation over 5,000% (a university textbook costing $25 pesos in August would cost more than $1,250 pesos the following August). Amid Alfonsín's inability to resolve these legacies of military rule, Argentines elected Carlos Menem, the candidate of Perón's Justicialist Party in 1989. Alfonsín surrendered power early so that Menem could more quickly establish policies to control an inflation rate so high it had triggered food riots. Menem changed course and pardoned all of the convicted members of the military Juntas and others convicted for human rights violations. He also began a wave of free-market reforms, privatizing the state's extensive business holdings and attracting an influx of foreign capital.

The free-market reforms fueled a temporarily successful currency stabilization plan that established parity between the dollar and the peso. The privatizations and the strong currency created an illusion of stability and prosperity that was a welcome respite from the upheaval of recent decades. Yet by 2000, the influx of capital declined as the privatizations ran their course, leaving Argentines with increasingly expensive utilities and services provided now by foreign companies, along with an overvalued peso that caused investor flight, prompting an economic and political collapse at the end of 2001. Where $1 dollar had bought $1 peso, almost overnight $1 dollar bought $3 pesos – a ruinous change for members of Argentina's middle class, whose salaries were in pesos but whose mortgages were in dollars. Currency simply disappeared and both private businesses and local governments were reduced to paying salaries in scrip that employees redeemed at a discount at whatever markets would accept them.

Menem's successor, Fernando de la Rua, was unable to stem the political and economic crisis and resigned in December 2001. Over the following month, five separate people held the presidency of Argentina, sometimes for less than a week at a time – no one could build a credible political base upon which to address the economic collapse. Ultimately, it was the economy that saved politics: the devaluation of the peso made agricultural exports more competitive, and an export boom righted the economy. After 2003, a new Justicialist president, Néstor Kirchner, again pressed the questions of human rights. He voided not just the amnesty granted by Menem but also the Obediencia Debida and Punto Final laws. Members of the Juntas were again sentenced and imprisoned. A new wave of prosecutions unfolded across the country. Kirchner purged the armed forces of senior officers who had served during the Dirty War. His wife, Cristina Fernández de Kirchner, succeeded him as president in 2007 and began to reverse the privatizations of the previous decade. The distance Argentina traveled from the economic and political upheaval of the 1970s and 1980s suddenly seemed not so great.

Brazil followed a course of stabilization and reform similar to Argentina's. The currency was stabilized through the 1994 Real Plan, which tied the real to the dollar as part of a reform that included more limited privatizations than in Argentina. Brazil faced an earlier and less abrupt currency devaluation in 1998. The president who conducted these reforms, Fernando Henrique Cardoso, was an architect of dependency theory in the 1960s, before being coerced into exile by the dictatorship. Returning to Brazil, he proved to be the country's most effective proponent of the free market. He was succeeded as president in 2003 by unionist and Workers' Party leader Lula da Silva. Though Lula da Silva had long campaigned on promises such as reversing the privatizations and renouncing the country's debt, he won election on a pledge to respect his predecessor's economic course. In Brazil (as in Chile), the political left became a steward of the free market, private enterprise and currency stabilization.

At the same time, the Cardoso and Lula da Silva governments made gains in social inclusion. Cardoso became the first president to acknowledge Brazilian racial discrimination, and began implementing quota and affirmative action programs intended to integrate long-excluded black and indigenous Brazilians into universities and government. Lula da Silva consolidated into federal policy a number of experiments through conditional cash transfer programs such as *Bolsa Familia*. Through Bolsa Familia, poor families who keep their children in school and make use of public health resources receive stipends from the government, a model of social programming intended to both meet the immediate consequences of poverty and address the long-term needs for alleviating poverty through education. The program has contributed to the first persistent decrease in social inequality in modern Brazilian history.

If in 1976 it was fitting to label South America the "Graveyard of Democracy," by 1990 this ceased to be the case: every country that had been under military rule was governed by a democratically elected president. Between 2006 and 2010, Argentina, Brazil, and Chile elected women presidents, two of whom had been imprisoned and tortured under military rule. Each country gradually unraveled the vestiges of military rule. The reduction of the constitutional influence of the armed forces in Chile is one example. At the same time, the countries have brought greater scrutiny to the armed forces for past actions, as Nestor Kirchner did in revoking the Obediencia Debida and Punto Final laws. The Brazilian Congress established a truth commission that began work in 2012.

Alongside this long transition, the challenge of producing historical understanding of these regimes unfolds. As archives are opened, as testimony is gathered, as memoirs emerge, the questions historians ask – through fields of scholarship described in the pages that follow – have begun to bring intentionally obscured histories to light.

Notes

1   Cited in Calveiro, *Poder y Desaparición: Los campos de concentración en Argentina* (Colihue, 2006), 9–10.
2   Marguerite Feitlowitz, *A Lexicon of Terror* (Oxford University Press, 1999), 17.
3   See for instance Juan Linz and Alfred Stepan, *Problems of Democratic Transition and Consolidation: Southern Europe, South America, and Post-Communist Europe* (Johns Hopkins University Press, 1996).
4   Feitlowitz, *A Lexicon of Terror*, 16.

Sources

Today the most exciting studies of the Argentine, Brazilian, and Chilean dictatorships are being produced in those countries. This has not always been the case. In the 1970s and 1980s, the strongest work was being produced abroad. One of the things these dictatorships "disappeared" was their countries' ability to write their own history. The regimes denied or obscured many of their own actions – both their acts of repression and their policy debates. Public policies were conducted without public accountability and often hidden from view. The ability of scholars to interrogate aspects of their country's recent experience, or even to apply certain kinds of theories or methodologies to their work was often harshly suppressed.

Many scholars were exiled, often under considerable hardship and duress. They found refuge, often in the United States, Mexico, and Europe, where they found the freedom to analyze and debate the regimes (O'Donnell, Calveiro, and Cardoso are examples). Scholars from the United States and other countries helped fill the void. Foreign scholars were not free from pressure from the dictatorships, which detained, sought to discredit, or refused entry to scholars they mistrusted. Latin American universities were starved of research funding in controversial areas, and that funding would be redirected to uncontroversial areas more consistent with the aims of the regimes, such as engineering, physics, or free-market economics.

Beginning in the 1990s, this situation reversed itself. In the course of the transition to democracy, history is being rescued from its disappearance. National scholars have regained the space to research subjects

Dictatorship in South America, First Edition. Jerry Dávila.
© 2013 Jerry Dávila. Published 2013 by Blackwell Publishing Ltd.

related to the dictatorships, are securing access to once hidden records, and increasingly receive the support to conduct new research. They are again the front line of interpretation of their recent past, and the products of this research are incisive and far ranging.

That is not to say that U.S.-based scholars have not continued to have a strong impact on the study of these histories, particularly in examining the history of particular institutions under military rule or considering the experience of social movements. Indeed, what has emerged is a transnational dialogue about dictatorship, resistance and re-democratization that is one of the dynamic areas of scholarly production.

Human Rights

This area of scholarship is anchored by the three Nunca Más reports produced in the aftermath of the dictatorships. The first was *Nunca Más: The Report of the Argentine Nacional Commission on the Disappeared* (Farrar Strauss Giroux, 1986). A similar report was published by the Chilean Rettig Commission in 1990: *Nunca Más en Chile: Síntesis corregida y actualizada del Informe Rettig* (LOM, 1991/9). The Rettig Commission's work was complemented in 2003 by a second official inquiry conducted by the Valech Commission, which recorded testimony about torture and political imprisonment. In Brazil, an official report was not produced as part of the initial transition to democracy. Instead, the Archdiocese of São Paulo produced a volume based on its extensive records on human rights violations under military rule, *Torture in Brazil: A Shocking Report on the Pervasive Use of Torture by Brazilian Military Governments, 1964–1979* (Texas [1979], 1998). An official inquiry was only completed in 2007, and was published as Comissão Especial sobre Mortos e Desaparecidos Políticos, *Direito à Memória e à Verdade* (Secretaria Especial dos Direitos Humanos da Presidência da República, 2007). The Brazilian report is available online, in Portuguese.[1] The Argentine *Nunca Más* report[2], the Chilean *Rettig Commission Report*,[3] and *Valech Commission Report*[4] as well as the Archdiocese of São Paulo's *Torture in Brazil*[5] report are all available online through the United States Institute of Peace.

The role of the U.S. government in support of these regimes can be accessed in detail. The congressional Church Committee Report (1975), examining the Nixon administration's efforts to undermine the Salvador

Allende government in Chile is available through the U.S. Department of State website.[6] The National Security Archive, a non-profit research organization, provides electronic access to a rich collection of declassified documents related to U.S. policy in Latin America during the era of military rule, particularly the Nixon effort to undermine Allende, support for the Pinochet regime and the Brazilian military coup, Operation Condor, human rights violations in Argentina, and other subjects.[7]

Finally, there is a remarkable website which was created in Argentina but now includes other Latin American countries, that functions as a kind of Facebook for the disappeared. The site, Desaparecidos.org, has information on victims of repression, the largest collection of which focuses on Argentina.[8] The pages on disappeared persons provide a forum for relations to add information about their background, the circumstances of their detention and their disappearance.

Desaparecidos plays many roles. It provides a means for surviving detainees to help trace the trajectories of the disappeared after they were detained – where they were held, where they were last seen, who was responsible for their disappearance. It also makes the disappeared and the crime of their disappearance visible.

Studies of human rights in Argentina, Brazil, and Chile often adopt a transnational perspective. Some, like *Human Rights and Transnational Solidarity in Cold War Latin America*, ed. Jessica Stites Mor (University of Wisconsin Press, 2013), and Marguerite Guzman Bouvard's *Revolutionizing Motherhood: The Mothers of the Plaza de Mayo* (Rowman & Littlefield, 2002) trace the internationalization of human rights advocacy in opposition to military rule. Among studies that consider human rights across multiple countries, see Kathryn Sikkink, *The Justice Cascade: How Human Rights Prosecutions Are Changing World Politics* (Norton, 2011); Priscilla Hayner's *Unspeakable Truths: Transitional Justice and the Challenge of Truth Commissions* (Routledge, 2001); Thomas Wright, *State Terrorism in Latin America: Chile, Argentina and International Human Rights* (Rowman & Littlefield, 2007); and Edward Cleary, *The Struggle for Human Rights in Latin America* (Praeger, 1997).

United States–Latin America Relations

On the Iran–Contra Affair, see the account by federal prosecutor Lawrence Walsh, *Firewall: The Iran–Contra Conspiracy and Cover-Up* (Norton,

1998), as well as accounts by journalists Theodore Draper, *A Very Thin Line: The Iran–Contra Affairs* (Hill & Wang, 1991), and Robert Parry, *Lost History: Contras, Cocaine, the Press & "Project Truth"* (Media Consortium, 1999). See also Peter Kornbluh, *The Iran–Contra Scandal (The National Security Archive Document* (New Press, 1993).

There are a number of strong studies of U.S. relations with the dictatorships addressed here. Gregory Weeks, *U.S. And Latin American Relations* (Longman, 2007) offers a rich overview, as do Lars Schoultz, *Beneath The United States: A History of U.S. Policy Toward Latin America* (Harvard University Press, 1998), *National Security and United States Policy toward Latin America* (Princeton University Press, 1987), and *Human Rights and United States Policy Toward Latin America* (Princeton University Press, 1981); as well as Brian Loveman, *No Higher Law: American Foreign Policy and the Western Hemisphere since 1776* (University of North Carolina Press, 2010).

Eduardo Galeano, *The Open Veins of Latin America* [1973] (Monthly Review Press, 1997) is a classic reflection on the relationship between the United States and Latin America written through the perspective of dependency theory. Two provocative texts examine the assertion of U.S. hegemony through free-market economic policies: Naomi Klein, *The Shock Doctrine: The Rise of Disaster Capitalism* (Picador, 2007) and Greg Grandin, *Empire's Workshop: Latin America, the United States, and the Rise of the New Imperialism* (Owl, 2006).

A series of studies by Stephen Rabe examine U.S. Cold War ideology and its impact in Latin America: *Eisenhower and Latin America: The Foreign Policy of Anticommunism* (University of North Carolina Press, 1988), *The Most Dangerous Area in the World: John F. Kennedy Confronts Communist Revolution in Latin America* (University of North Carolina Press, 1999), and *The Killing Zone: The United States Wages Cold War in Latin America* (Oxford University Press, 2011). Lesley Gill, *The School of the Americas: Military Training and Political Violence in the Americas* (Duke University Press, 2004) and William Blum, *Killing Hope: U.S. Military and CIA Interventions Since World War II* (Common Courage, 1995) examine the role of the U.S. armed forces and intelligence services in training Latin American regimes in torture and other counterinsurgency methods.

There is also a vein of scholarship that looks at efforts in the United States to protect human rights and oppose military rule in Latin America, notably James Green, *We Cannot Remain Silent: Opposition to the Brazil-*

ian Military Dictatorship in the United States (Duke University Press, 2010); and Kathryn Sikkink, *Mixed Signals: U.S. Human Rights Policy and Latin America* (Cornell University Press, 2004).

International and Comparative

Brian Loveman's edition of Che Guevara's *Guerrilla Warfare* (Bison, 1985) includes a collection of essays examining his influence on revolutionary movements across Latin America.

Scholarship that considers two or more these dictatorships together, or situates them in their international context help define questions that we can bring to national experiences. One of the most influential of these is Guillermo O'Donnell's *Modernization and Bureaucratic Authoritarianism: Studies in South American Politics* (University of California Press, 1973), which focuses on Argentina, but situates its experience in a comparative context within which the Brazilian military regime plays an important role. See also Kathryn Sikkink, *Ideas and Institutions: Developmentalism in Brazil and Argentina* (Cornell University Press, 1991).

Some of these studies focus on specific aspects of military rule, such as Anthony Pereira's *Political (In)Justice: Authoritarianism and the Rule of Law in Brazil, Chile and Argentina* (Pittsburgh, 2005), which focuses on the role of the courts under dictatorship. Geraldo Munck, *Authoritarianism and Democratization: Soldiers and Workers in Argentina, 1976–1983* (Penn State University Press, 1988) places the experience of Argentine workers in an international context, bridging the approaches of O'Donnell and Pereira.

Patrice McSherry's *Predatory States: Operation Condor and Covert War in Latin America* (Rowman & Littlefield, 2005) and John Dinges' *The Condor Years: How Pinochet and His Allies Brought Terrorism to Three Continents* (New Press, 2005) examine the coordination of repression among the intelligence services of the dictatorships.

Several studies treat all three regimes, including Paul Lewis, *Authoritarian Regimes in Latin America: Dictators, Despots and Tyrants* (Rowman & Littlefield, 2005); Alain Roquie, *The Military and the State in Latin America* (University of California Press, 1989); Brin Loveman, *For la Patria: Politics and the Armed Forces in Latin America* (Rowman & Littlefield, 1999); *The Politics of Antipolitics: The Military in Latin America,* ed. Thomas Davies and Brian Loveman (Rowman & Littlefield, 1997); *The New Authoritarianism in Latin America*, ed. David Collier (Princeton University Press, 1980); Karen Remmer, *Military Rule in Latin America* (Westview, 1991); Juan Linz, *Totalitarian and Authoritarian Regimes* (Lynne Rienner, 2000); and Alfred Stepan, *Rethinking Military Politics* (Princeton University Press, 1988). There is a series entitled *The Breakdown of Democratic Regimes*, edited by Linz and Stepan, which includes a volume on Chile by Arturo Valenzuela (Johns Hopkins University Press, 1978).

Transition politics are themselves the subject of a rich vein of comparative and transnational work. Juan Linz and Alfred Stepan, *Problems of Democratic Transition and Consolidation: Southern Europe, South America, and Post-Communist Europe* (Johns Hopkins University Press, 1996) reflects the possibilities of comparison between the Latin American experience with re-democratization and that of other regions. Guillermo O'Donnell, Philippe Schmitter, and Lawrence Whitehead's edited volume on re-democratization in Latin America, *Transitions from Authoritarian Rule, Volume 2, Latin America* (Johns Hopkins University Press, 1986), is part of a comparative four-volume series that links the South American experience to that of transitions from corporatist regimes in Southern Europe. See also Jorge Castañeda, *Utopia Unarmed: The Latin American Left After the Cold War* (Vintage, 1993).

Several essays by Joseph Love are helpful for understanding the life of structuralism and dependency theory in Latin America: "Economic Ideas and Ideologies in Latin America Since 1930," *Cambridge History of Latin America*, vol. VI, part 1, ed. Leslie Bethell (Cambridge University Press, 1994), 393–460; "Raúl Prebisch and the Origin of the Doctrine of Unequal Exchange," *Latin American Research Review*, 15:3 (1980), 45–72; "The Origins of Dependency Analysis," *Journal of Latin American Studies*, 22:1 (1990), 143–8; and "The Rise and Decline of Economic Structuralism in Latin America: New Dimensions," *Latin American Research Review*, 40:3 (2005), 100–25. A conservative assessment of dependency theory is offered in Robert Packenham, *The Dependency Movement: Scholarship and Politics in Development Studies* (Harvard University Press, 1992). On Raúl Prebisch, see Edgar Dosman, *The Life and Times of Raúl Prebisch* (McGill-Queen's University Press, 2010).

Among works on dependency theory, see Andre Gunder Frank, *Capitalism and Underdevelopment in Latin America: Historical Studies of Chile and Brazil* (Monthly Review Press, 1967), Fernando Henrique Cardoso and Enzo Faletto, *Dependency and Development in Latin America* (University of California Press, 1979), Celso Furtado, *Economic Development of Latin America* (Cambridge University Press, 1970), and Peter Evans, *Dependent Development: The Alliance of Multinational, State and Local Capital in Brazil* (Princeton University Press, 1969).

Argentina

Argentina's long and dark history of military rule has made it the subject of some of the strongest scholarship on dictatorship. The Argentine experience anchors many of the comparative studies and has provided much of the theoretical understanding, for instance work by O'Donnell and Sikkink. Two studies by Paul H. Lewis examine the political and economic currents that culminated in the Dirty War: *The Crisis of Argentine Capitalism* (University of North Carolina Press, 1990) and *Guerrillas and Generals: The "Dirty War" in Argentina* (Praeger, 2001). Klaus Freidrich Veigel, *Dictatorship, Democracy, and Globalization: Argentina and the Cost of Paralysis, 1973–2001* (Penn State University Press, 2012) examines the tension between economic and political instability. On the Junta's involvement in Central America, see Ariel Armony, *Argentina, the United States, and the Anti-Communist Crusade in Central America, 1977–1984* (Ohio University Press, 1997), and on the Falklands/Malvinas War, Alejandro Dabat and Luis Lorenzano, *Argentina: The Malvinas and the End of Military Rule* (Verso, 1984).

Two histories that trace Argentina's twentieth century are David Rock, *Argentina: 1516–1987: From Spanish Colonization to Alfonsín* (University of California Press, 1987) and Luis Alberto Romero, *A History of Argentina in the Twentieth Century* (Penn State University Press, 2002). On Juan and Evita Perón, see Raanan Rein, *The Franco-Perón Alliance: Relations Between Spain and Argentina, 1946–1955* (University of Pittsburgh Press, 1993) and *Argentina, Israel and the Jews: Perón, the Eichmann Capture and After* (University Press of Maryland, 2002); Mark Healey, *The Ruins of the New Argentina: Peronism and the Remaking of San Juan after the 1944 Earthquake* (Duke University Press, 2011); Joseph Page, *Perón: A Biography* (Random House, 1983); Mariano Ben Plotkin, *Mañana es San Perón: A Cultural History of Peronism in Argentina* (Scholarly Resources, 2002); and Nicholas Fraser and Marysa Navarro *Evita: The Real Life of Eva Perón*, 4th edn. (Norton, 1996). A compelling fictional account of Perón's last days is Tomás Eloy Martinez's *The Perón Novel* (Vintage, 1998).

On Peronism in Argentine unions both during his presidency and under de-Peronization, see Daniel James' *Resistance and Integration: Peronism and the Argentine Working Class, 1946–1976* (Cambridge University Press, 1988) and James McGuire's *Peronism Without Perón: Unions, Parties and Democracy in Argentina* (Stanford University Press, 1999). On the influence of Peronism on education, see Mónica Esti Rein, *Politics and Education in Argentina, 1946–1962* (M.E. Sharpe, 1998).

Excellent analyses of the symbolism employed by the Argentine Junta and its system of repression can be found in Marguerite Feitlowitz, *A Lexicon of Terror: Argentina and the Legacies of Torture* (Oxford University Press, 1999) and Diana Taylor, *Disappearing Acts: Spectacles of Gender and Nationalism in Argentina's "Dirty War"* (Duke University Press, 1997). On the Montoneros, see *Soldiers of Perón: Argentina's Montoneros* (Oxford University Press, 1983). For an account of the tactics of disappearance, see Argentine journalist Horacio Verbitsky, *Confessions of an Argentine Dirty Warrior, A Firsthand Account of Atrocity* (New Press, 2005). On Argentina's transition to democracy, see Patrice McSherry, *Incomplete Transition: Military Power and Democracy in Argentina* (Palgrave, 1997); as well as Luis Roniger and Mario Sznajder, *The Legacy of Human Rights Violtions in the Southern Cone: Argentina, Chile and Uruguay* (Oxford University Press, 1999).

There are several memoirs and novels that offer a rich window into experiences under dictatorship in Argentina. These include Alicia Portnoy, *The Little School: Tales of Disappearance and Survival* (Cleis, 1998); Jacobo Timermann, *Prisoner Without a Name, Cell Without a Number* (University of Wisconsin Press, 2002); Andrew Graham-Yooll, *A State of Fear: Memories of Argentina's Nightmare* (Eland [1986], 2009); and Gloria Lisé, *Departing at Dawn: A Novel of Argentina's Dirty War* (Feminist Press, 2009).

Spanish language sources

These studies are produced in both Argentina and Mexico, where many Argentine exiles settled. An especially influential study is Marcos Novaro and Vicente Palermo's *La dictadura militar, 1976/1983: Del golpe de estado a la restauración democrática* (Paidós, 2003). Two collections of essays from the *Nueva Historia Argentina* series capture key questions of the 1955–2001 period: *Violencia, Proscripción y Autoritarismo (1955–1976)*, ed. Daniel James (Sudamericana, 2003) and *Dictadura y Democracia (1976–2001)*, ed. Juan Suriano (Sudamericana, 2005). On the years leading to the Proceso, the 1976 coup and its aftermath, see María Matilde Ollier, *Golpe o revolución: La violencia legitimada, Argentina 1966/1973* (Eduntref, 2005) and *Argentina, 1976: Estudios en torno al golpe de Estado*, ed. Clara Lida, Horacio Crespo and Pablo Yankelevich (Colégio de México, 2007).

There are several reflections on the nature of authoritarianism and political contestation in Argentina that have been particularly influential in framing the historical memory of military rule. These include Pilar Calveiro's *Poder y Desaparición: Los campos de concentración en Argentina* (Colihue, 2006) and *Politica y/o Violencia: Una aproximación a la guerrilla de los años 70* (Norma, 2005); Hugo Vezzetti, *Passado y Presente: Guerra, dictadura y sociedad en la Argentina* (Siglo XXI, 2003); and Elizabeth Jelin *Los trabajos de la memoria* (Siglo XXI, 2002).

Among the extensive literature on radical movements, see Eduardo Anguita and Martín Caparrós, *La Voluntad: Una historia de la militancia revolucionaria en la Argentina*, volumes 1–3 (Norma, 1998); Marcelo Larraquy, *De Perón a Montoneros: Historia de la violencia política en la Argentina* (Agular, 2010); Felipe Celesia and Pablo Waisberg's biography of Montoneros leader Mário Firmenich, *Firmenich: la historia ajás contada del jefe montonero* (Aguilar, 2010); and Lucas Lanusse, *Montoneros: El mito de sus 12 fundadores* (Vergara, 2005). For a conservative journalist's perspective on the political and economic chaos that accompanied military rule, see Juan Yofre, *"Nadie Fue:" Crónica, documentos y testimonios de los últimos meses, días y horas de Isabel Perón en el Poder* (Sudamericana, 2008) and *"Fuimos Todos": Cronología de un Fracaso, 1976–1983* (Sudamericana, 2007).

There are journalists' accounts of major events in Argentina: Horacio Verbitsky on the Ezeiza massacre carried out during Perón's return in 1973, *Ezeiza* (Contrapunto, 1985), and the Falklands War: and *Malvinas: La últina batalla de la Tercera Guerra Mundial* (Sudamericana, 2002). Ricardo Gotta's *Fuimos Campeones: La Dictatura, el Mundial 78, y erl misterio del 6 a 0 a Perú* (Edhasa, 2008) places the 1978 World Cup in its political and social context.

Brazil

The classic study of the Brazilian dictatorship remains Thomas Skidmore, *The Politics of Military Rule in Brazil, 1964–1985* (Oxford University Press, 1990). *The Politics of Military Rule* offers analysis of the internal politics of the regime as well as the country's economic trajectory. This volume succeeds Skidmore, *Politics in Brazil: An Experiment in Democracy, 1930–1964* (Oxford University Press, 1967) that was researched in the years following the 1964 coup. Similarly influential is Maria Helena Moreira Alves' *State and Opposition in Military Brazil* (University of Texas Press, 1988) – it was her brother, Márcio Moreira Alves, who delivered the 1968 congressional address denouncing the dictatorship that unleashed the regime's backlash culminating in Institutional Act 5.

Kenneth Serbin, *Secret Dialogues: Church–State Relations, Torture, and Social Justice in Authoritarian Brazil* (University of Pittsburgh Press, 2000) examines the role of the Catholic Church under military rule. Andrew Kirkendall, *Paulo Freire and the Cold War Politics of Literacy* (University of North Carolina Press at Chapel Hill, 2010) traces the influence of Freire's pedagogy of liberation. Published at the height of repression, the essays edited by Alfred Stepan, *Authoritarian Brazil: Origins, Policies, and Future* (Yale University Press, 1973) debate the economics and politics of the regime. For the Brazilian economy under military rule, see Werner Baer, *The Brazilian Economy*, 6th edn. (Lynne Rienner, 2006).

Jeffrey Lesser, *A Discontented Diaspora: Japanese Brazilians and the Meanings of Ethnic Militancy, 1960–1980* (Duke University Press, 2007) as well as Sonia Alvarez, *Engendering Democracy in Brazil: Women's Movements in Transition Politics* (Princeton University Press, 1990) reflect the value of looking at military rule through the perspectives of women and ethnic minorities. A similar approach examining the changes military rule brought to the experience of rural workers is Thomas Rogers, *The Deepest Wounds: A Labor and Environmental History of Sugar in Northeast Brazil* (University of North Carolina Press, 2010), while Shelton Davis, *Victims of the Miracle: Development and the Indians of Brazil* (Cambridge University Press, 1977) and Seth Garfield, *Indigenous Struggle at the Heart of Brazil: State Policy, Frontier Expansion, and the Xavante Indians, 1937–1988* (Duke University Press, 2001) examine indigenous experiences with dictatorship.

On counterculture during the dictatorship, see Christopher Dunn, *Brutality Garden: Tropicália and the Emergence of a Brazilian Counterculture* (University of North Carolina Press, 2001). There are several studies that engage historical memory, such as Victoria Langland's study of the student movement, *Speaking of Flowers: Student Movements and the Molding of 1968 in Military Brazil* (Duke University Press, 2013); Lina Sattamini, *A Mother's Cry: A Memoir of Politics, Prison, and Torture under the Brazilian Military Dictatorship*; Lawrence Weschler, *A Miracle, A Universe: Settling Accounts with Torturers* (Chicago University Press, 1998); *Violence Workers: Police, Torturers and Murderers Reconstruct Brazilian Atrocities*, ed. Martha Huggins, Mika Haritos-Fatouros, and Philip Zimbardo (University of California Press, 2002); and Rebecca Atencio, "A Prime Time to Remember: Memory Merchandising in Globo's *Anos Rebeldes*," in *Accounting for Violence: The Memory Market in Latin America*, ed. Ksenija Bilbija and Leigh Payne (Duke University Press, 2011).

On the transition to democracy and the emergence of the PT, see Margaret Keck, *The Worker's Party and Democratization in Brazil* (Yale University Press, 1992); Emir Sader and Ken Silverstein, *Without Fear of Being Happy: Lula, the Workers Party and Brazil* (Verso, 1991); Wendy Hunter, *The Transformation of the Workers' Party in Brazil, 1989–2009* (Cambridge University Press, 2010); Angus Wright and Wendy Wolford, *To Inherit the Earth: The Landless Movement and the Struggle for a New Brazil* (Food First, 2003); and *Brazil: A Century of Change*, ed. Ignacy Sachs, Jorge Wilheim, and Paulo Sergio Pinheiro (University of North Carolina Press, 2009). On the 1988 Constitution and civil rights, see Jan Hoffman French, *Legalizing Identities: Becoming Black or Indian in Brazil's Northeast* (University of North Carolina Press, 2009). An insightful look into the limits of re-democratization is Enrique Desmond Arias, *Drugs & Democracy in Rio de Janeiro: Trafficking, Social Networks & Public Security* (University of North Carolina Press, 2006).

Portuguese language sources

An influential analysis of the regime and its context is found in the four-volume study by journalist Elio Gaspari, based on his reading of the papers of the private secretary of Ernesto Geisel and the regime's chief intellectual strategist, General Golbery Couto e Silva. The series, *A Ditadura Envergonhada, A Ditadura Escancarada, A Ditadura Derrotada,* and *A Ditadura Ecurralada* (Companhia das Letras, 2002–4). See also Carlos Fico, *Reinventando o otimismo: Ditadura, propaganda e imaginário social no Brasil* (Fundação Getúlio Vargas, 1997), on propaganda; *Como eles agiam: Os subterrâneos da Ditadura Militar – Espionagem e polícia política* (Record, 2001) on espionage and surveillance; *O Grande Irmão: Da operação brother sam aos anos de chumbo* (Civilização Brasileira, 2008) on the role of the United States; and the historiographic *Além do golpe: Versões e controvérsias sobre 1964 e a Ditadura Militar* (Record, 2004). The breadth of this historiography is evident in *O Brasil Republicano, livro 4: O tempo da ditadura – regime militar e movimentos socials em fins do século XX*, ed. Jorge Luiz Ferreira and Lucilia de Almeida Neves Delgado (Civilização Brasileira, 2003).

Memoirs of opponents to military rule, include Fernando Gabeira, involved in the kidnapping of the U.S. Ambassador, *O que é isso, companheiro?* (Encanto das Letras, 1979), as well as Alfredo Sirkis, involved in the kidnapping of the Swiss and German ambassadors, *Os Carbonários* (Record, 1981). There is a ranging memoir by Maria do Carmo Brito, *Uma tempestade como a sua memória: A história de Lia* (Record, 2003). There are biographies of guerrilla movement leaders, such as Wilma Antunes Maciel's *O Capitão Lamarca e a VPR* (Alameda, 2006), on Carlos Lamarca, and several biographies of Carlos Marighella, including Christiane Nova's *Carlos Marighella: O homem por tras do mito* (UNESP, 1999).

There are memoirs presenting the viewpoint of members of the regime, including an oral history with Ernesto Geisel by Celso Castro and Maria Celina D'Araujo, *Ernesto Geisel: Depoimento* (FGV, 1997). Castro, D'Araujo and Gláucio Ary Dillion have published a series of oral histories with members of the armed forces, *Visões do Golpe: A Memória Militar sobre 1964* (Relumé-Dumará, 1994), *Os Anos de Chumbo: A Memória Militar sobre a Repressão* (Relumé-Dumará, 1994), and *A volta aos quartéis: A Memória Militar sobre a Abertura* (Relumé-Dumará, 1995). A good representation of the thinking of military hardliners can be found in Sylvio Frota's memoir *Ideais traídos: Brasil acima de tudo* (Zahar, 2006).

Chile

Some of the richest work on the Pinochet regime has been written by scholars who played important roles in the transition to democracy and the Concertación governments of the 1990s. Carlos Huneeus, author of the detailed *The Pinochet Regime* (Lynne Rienner, 2007) was an activist in the Christian Democratic Party during the transition. Political scientist Juan Gabriel Valdez, author of *Pinochet's Economists: The Chicago School of Economics in Chile* Cambridge, 1995), was an exile in Washington, DC, who typically rode to work with Orlando Letelier and only by coincidence was not in Letelier's car when it was bombed by the DINA. He worked on media campaigns for the No! campaign and later served as foreign minister.

A rich analysis of politics and economics in Chilean history is Brian Loveman, *Chile: The Legacy of Hispanic Capitalism* 3rd edn. (Oxford University Press, 2001). The Chilean dictatorship was more successful than its counterparts at shielding its decision-making and its internal divisions from public view. It was also the most ideologically committed of the regimes, in its embrace of both corporatism and the free market. As a result, some of the most influential studies of the regime are those which find ways to lift the curtain, such as Robert Barros' *Constitutionalism and Dictatorship: Pinochet, the Junta and the 1980 Constitution* (Cambridge University Press, 2002).

There are also excellent studies of Chilean society during and before the dictatorship, including Pamela Constable and Arturo Valenzuela's *A Nation of Enemies: Chile Under Pinochet* (Norton, 1991); Arturo Valenzuela's *The Breakdown of Democratic Regimes: Chile* (Johns Hopkins University Press, 1978), part of the series organized by Linz and Stepan; Peter Winn's *Weavers of the Revolution: The Yarur Workers and Chile's Road to Socialism* (Oxford, 1986); and the volume organized by Peter Winn, *Victims of the Chilean Miracle: Workers and Neoliberalism in the Pinochet Era, 1973–2002* (Duke University Press, 2004).

On the regime and economic policy, see Genaro Arriagada, *Pinochet: The Politics of Power* (Unwin Hyman, 1988); Mary Helen Spooner, *Soldiers in a Narrow Land: The Pinochet Regime in Chile* (University of California Press, 1999); Patricio Silva, *In the Name of Reason: Technocrats and Politics in Chile* (Penn State University Press, 2008); and the document collection by Peter Kornbluh, *The Pinochet File: A Declassified Dossier on Atrocity and Accountability* (New Press, 2004).

There are several accounts of life during military rule, including Patricia Politzer's *Fear in Chile: Lives Under Pinochet* (New Press, 2001); Heraldo Muñoz's *The Dictator's Shadow: Life Under Augusto Pinochet* (Pluto, 2008); and Diana Kay, *Chileans in Exile: Private Struggles, Public*

Lives (Longwood Academic, 1987); as well as Steve J. Stern's three-volume series on historical memory examines the social rifts caused by Chile's experience with authoritarianism: *Remembering Pinochet's Chile: On the Eve of London, 1998* (Duke University Press, 2006), *Battling for Hearts and Minds: Memory Struggles in Pinochet's Chile, 1973–1988* (Duke University Press, 2006), and *Reckoning with Pinochet: The Memory Question in Democratic Chile, 1989–2006* (Duke University Press, 2010).

On the transition to democracy, see Gregory Weeks, *The Military and Politics in Postauthoritarian Chile* (University of Alabama University, 2003); Diane Haughney, *Neoliberal Economics, Democratic Transition, and Mapuche Demands for Rights in Chile* (University Press of Florida, 2006); *The Struggle for Democracy in Chile, 1982–1990*, ed. Paul Drake and Ivan Jasic (Nebraska University Press, 1991); *After Pinochet: The Chilean Road to Democracy and the Market*, ed. Silvia Borzutzky and Lois Oppenheim (University Press of Florida, 2006); Philip Oxhorn, *Organizing Civil Society: The Popular Sector and the Struggle for Democracy in Chile* (Penn State University Press, 1995); Kenneth Roberts, *Deepening Democracy? The Modern Left and Social Movements in Chile and Peru* (Stanford University Press, 1998); *From Dictatorship to Democracy: Rebuilding Political Consensus in Chile*, ed. Joseph Tulchin and Augusto Varas (Lynne Rienner, 1991); Peter Siavelis, *The President and Congress in Post-Authoritarian Chile* (Penn State University Press, 2000); Luis Roniger and Mario Sznajder, *The Legacy of Human Rights Violtions in the Southern Cone: Argentina, Chile and Uruguay* (Oxford University Press, 1999); and Manuel Antonio Garreton, *Incomplete Democracy: Political Democratization in Chile and Latin America*; and Paul Posner, *State, Market and Democracy in Chile: The Constraint of Popular Participation* (Palgrave, 2008).

Spanish language sources

A rich vein of work on the Pinochet regime examines the ideology and political processes of the regime. Two studies of the intellectual architect of the 1980 Constitution and the idea of a "protected democracy," are Jaime Guzmán, are Renato Cristi, *El pensamiento político de Jaime Guzmán: Autoridad y Libertad* (LOM, 2000) and Belén Moncada Durriti, *Jaime Guzmán: Una democracia contrarrevolucionaria, el político, de 1964 a 1980* (Ril, 2006). Verónica Valdivia examines the emergence of right-wing ideology in 1960s Chile: *Nacionales y gremialistas: El "parto" de la nueva derecha política chilena, 1964–1973* (LOM, 2008). Humberto Lagos Schuffeneger examines the discourse employed by Pinochet to present himself as the expression of divine will: *El general Pinochet y el mesianismo político* (LOM, 2001).

Several studies engage experience of opposition to Pinochet, including Patricio Rivas, *Chile, un largo septiembre* (LOM, 2007); *El movimiento de derechos humanos en Chile, 1973–1990*, ed. Patricio Orellana and Elizabeth Q. Hutchison (CEPLA, 1991); *Exilio, derechos humanos y democracia: El exilio chileno en Europa*, ed. Fernando Montupil I (Caupolicán, 1993); and the series *Su revolución contra nuestra revolución, Vol. I: Izquierdas y derechas en el Chile de Pinochet (1973–1981)* (LOM, 2006), and *Vol II: La pugna marxista-gremialista en los ochenta* (LOM, 2008), ed. Veróniva Valdivia, Rolando Álvarez, Julio Pinto, Karen Donoso, and Sebastián Leiva.

On the regime politics, see Enrique Cañas Kirby, *Proceso político en Chile, 1973–1990* (Andrés Bello, 1996); and Eugenio Tironi, *Autoritarismo, Modernización y Marginalidad: El caso de Chile, 1973–1989* (SUR, 1990). Pilar Vergara examines social policy in *Políticas hacia la extrema pobreza en Chile, 1973–1988* (FLACSO, 1990). On the transition to democracy, with its continuities and ruptures, see *El gobierno de Ricardo Lagos: La nueva vía chilena hacia el socialismo*, ed. Robert Funk (Diego Portales, 2006) and Manuel Riesco, *Se derrumba un mito: Chile reforma sus sistemas privatizados de educación y previsión* (LOM 2007).

Notes

1 http://portal.mj.gov.br/sedh/biblioteca/livro_direito_memoria_verdade/livro_direito_memoria_verdade_sem_a_marca.pdf, accessed October 14, 2012.

2 www.usip.org/publications/truth-commission-argentina, accessed October 14, 2012.

3 www.usip.org/publications/truth-commission-chile-90, accessed October 14, 2012.

4 www.usip.org/publications/commission-inquiry-chile-03, accessed October 14, 2012.

5 www.usip.org/publications/commission-inquiry-brazil, accessed October 14, 2012.
6 http://foia.state.gov/reports/churchreport.asp, accessed October 14, 2012.
7 www.gwu.edu/~nsarchiv/NSAEBB/index.html, accessed October 14, 2012.
8 www.desaparecidos.org/eng.html, accessed October 14, 2012.

Index

AC/DC, 153
Africa, decolonization movements, 15, 52, 140
Agosti, Orlando, 117, 129
Agostinho Neto, António, 146
Aleixo, Pedro, 40
Alessandri, Arturo, 164
Alfonsín, Raúl, 123, 134, 153, 181–2
Algeria, 46, 116
Allende, Salvador, 7, 10, 13, 15, 17, 83–93, 100, 103, 113, 157–9, 164
Alliance for Progress, 16–17, 26
Alves, Márcio Moreira, 38–9
Amazon, 50–1
Angola, 46, 140, 146
Araguaia, 47
Aramburu, Pedro, 61–2, 64–5, 68, 75
Arbenz, Jacobo, 14
Arellano, Sergio, 93
Argentina
    "Argentine Revolution" Dictatorship, 63–5, 68, 114
    caras pintadas, 182
    Cordobazo, 63–5, 114
    de-Peronization, 61–2, 66
    Infamous Decade, 59
    Institute for Promotion of Trade (IAPI), 60
    Junta, 112, 123, 127, 129, 131
    labor unions, 58–9, 62–3, 65, 70

Ley de Obediencia Debida, 182, 185
Ley del Punto Final, 182, 185
    "Liberating Revolution" Dictatorship, 61–62
    Ministry of Social Welfare, 70–2, 74, 76–7
    National Labor Federation (CGT), 64, 72, 76
    "Process of National Reorganization" Dictatorship (Proceso), 57–8, 112
    rodrigazo, 76
    Social Pact, 73–4, 76
    Trials of the Juntas, 181–3
    Viborazo, 64
Argentine police and intelligence services
    Argentine Anticommunist Alliance (AAA), 73, 77, 118
    Buenos Aires Provincial Police, 119, 121
    Campo de Mayo detention hospital, 119
    La Perla detention center, 133
    Naval Mechanics School (ESMA), 120–1, 126, 133
    Operation Independence, 78
    Patota, 118, 120
Argentine political parties and movements
    Communist Party, 112
    Justicialist Party, 60, 63, 75, 182–3
    Permanent Assembly for Human Rights, 123
    Peronist Feminine Party, 61

Dictatorship in South America, First Edition. Jerry Dávila.
© 2013 Jerry Dávila. Published 2013 by Blackwell Publishing Ltd.

Argentine political parties and movements
(*cont'd*)
  Peronist Youth, 66, 72
  Radical Civic Union (UCR), 59, 62, 134,
    181
  Service for Peace and Justice, 123
Argentine revolutionary movements
  Liberating Armed Forces (FAL), 66
  Montoneros, 64–6, 68, 72, 74–5, 79, 113,
    115, 117–18, 120, 165
  Peronist Armed Forces (FAP), 66
  Revolutionary Armed Forces (FAR), 56,
    66, 68, 115
  Revolutionary Army of the People
    (ERP), 55–8, 66, 68, 78, 80, 115, 118,
    120, 133
Arinos, Afonso, 26
Arns, Cardinal Evaristo, 37, 142–4
Astiz, Alfredo, 133
Austrian School economics, 99
Aylwin, Patricio, 175

Bachelet, Alberto, 98
Bachelet, Michelle, 98, 176, 181
Barros, Adhemar de, 45
Beagle Channel Conflict, 130–1, 133
Belgrano, 132
Bignone, Reynaldo, 134, 179
Boff, Leonardo, 150
Bolivia, 16, 99, 116, 130, 137
Born, Juan and Jorge, 68, 76, 79, 165
Brazil
  Abertura, 138, 146–8
  April Package, 148
  armed forces, 20–3
  base reforms, 27, 41, 95
  black population, 51, 154, 183
  Bolsa Familia, 183–4
  Constitution of 1988, 154, 177
  indigenous population, 51, 154, 183
  Institutional Act 1, 31
  Institutional Act 2, 34
  Institutional Act 3, 35
  Institutional Act 4, 35
  Institutional Act 5, 39–41, 63, 138, 145,
    148–9

  labor movement, 148–9
  National Council of Bishops (CNBB),
    37
  National Development Bank (BNDE),
    49
  National Student Union (UNE), 37, 41,
    95
  steel industry, 22–3
  tenente revolts, 21–2, 53
Brazilian police and intelligence services
  Air Force Intelligence Service (CISA),
    44
  Army Intelligence Service (CIE), 44, 47
  Center for Naval Intelligence
    (CENIMAR), 44
  Department of Intelligence Operations–
    Center for Internal Defense
    Operations (DOI–CODI), 44, 142,
    144, 146, 149
  Department of Political and Social
    Police (DOPS), 44, 46, 51, 146, 149
  National Intelligence Service (SNI), 29,
    44, 148
  Operation Bandeirantes (OBAN), 44–5
Brazilian political parties and movements
  Brazilian Communist Party (PCB), 22,
    40, 143, 149
  Brazilian Democratic Union Party
    (MDB), 35, 147, 152
  Brazilian Workers Party (PTB), 149
  Communist Party of Brazil (PC do B),
    47
  Democratic Workers Party (PDT), 46,
    149
  Marxist Workers' Political Operation
    (POLOP), 45–46
  National Democratic Union Party
    (UDN), 26
  National Renovation Party (ARENA),
    35, 148, 152
  Worker's Party (PT), 149–50
Brazilian revolutionary movements
  Movement for Revolutionary Action
    (MAR), 42–3
  National Command for Liberation
    (COLINA), 45–6

National Liberation Alliance (ALN), 43
National Revolutionary Movement
(MNR), 42
Popular Action (AP), 41
Popular Revolutionary Vanguard
(VPR), 42, 44–6
Revolutionary Armed Vanguard (VAR–
Palmares), 42, 45–6
Brazil: Never Again, 4
Brito, Maria do Carmo, 45
Brizola, 29, 42, 149
Büchi, Hernán, 170, 175
Bulhões, Octavio, 32
Bush, George W., 108

Câmara, Dom Helder, 37, 143
Cámpora, Héctor, 66, 68, 70, 72, 115
Campos, Francisco, 157
Campos, Roberto, 32
Campos-Bulhões Plan, 32, 48, 52, 63, 127
Camps, Ramón, 119, 121, 181
Cardoso, Fernando Henrique, 12, 183
Carter, Jimmy, 18, 130
Castelo Branco, Humberto, 25, 31–5, 40,
43, 138, 146–7
Castro, Fidel 15–16, 79, 88–9
Castro, Sérgio de, 70
Catholic Church, 151, 179
Conference of Latin American Bishops,
37
in Argentina, 61, 113, 121–3
in Brazil, 37, 142–5, 149
in Chile, 86, 166–8, 172
liberation theology, 37, 121, 149
Pastoral Commission for Peace and
Justice (Brazil), 143
Catholic (Pontificate) University of Chile,
99, 165
Cato Institute, 109
Cavallo, Domingo, 129
Central America, 14, 37, 79, 116, 130–2,
134
Cerda, Luis Escobar, 170
Chicago Boys, *see* Chilean free-market
reforms
Chicago School economics, 99–100, 109

Chile
1978 referendum, 160–1, 163, 169
1980 plebiscite, 163, 169
1988 plebiscite, 162, 171, 173
Chacarillas Address, 159, 161
Constitution of 1980, 156, 164, 168–9,
171, 175, 177, 180–1
Democratic Manifesto, 172
Junta, 83, 91, 97, 156–62, 175
Las Condes, 101, 106–7
Ministry of the Family, 86
National Accord for Transition to Full
Democracy, 173
National Copper Corporation
(CODELCO), 103
National Health Service, 102
National Stadium, 93–6
Tanquetazo, 90
Valdivia Proclamation, 171
Chilean free-market reforms, 83
Central Bank, 109
Chicago Boys, 99–110, 169–71
Institutional Health Providers
(ISAPREs), 102, 106
Pension Fund Administrators (AFPs),
101
school vouchers and privatizations, 102,
106
Chilean police and intelligence services
Caravan of Death, 94
Dawson Island Prison Camp, 94–5
Directorate of National Intelligence
(DINA), 98, 158–9, 161, 165, 168,
176
National Intelligence Service (SNI), 159
Vila Grimaldi Prison Camp, 98
Chilean political parties and movements
Arpilleristas, 166–8
Christian Democratic Party (PDC), 10,
84, 160, 166, 173, 175–6
Communist Party (PCC), 84, 91, 165,
172–5
Concertación, 174–5, 180–1
Conservative Party, 84
Democratic Alliance (AD), 172–4
Democracy and Progress, 175

Chilean political parties and movements
(*cont'd*)
  Ecumenical Committee for Peace
    (COPACHI), 167–8
  Families of the Detained and
    Disappeared, 166–7, 172
  Fatherland and Freedom, 87
  Independent Democratic Union (UDI),
    174
  Liberal Party, 84
  National Renewal, 174
  Popular Democratic Movement (MDP),
    172
  Popular Unity (UP), 84–5, 87, 90–1,
    164–5
  Popular Unity Action Movement
    (MAPU), 85, 91
  Revolutionary Leftist Movement (MIR),
    85, 81
  Socialist Party, 84, 168, 172, 176
  Vicariate of Solidarity, 168
Chilean revolutionary movements
  Manuel Rodriguez Patriotic Front
    (FPMR), 165
  Revolutionary Leftist Movement (MIR),
    164–5, 173
China, 140
Church, Frank, 18, 97
Cold War, 13, 22
Containment Doctrine, 13, 16
Contras (Nicaragua), 130
Contreras, Carlos Cáceres, 170
Contreras, Manuel, 98, 159, 161, 176
Costa Gavras, 17
Costa Méndez, Nicanor, 134–5
Costa e Silva, Artur da, 30, 35–6, 39–41,
    48
Cuba, 15–16, 27, 29, 64, 67, 79, 89, 103,
    134, 140, 146, 165
Czechoslovakia, 85

D'Ávila, Ednardo, 146
Debray, Régis, 16
debt crisis, 128, 134, 138–9, 150–4,
    169–70, 180
Delfim Neto, Antonio, 48–9, 139, 150–1

dependency theory, 11–12, 24, 37, 83,
    183
developmentalism, 9–10, 20, 24–6, 139,
    141
Dominican Republic, 15, 32, 83
Domon, Alice, 121, 123, 133
Duquet, Leonine, 121, 123, 133
Duvalier, Baby Doc, 83
Duvalier, Papa Doc, 83

Eastern Europe, 85, 140, 180
Economic Commission for Latin America
    (ECLA), 11, 17, 83
Eisenhower, Dwight, 26
El Salvador, 130, 144
Esquivel, Adolfo Pérez, 123
Evita, *see* Perón, Eva
Ezeiza Massacre, 72–3, 75

Falklands and South Georgia Islands, 116,
    126, 130–5, 151, 176
Fernández de Kirchner, Cristina, 183
Fernández, Sergio, 161–2, 164
Figueiredo, João Baptista, 44, 134, 148–50
Firmenich, Mário, 77
Fleury, Sérgio, 44
foco theory (*foquismo*), 16, 47, 78
Ford, Gerald, 17
Ford Motor Co., 15, 44, 121
France, 116
Franco, Francisco, 61, 157–8
Frei Montalva, Eduardo, 85, 160, 163, 166,
    173
Frei-Tagle, Eduardo, 83, 176, 181
Freire, Paulo, 37, 150
Frenz, Helmut, 167
Fresno, Francisco, 173
Freyre, Gilberto, 28
Friedman, Milton, 99–101, 108, 170
Frondizi, Arturo, 62
Frota, Sylvio, 146–7
Furtado, Celso, 12, 27, 31

Galtieri, Leopoldo, 129–34
Geisel, Ernesto, 18, 44, 137–41, 145–8, 177
Gelbard, José, 73

General Electric Co., 22
General Motors Co. 15, 44
Germany (East), 165
Germany (West), 140
Gordon, Lincoln, 28
Goulart, João, 6, 27–31, 41, 95
Grandmothers of the Plaza de Mayo, 120, 122
Great Britain, 116, 131–4
Gremialistas, 99, 157, 159–62, 177
Grenada, 15
Guatemala 3, 14, 16, 130
Guerreiro, Ramiro Saraiva, 134
Guevara, Che, 16, 40, 45, 55, 62, 67, 78–9, 103–4
Guido, José Maria, 62
Guyana, 140
Guzmán, Jaime, 157–9, 162–3, 165, 175

Haig, Alexander, 133
Haiti, 83
Harper, Ben, 167
Hayek, Friedrich von, 99–101
Herzog, Vladimir, 143–6
human rights, 18, 122–4, 130, 145, 149–50, 154, 158, 168, 172, 183
Humeres, Héctor, 161

Illia, Arturo, 62
Import Substitution Industrialization (ISI), 11
indexation, 48, 127
inflation, 26, 32–3, 53, 100, 108, 126–30, 132, 152–4, 182
International Monetary Fund (IMF), 26–7, 33
International Telephone and Telegraph (ITT), 15, 97
Iran-Contra Affair, xiii, 18
Iranian Revolution, 139
Iraq, 140
Israel, 52, 139–40
Italy, 157

Jara, Victor, 96
Jarpa, Sergio Onofre, 172

Johnson, Lyndon, 29
Juan Carlos II, 158

Kamayana, Suely Yumiko, 45, 47
Kirchner, Néstor, 183, 185
Kissinger, Henry, 17–18, 86, 97, 125–6, 141
Kubitschek, Juscelino, 24–7, 31, 62

Lagos, Ricardo, 164, 176, 181
Lamarca, Carlo, 42, 44–5
land reform, 12, 27, 31, 37, 84–5, 91, 116, 166
Lanusse, Alejandro, 65–6, 68
Lavín, Joaquín, 105–10, 181
Leigh, Gustavo, 90–1, 161, 165, 174
Leme, Alexandre Vannuchhi, 142–3
Letelier, Orlando, 95, 98, 158–61, 169
Levingston, Roberto, 65
liberation theology, *see* Catholic Church, 37
literacy, 15, 17, 21, 24, 27, 37, 41, 49
Lybia, 140

Macedo Soares, Edmundo, 22–3
Maluf, Paulo, 152–3
Malvinas, *see* Falklands and South Georgia Islands
Marighella, Carlos, 43–44
Marinho, Roberto, 50
Martinez de Hoz, 117, 126–9
Marxism, 11–15, 67, 115, 140, 146, 163
Massera, Emilio, 117, 125, 181
Matthei, Fernando, 162, 169, 174
Mazzilli, Ranieri, 29–31
Médici, Emilio Garrastazu, 17, 48–51, 138–9
Mendoza, Cesar, 91, 161–2
Menem, Carlos, 63, 182
Menéndez, Mario, 133
Merino, José, 90–1, 161–2
Mexico, 135, 140, 150–1, 165, 169
Middle East, 140
Mitrione, Dan, 17
modernization theory 11
Moffit, Ronni, 99, 158

206   *Index*

Moore, Jeremy, 134
Mothers of the Plaza de Mayo, 122–3, 133

National Commission on Disappeared Persons (CONADEP), Argentina, 119, 121
Neves, Tancredo, 152
Nicaragua, 83, 130
Nixon, Richard, 17–18, 85–8
Noriega, Manuel, 83
Nunca Más (Argentina), 4, 119, 121
Nunca Más en Chile, 96

O'Donnell, Guillermo, 6–8
oil, 12, 52
    oil embargo of 1973, 18, 52, 73, 76, 138, 141, 150
    Petrobrás, 12, 139
    petrodollars, 139, 151
    second oil shock of 1979, 109, 150, 169
Onganía, Juan Carlos, 63, 65
Operation Condor, 82, 98–9, 116
Osinde, Jorge, 72
Osawa, Mário, 44, 46–7

Panama, 15, 72, 74, 83
Paraguay, 61, 83, 99, 137
Pedro II, 21
Perón, Eva (Evita), 59–62, 64, 66, 68, 72
Perón, Maria Estela (Isabelita), 68, 72, 74–7, 80, 112
Perón, Juan, 6, 10, 12, 14, 58–66, 68–75, 77, 80, 114, 125
Peru, 125–6, 137
Piñera, José, 101, 108
Piñera, Sebastián, 181
Pinochet, Augusto, 17, 82–3, 90, 93–103, 113–14, 130, 132, 137, 156–62, 167–76, 180
populism, 9–10, 24, 84, 138
Portugal, 140, 157
Positivism, 21, 53
Potestad marital, 166

Prats, Carlos, 90, 98
Prebisch, Raúl, 11–14, 60
PRO-ALCOOL, 139

Quadros, Jânio, 26–7

Rauff, Walter, 94
Rega, José López, 69–77
Reagan, Ronald, 18, 130, 134, 173
Rettig Commission Report, 4, 96, 176
Riocentro Bombing, 147
Rock in Rio, 153
Rodrigo, Celestino, 76
Romero, Óscar, 144
Rousseff, Dilma, 45

Salazar, Antonio, 157
Sallustro, Oberdan, 55–8, 66
Sandinistas, 130
Santucho, Mario, 68, 78
Sarney, José, 152–4
Schneider, René, 86, 90–1
Scorpions, The, 153
Scott, James, 7–8
Serra, José, 95
Silva, Golbery do Couto e, 20, 29, 44
Silva, Luiz Inácio (Lula) da, 46, 148–9, 183–4
Silva, Raúl, 167, 173
Silveira, Antonio Azeredo da, 140–1
Sobel, Henry, 143–4
Somoza, Antastácio, 83
South Africa, 140
Souto, Edson Luis de Lima, 36
Soviet Union, 15, 115, 140, 165, 180
Stroessner, Alfredo, 83
structuralism, 11–12, 37
Spain, 61, 72, 82, 157–8
Syria, 52

television, 86, 125, 152, 174
    Globo (Brazil), 50
Thatcher, Margaret, 82, 132
Timmerman, Jacobo, 119
Toha, José, 95

Trujillo, Rafael, 83
Tucumán, 78, 114, 117, 133
Tupamaros (Uruguay) 17

United States, 13–19, 22–3, 85, 93, 150,
    170, 179
  aid to Brazilian Coup, 28
  Central America Interventions, 131–2,
    135
  Central Intelligence Agency (CIA), 17,
    87, 98, 167
  Federal Bureau of Investigation (FBI),
    17, 158, 161
  influence of Chilean free-market
    reforms, 108–9
  "Invisible Blockade" of Chile, 87–8
  School of the Americas, 74
  support for Argentine Junta, 113, 116,
    127, 132
  support for Pinochet, 97–8
United Nations
  General Assembly, 158, 160
  Commission on Human Rights, 158
  Resolution 3379 (Zionism), 139–41

University of Chicago, 99
Uruguay, 17, 42, 99
USAID, 17

Vargas, Getúlio, 10, 14, 21–2, 24
Vatican, 130
Velloso, João Reis, 139
Videla, Jorge, 4, 78, 80, 115, 117, 122–30,
    181
Vietnam, 18, 116
Villar, Alberto, 74
Viola, Roberto, 129–130
Volkswagen of Brazil, 23
Volta Redonda, 23

Walters, Vernon, 28
World Cup, 1970, 46, 49, 138
World Cup, 1978, 117, 120, 124–6, 131
Wright, James, 144

Yom Kippur War, 52
Yrigoyen, Hipólito, 59

Zaire, 16, 140